PENGUIN BOOKS

THE ENGLISH LANGUAGE

David Crystal was born in 1941 and spent the early years of his life in Holyhead, North Wales. He went to St Mary's College, Liverpool, and University College, London, where he read English and obtained his Ph.D. in 1966. He became lecturer in linguistics at University College, Bangor, and from 1965 to 1985 was at the University of Reading, where he was Professor of Linguistic Science for several years. He is currently an Honorary Professor at University College, Bangor. His research interests are mainly in English language studies, and in the clinical and remedial applications of linguistics in the study of language handicap. He is also interested in developing the relationship between linguistics and language teaching in schools.

David Crystal has published numerous articles and reviews, and is the author of *Linguistics, Language and Religion, What is Linguistics? Prosodic Systems and Intonation in English, Linguistics* (Penguin 1971, second edition 1985), *The English Tone of Voice, Child Language Learning and Linguistics, Working with LARSP, Introduction to Language Pathology, A Dictionary of Linguistics and Phonetics, Clinical Linguistics, Directions in Applied Linguistics, Profiling Linguistic Disability, Linguistic Encounters with Language Handicap, Who Cares about English Usage?* (Penguin 1984), *Listen to Your Child* (Penguin 1986), *Rediscover Grammar. The Cambridge Encyclopedia of Language, The English Language* (1988) and *Pilgrimage* (1988). He is co-author of *Systems of Prosodic and Paralinguistic Features in English, Investigating English Style, Advanced Conversational English, The Grammatical Analysis of Language Disability, Skylarks* (a language development programme) and *Databank* (a remedial reading series) and the editor of *Eric Partridge: In His Own Words* and *Linguistic Controversies*. He is also the editor of *Linguistics Abstracts* and *Child Language Teaching and Therapy*, and the consultant editor of *English Today*.

David Crystal now lives in Holyhead, where he works as a writer, lecturer and consultant on language and linguistics. He is also a frequent radio broadcaster.

DAVID CRYSTAL

The English Language

ℰ ℰ ℰ ℰ ℰ

PENGUIN BOOKS

PENGUIN BOOKS

Published by the Penguin Group
Penguin Books Ltd, 27 Wrights Lane, London W8 5TZ, England
Viking Penguin, a division of Penguin Books USA Inc.
375 Hudson Street, New York, New York 10014, USA
Penguin Books Australia Ltd, Ringwood, Victoria, Australia
Penguin Books Canada Ltd, 2801 John Street, Markham, Ontario, Canada L3R 1B
Penguin Books (NZ) Ltd, 182–190 Wairau Road, Auckland 10, New Zealand

Penguin Books Ltd, Registered Offices: Harmondsworth, Middlesex, England

First published in Pelican Books 1988
Reprinted in Penguin Books 1990
3 5 7 9 10 8 6 4 2

Maps by Phillip Patinall

Printed in England by Clays Ltd, St Ives plc
Filmset in Monophoto Ehrhardt

ʊ ʊ ʊ ʊ ʊ ʊ ʊ ʊ ʊ ʊ

Contents

	List of Maps	vii
	Acknowledgements	viii
	Introduction	ix
Chapter 1	The English Language Today	1
	Pidgins and Creoles	12
PART I	THE STRUCTURE OF ENGLISH	17
Chapter 2	Grammar	19
	Grammar and You	30
Chapter 3	Vocabulary	32
	How Large is Your Vocabulary?	44
Chapter 4	Pronunciation	50
	Received Pronunciation	62
Chapter 5	Spelling	66
	Spelling Reform	79
PART II	THE USES OF ENGLISH	83
Chapter 6	Language Variety	85
	Trucker Talk	102
Chapter 7	English at Play	105
	Sound Symbolism	122
Chapter 8	Personal English	125
	Statistical Laws?	138

PART III   THE HISTORY OF ENGLISH   143
   Chapter 9   Old English   145
           Casting the Runes   161
   Chapter 10 Middle English   166
           The Origins of Modern Standard English   185
   Chapter 11 Early Modern English   189
           Words Then and Now   211
   Chapter 12 English Around the World   215
           British and American English   246
   Chapter 13 English Today   251
           Plain English   266
   Chapter 14 English Tomorrow   273
   Appendix A Some Events in English Language History   277
   Appendix B A Guide to the Guides   280
   Appendix C Data Sources   283
           Index   285

ɞ ɞ ɞ ɞ ɞ ɞ ɞ ɞ ɞ ɞ

List of Maps

English in the World   8–9
Three British accent boundaries   87
Regional forms of 'newt'   91
Old English dialects   156
Scandinavian parish names   158
Family names ending in –son   159
Middle English dialects   186
Linguistic influences in Scotland and Ireland   220
English settlements on the east coast of America   223
American dialect divisions   225
English-speaking immigration in Canada   233
English-speaking areas in the Caribbean   236
Australia and New Zealand   239
South Africa   243

ʊ ʊ ʊ ʊ ʊ ʊ ʊ ʊ ʊ ʊ

Acknowledgements

I am most grateful to the following sources for permission to use their material in this book: BBC Hulton Picture Library, for the picture of Noah Webster; the Bodleian library and Curators for MS Laud. Misc. 636, folio 89 verso (the Peterborough Chronicle); the British Library, for the opening page of the Beowulf manuscript, Psalm 23 from the King James Bible, pages from the Shakespeare First Folio and the page from Johnson's *Dictionary*; The Fotomas Index, for the facsimile illumination of Geoffrey Chaucer, the opening lines of *The Squire's Tale*, as recorded in the Ellesmere manuscript (photograph John R. Freeman) and the picture of Samuel Johnson; Orient Longman Limited, for the extract from Kamala Das, taken from *The Old Playhouse and Other Poems* (1973); Her Majesty's Stationery Office, for the use of National Savings standard letter SB205B; the University of Leeds, for the use of the dialect map of *newt* from the Survey of English Dialects; Manchester University Press, for the Shaw alphabet key and extract, taken from W. Haas, ed., *Alphabets for English* (1969); Bengt Odenstedt, University of Umeå, for the drawing of the Undley bracteate; Picture Point, for the photograph of Ye Old Fighting Cocks; and Clement Wood, for 'Death of a Scrabble-master', in W. R. Espy, *Another Almanac of Words at Play* (Crown Publishers).

Acknowledgement is also made to the following sources: *Rot Sefti Long Niugini* (Department of Information, Port Moresby, Papua New Guinea); John Geipel, *The Viking Legacy* (David and Charles Publishers); the *Sun* and *Star* newspapers; Loreto Todd, *Modern Englishes* (Blackwell); the Plain English Campaign; Dr Seuss, *The Cat in a Hat* (Random House); F. J. Schonell, *The Essential Spelling List* (Macmillan); the *Guardian*; A. A. Milne, *Winnie the Pooh*; Ernest Wright, *Gadsby*. The *Punch* cartoons are reproduced by kind permission of *Punch*.

Thanks also to Charles Barber, Tom McArthur, Bengt Odenstedt, Matti Rissanen, and Loreto Todd for information and comments received while this book was in preparation.

ᘒ ᘒ ᘒ ᘒ ᘒ ᘒ ᘒ ᘒ ᘒ ᘒ

Introduction

This book is a mixture of what, in the world of travel, tourists would expect to find in a 'guide' or a 'companion'. In the main, it provides a systematic account of the most important characteristics of the English language, such as you would hope to receive from a professional guide. At the same time, it includes a number of special features and illustrations which are off the beaten track, and which would be more likely to come from a knowledgeable companion. In exploring a new country, both kinds of approach have their value; and so I believe it is in exploring a language. In the space available, I have been able to cover most of the topics that would be considered central, or orthodox, in any account of English; but I have devoted a great deal of space, especially in the panels and end-of-chapter features, to topics which have no other justification than that I find them fascinating. My hope is that my tastes and yours will coincide, at least some of the time.

I have organized the book so that it can be dipped into. The chapters are numbered in sequence, but each is self-contained, and they do not have to be read in order. There is an element of the country ramble in this account of the language. Some parts can be read quickly; others invite you to pause and consider – and at times to act.

There are three main parts. Part I (Chapters 2–5) is anatomical, dealing with the structure of the language – its grammar, vocabulary, sounds and spellings. Part II (Chapters 6–8) is physiological: it shows the language in use in a wide variety of settings. And Part III (Chapters 9–14) is historical. Here we do not have an appropriate biological term, for a language does not grow like a plant or person. Part III traces the development of English from Anglo-Saxon times to the present day, and its movement out of England to all parts of the globe.

There are three appendices. Appendix A provides a chronology of the language – a résumé of the significant dates in English language history. Appendix B lists recent books about English, with some comments about their coverage or emphasis. And Appendix C gives in full any references made in the body of the text. The whole is preceded by a general chapter reviewing the current state of English world-wide.

1

ʊ ʊ ʊ ʊ ʊ ʊ ʊ ʊ ʊ ʊ

The English Language Today

In the glorious reign of Queen Elizabeth (the first, that is, from 1558 to 1603), the number of English speakers in the world is thought to have been between five and seven million. At the beginning of the reign of the second Queen Elizabeth, in 1952, the figure had increased almost fiftyfold: 250 million, it was said, spoke English as a mother tongue, and a further 100 million or so had learned it as a foreign language.

Thirty-five years on, the figures continue to creep up. The most recent estimates tell us that mother-tongue speakers are now over 300

'Would you like an English "You're too late for breakfast" or a Continental "You're too late for breakfast"?'

Punch Extra, 20 June 1984, p. 13

million. But this total is far exceeded by the numbers of people who use English as a foreign language – at least a further 400 million, according to the most conservative of estimates, and perhaps a further billion, according to radical ones. 'Creep', perhaps, is not quite the right word, when such statistics are introduced.

What accounts for the scale of these increases? The size of the mother-tongue total is easy to explain. It's the Americans. The estimated population of the USA was just under 239 million in 1985, of whom about 215 million spoke English as a mother tongue. The British, Irish, Australians, New Zealanders, Canadians, and South Africans make up most of the others – but even combined they don't reach 100 million. There's no doubt where the majority influence is. However, these figures are growing relatively slowly at present – at an average rate of about half a per cent per annum. This is not where the drama lies.

A much more intriguing question is to ask what is happening to English in countries where people *don't* use it as a mother tongue. A highly complicated question, as it turns out. Finding out about the number of foreigners using English isn't easy, and that is why there is so much variation among the estimates. There are hardly any official figures. No one knows how many foreign people have learned English to a reasonable standard of fluency – or to any standard at all, for that matter. There are a few statistics available – from the examination boards, for example – but these are only the tip of a very large iceberg.

ENGLISH AS A 'SECOND' LANGUAGE

The iceberg is really in two parts, reflecting two kinds of language learning situation. The first part relates to those countries where English has some kind of special status – in particular, where it has been chosen as an 'official' language. This is the case in Ghana and Nigeria, for example, where the governments have settled on English as the main language to carry on the affairs of government, education, commerce, the media, and the legal system. In such cases, people have to learn English if they want to get on in life. They have their mother tongue to begin with – one or other of the local languages – and they start learning English, in school or in the street, at an early age. For them, in due course, English will become a language to fall back on, when their mother tongue proves to be inadequate for communication – talking to people from a different tribal background, for example, or to people from outside the country. For them, English becomes their 'second' language.

Why do these countries not select a local language for official use? The problem is how to choose between the many indigenous languages, each of which represents an ethnic background to which the adherents are fiercely loyal. In Nigeria, for example, they would have to choose between Hausa, Yoruba, Ibo, Fulani, and other languages belonging to different ethnic groups. The number of speakers won't decide the matter – there are about as many speakers of Hausa as there are of Yoruba, for instance. And even if one language did have a clear majority, its selection would be opposed by the combined weight of the other speakers, who would otherwise find themselves seriously disadvantaged, socially and educationally. Inter-tribal tension, leading to unrest and violence, would be a likely consequence. By giving official status to an outside language, such as English, all internal languages are placed on the same footing. Everyone is now equally disadvantaged. It is a complex decision to implement, but at least it is fair.

To talk of 'disadvantaged', though, is a little misleading. From another point of view, the population is now considerably 'advantaged', in that they thereby come to have access to a world of science, technology, and commerce which would otherwise not easily be available to them.

But why English? In Ghana, Nigeria, and many other countries, the choice is motivated by the weight of historical tradition from the British colonial era. A similar pattern of development can be observed in countries which were influenced by other cultures, such as the French, Spanish, Portuguese, or Dutch. French, for example, is the official language in Chad; Portuguese in Angola. But English is an official or semi-official language in over sixty countries of the world (see p. 5) – a total which far exceeds the range of these other languages.

Does this mean that we can obtain an estimate of the world's second-language English speakers simply by adding up the populations of all the countries involved? Unfortunately, it isn't so easy.

Most of these countries are in underdeveloped parts of the world, where educational opportunities are limited. The country may espouse English officially, but only a fraction of the population may be given an opportunity to learn it. The most dramatic example of this gap between theory and practice is India.

In 1985, the population of India was estimated to be 768 million. English is an official language here, alongside Hindi. Several other languages have special status in their own regions, but English is the language of the legal system; it is a major language in Parliament; and it is a preferred language in the universities and in the all-India competitive exams for senior posts in such fields as the civil service and engineering. Some 3,000 English newspapers are published throughout the country. There is thus great reason to learn to use the language well. But it is thought that those with an educated awareness of English may be as little as 3 per cent of the population. Perhaps 10 per cent or more, if we recognize lower levels of achievement, and include several varieties of pidgin English (see pp. 12–16). In real terms, the English speakers of India may only number 70 millions – a small amount compared with the total population. On the other hand, this figure is well in excess of the population of Britain.

When all the estimates for second-language use around the world are added up, we reach a figure of around 300 million speakers – about as many as the total of mother-tongue users. But we have to remember that most of these countries are in parts of the world (Africa, South Asia) where the population increase is four times as great as that found in mother-tongue countries. If present trends continue, within a generation mother-tongue English use will have been left far behind.

ENGLISH AS A 'FOREIGN' LANGUAGE

The second part of the language-learning iceberg relates to people who live in countries where English has no official status, but where it is learned as a foreign language in schools, institutes of higher education, and through the use of a wide range of 'self-help' materials. There are only hints as to what the numbers involved might be. Even in the statistically aware countries of Western Europe, there are no reliable figures available for the number of people who are learning

English in the world

English is an official language, or has a special status, in over 60 of the world's territories, listed below (with population estimates, in most cases for 1985). Countries with a major mother-tongue English population are marked *. Note that there are several other countries where English has no official status, but where there are none the less substantial numbers of second-language speakers, such as Bangladesh, Bhutan, Brunei, Malaysia, Nepal, and Sri Lanka.

1. Australia*	15,749,000	27. Nauru (with	
2. Bahamas*	230,000	Nauruan)	8,000
3. Barbados*	252,700	28. New Zealand*	3,291,300
4. Belize*	166,400	29. Nigeria	96,015,000
5. Bermuda*	56,700	30. Pakistan (with Urdu)	100,356,000
6. Botswana	1,082,000	31. Papua New Guinea	3,345,000
7. Cameroon (with		32. Philippines (with	
French)	9,635,000	Filipino)	54,669,000
8. Canada (with		33. Puerto Rico (with	
French)*	25,427,000	Spanish)	3,311,100
9. Dominica*	77,400	34. Saint Christopher	
10. Fiji	692,000	and Nevis*	47,000
11. Gambia	749,200	35. Saint Lucia*	137,600
12. Ghana	12,815,300	36. Saint Vincent and the	
13. Grenada*	96,000	Grenadines*	105,000
14. Guyana*	953,000	37. Senegal (with	
15. Hong Kong (with		French)	6,520,000
Chinese)	5,415,000	38. Seychelles (with	
16. India (with Hindi,		French)	65,100
and several local		39. Sierra Leone	3,930,000
languages)	768,000,000	40. Singapore (with	
17. Ireland (with Irish)*	3,614,000	Chinese, Malay,	
18. Jamaica*	2,343,700	Tamil)	2,558,200
19. Kenya (with Swahili)	20,312,000	41. Solomon Is.	267,270
20. Kiribati	65,000	42. South Africa (with	
21. Lesotho (with Sotho)	1,499,600	Afrikaans)*	27,424,000
22. Liberia	2,232,000	43. Suriname (with	
23. Malawi (with Chewa)	7,058,800	Dutch)	395,000
24. Malta (with Maltese)	333,000	44. Swaziland (with	
25. Mauritius	1,024,900	Swazi)	647,400
26. Namibia (with		45. Tanzania (with	
Afrikaans)	1,097,000	Swahili)	21,730,000

46. Tonga (with Tongan)	97,050	53. Western Samoa (with Samoan	160,000
47. Trinidad and Tobago*	1,189,000	54. Zambia	6,666,000
48. Tuvalu	8,580	55. Zimbabwe	8,100,000
49. Uganda	14,716,100	And many other British and US dependencies (e.g. Gibraltar, Falkland Is., US Pacific Territories)	
50. United Kingdom*	56,518,000		
51. United States of America*	238,740,000		
52. Vanuatu (with French)	140,000		300,000

English as a foreign language – or any other language, for that matter. In a continent such as South America, the total is pure guesswork.

The total most often cited in the mid-1980s was 100 million, based largely on the figures available from English-language examining boards, estimates of listeners to English-language radio programmes, sales of English-language newspapers, and the like. But this figure did not take into account what is currently happening in the country where data about anything has traditionally been notoriously difficult to come by: China.

In China, there has been an explosion of interest in the English language in recent years. One visitor returned to China in 1979, after an absence of twenty years, and wrote: 'in 1959, everyone was carrying a book of the thoughts of Chairman Mao; today, everyone is carrying a book of elementary English'. In 1983, it is thought, around 100 million people watched the BBC television series designed to teach the language, *Follow Me*. Considerable publicity was given in the Western media to the sight of groups of Chinese practising English-language exercises after work, or queuing to try out their English on a passing tourist. The presenter of *Follow Me*, Kathy Flower, became a national celebrity, recognized everywhere. And the interest continues, with new series of programmes being designed to meet the needs of scientific and business users. What level of fluency is being achieved by this massive influx of learners is unknown. But if only a fraction of China's population is successful, this alone will be enough to make the 100 million total for world foreign-language use a gross underestimate.

And why shouldn't they be successful, in China, Japan, Brazil, Poland, Egypt, and elsewhere? There is enormous motivation, given the way that English has become the dominant language of world communication. Textbooks on English these days regularly rehearse the litany of its achievements. It is the main language of the world's books, newspapers, and advertising. It is the official international language of airports and air traffic control. It is the chief maritime language. It is the language of international business and academic conferences, of diplomacy, of sport. Over two thirds of the world's scientists write in English. Three quarters of the world's mail is written in English. Eighty per cent of all the information stored in the electronic retrieval systems of the world is stored in English. And, at a local level, examples of the same theme can be found everywhere. A well-known Japanese company, wishing to negotiate with its Arabic customers, arranges all its meetings in English. A Colombian doctor reports that he spends almost as much time improving his English as practising medicine. A Copenhagen university student comments: 'Nearly everyone in Denmark speaks English; if we didn't, there wouldn't be anyone to talk to.'

Statistics of this kind are truly impressive, and could continue for several paragraphs. They make the point that it is not the number of mother-tongue speakers which makes a language important in the eyes of the world (that crown is carried by Chinese), but the extent to which a language is found useful outside its original setting. In the course of history, other languages have achieved widespread use throughout educated society. During the Middle Ages, Latin remained undisputed as the European language of learning. In the eighteenth century, much of this prestige passed to French. Today, it is the turn of English. It is a development which could be reversed only by a massive change in the economic fortunes of America, and in the overall balance of world power.

CONSEQUENCES

When a language, like a nation, exercises a new-found influence in world affairs, several things happen. People begin to study it in unprecedented detail. Research projects flourish. Scholars write grammars, dictionaries, and manuals of its style. They plan surveys of educated usage, and surveys of dialects. Courses in the teaching of the language proliferate, in a rapidly increasing number of (not always respectable) institutions. There is a general raising of

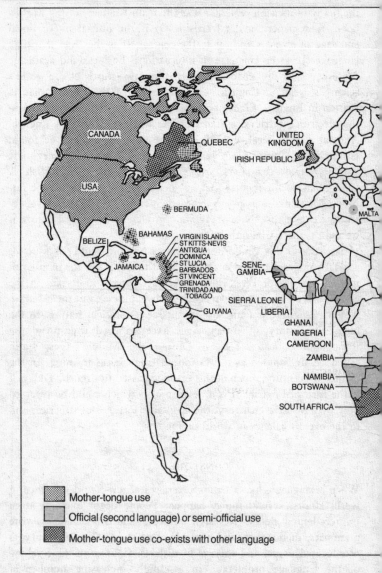

English in the world

PAKI-
STAN

INDIA

HONG KONG

PHILIPPINES

MALAY-
SIA

KENYA
UGANDA

SRI LANKA
SINGAPORE

SEYCHELLES

USA TERRITORIES

TANZANIA
MALAWI

PAPUA NEW
GUINEA

NAURU

KIRIBATI

MAURITIUS

SOLOMON
ISLANDS

TUVALU
WEST-
ERN
SAMOA

MBABWE
WAZILAND
ESOTHO

VANUATU

FIJI

AUSTRALIA

TONGA

COOK
ISLANDS

NEW ZEALAND

consciousness, with new language courses in schools, and popular programmes on radio and television. And there is a rapid growth in popular books and magazines about the language, to help people keep pace with developments – this book being the latest example.

People also become increasingly critical and concerned about language matters. It is, after all, *their* language which is the focus of attention; and while all mother-tongue speakers inevitably feel a modicum of pride (and relief) that it is their language which is succeeding, there is also an element of concern, as they see what happens to the language as it spreads around the world. Public anxiety is expressed. Changes are perceived as instances of deterioration in standards. Tension grows between those who wish simply to observe and explain the process of change, and those who wish to halt it. Such anxiety is most keenly felt in Britain, where, after centuries of dominance in the use of English, many people who take pride in their use of English find it difficult to come to terms with the fact that British English is now, numerically speaking, a minority dialect, compared with American, or even Indian, English.

These are matters which require careful and sympathetic discussion, as they relate to the biggest question of all hanging over the future of the English language at the end of the twentieth century. What will happen to the language, as it manifests its worldwide presence in the form of new varieties – not only in mother-tongue countries such as Australia and Canada, but also in second-language areas such as South Asia, West Africa, and the West Indies (see Chapter 12)? Each area presents a complex case, as speakers and writers struggle to find a way of communicating which they feel authentically expresses their identity. New authors in these areas may not wish to write in the vocabulary and grammar of British or American English. In many cases, such varieties symbolize an alien and alienating society, and they sense a need to find fresh language. The same point applies, even more dramatically, to new regional standards of pronunciation in everyday life, as in this case there are often real problems of mutual intelligibility between people who would all claim to be English-speaking.

Since these trends were first noted, there has been a great deal of pessimism about the future of the language. So far, however, it has been unfounded. In the mid nineteenth century, people were predicting that within 100 years British and American English would be mutually unintelligible. It hasn't happened. The same predictions continue to be made, but on a broader front, to include all the new major varieties, in India, West Africa, and elsewhere. So far, the problems are minor. Maybe one day, it is said, English will be transformed into a family of new languages – just as happened to Latin, less than 2,000 years ago, with the resulting emergence of French, Spanish, Portuguese, and the other Romance languages. Some people think that the process has already begun.

The history of language shows us that any such development would be entirely natural, and it could easily happen to English. On the other hand, there are strong counter-pressures in modern society which did not exist in earlier times. There is an urgent need to communicate at world level, where everyone involved has a vested interest in keeping at least one channel open, in the form of standard written English. And patterns of speech are bound to be affected by the unprecedented opportunity to talk to each other over long distances, in the form of radio, television, and telecommunications. It may be that these factors will balance the language's movement towards diversity. Or maybe they will not. What is going on in this area makes a fascinating topic of enquiry, but it is a complicated story that requires some linguistic background to be understood – which is what this book is about.

Pidgins and Creoles

Generations of children's comics and films have promoted a weird picture of what a pidgin language is. People remember 'Me Tarzan – you Jane', or other examples of primitive people barely able to communicate with each other. It can come as something of a shock, therefore, to realize that in many parts of the world pidgin languages are used routinely in such daily matters as news broadcasts, safety instructions, newspapers, and commercial advertising. And the more developed pidgin languages have been used for translations of Shakespeare and the Bible (see p. 14).

All pidgin languages originally start when people who don't have a common language try to communicate with each other. Most of the present-day pidgins grew up along the trade routes of the world – especially in those parts where the British, French, Spanish, Portuguese, and Dutch built up their empires. We talk of 'pidgin English', 'pidgin French', and so on, depending on which language the pidgin derived from.

Pidgin Englishes are mainly to be found in two big 'families' – one in the Atlantic, one in the Pacific. The Atlantic varieties developed in West Africa, and were transported to the West Indies and America during the years of the slave trade. In Africa, they are still widely used in the Gambia, Sierra Leone, Liberia, Ghana, Togo, Nigeria, and Cameroon. The Pacific varieties are found in a wide sweep across the south-western part of the ocean, from the coast of China to the northern part of Australia, in such places as Hawaii, Vanuatu, and Papua New Guinea. In the Americas, they are found, in a developed form (see below), in most of the islands and on the mainland, spoken largely by the black population. Estimates vary, but probably about thirty-five million people speak or understand one or other of these forms of English.

A page adapted from the Papua New Guinea road safety handbook, *Rot Sefti Long Niugini* (1972), written in the local pidgin language, Tok Pisin, with English translation

Sapos yu kisim bagarap kisim namba bilong narapela draiva, sapos yu ken, kisim naim bilong em na adres tu, na tokim polis long en. Noken paitim em o tok nogut long em.

If you have an accident, get the other driver's number, if possible his name and address and report it to the police. Do not fight him, or abuse him.

Pidgins often have a very short life span. While the Americans were in Vietnam, a pidgin English grew up there, but it quickly disappeared when the troops left. In a similar way, many pidgins which grew up for trading purposes have ceased to exist, because the

Pidgin translations

The Gospel According to St Mark

The beginning of the gospel of Jesus Christ, the Son of God. As it is written in the prophets, Behold, I send my messenger before thy face, which shall prepare thy way before thee. The voice of one crying in the wilderness, Prepare ye the way of the Lord, make his paths straight.

Tok Pisin

Dispela em i gutnius bilong Jisas Kraist, Pikinini bilong God. Dispela gutnius em I kamap pastaim olsem profet Aisaia I raitim: 'Harim, mi salim man bilong bringim tok bilong mi, na em I go paslain long yu. Em bai i redim rot bilong yu. Long graun i no gat man, maus bilong wanpela man i singaut, i spik. 'Redim rot bilong Bikpela. Stretim ol rot bilong en.'
Nupela Testamen Long Tok Pisin, British and Foreign Bible Society,
Canberra, 1969

Hamlet III, i

To be, or not to be – that is the question;
Whether 'tis nobler in the mind to suffer
The slings and arrows of outrageous fortune
Or to take arms against a sea of troubles
And by opposing end them?

Cameroon Pidgin English

Foh di foh dis graun oh foh no bi sehf – dat na di ting wei i di bring
  plenti hambag.
Wehda na sohm behta sehns sei mek man i tai hat
Foh di shap ston an shap stik dehm foh bad lohk wei dehm di wohri man
  foh dis graun,
Oh foh kari wowo ting foh fait dis trohbul wei i big laik sohlwata so?
Translated by R. Awa

And a nursery rhyme . . .

Dis smol swain i bin go fo maket.
Dis smol swain i bin stei fo haus.
Dis smol swain i bin chop sup witi fufu.
Dis smol swain i no bin chop no noting.
An dis smol swain i bin go wi, wi sotei fo haus.

countries which were in contact stopped trading with each other. On the other hand, if a trading contact is very successful, and contact builds up over the years, the people will very likely learn each other's language, and there will then be no reason for the continued use of the pidgin. Pidgin languages seem to be in a 'no win' situation, and it is rare to find one in existence for more than a century.

But it can happen. In multilingual parts of the world, the pidgin is found to be so useful that the peoples in contact find they cannot do without it. The pidgin becomes a common language, or *lingua franca*. This happened to Sabir, a pidginized form of French used along the Mediterranean coast from the Middle Ages until the twentieth century. It has happened in Nigeria. And above all, it has happened in Papua New Guinea, where Tok Pisin is known or used by over a million people – more than any other language in the country.

Of course, when a pidgin becomes widely used, its form changes dramatically. To begin with, pidgins are very limited forms of communication with few words, a few simple constructions (mainly commands), helped along by gestures and miming. Tarzan's style is not very far from reality, in such cases. But when a pidgin expands, its vocabulary increases greatly, it develops its own rules of grammatical construction, and it becomes used for all the functions of everyday life.

A very significant development can then take place. People begin to use the pidgin at home. As children are born into these families, the pidgin language becomes their mother tongue. When this happens, the status of the language fundamentally alters, and it comes to be used in a more flexible and creative way. Instead of being seen as subordinate to other languages in an area, it starts to compete with them. In such cases linguists no longer talk about pidgin languages, but about *creoles*. Creolized varieties of English are very important throughout the Caribbean, and in the countries to which Caribbean people have emigrated – notably Britain. Black English in the United States is also creole in origin (see p. 236).

There is often conflict between the creole and standard English in these places. The creole gives its speakers their linguistic identity, as an ethnic group. Standard English, on the other hand, gives them access to the rest of the English-speaking world. It is not easy for governments to develop an acceptable language policy when such fundamental issues are involved. Should road signs be in standard

English or in creole? Should creole-speaking school-children be educated in standard English or in creole? And which variety should writers use when contributing to the emerging literature of their country? Social and political circumstances vary so much that no simple generalization is possible – except to emphasize the need for standard English users to replace their traditional dismissive attitude towards creole speech with an informed awareness of its linguistic complexity as a major variety of modern English. We have to forget Tarzan.

Pronouns in Tok Pisin

Sometimes a pidgin language can develop forms that are *more* complex than those available in the standard language. An example is the range of personal pronouns used in Tok Pisin. There are two forms of 'we': the *inclusive* form means 'you and me'; the *exclusive* form means 'me and someone else'.

Tok Pisin	English origin	Modern meaning
me	me	I, me
yu	you	you
em	him, 'em (them)	he, she, it, him, her
yumi	you + me	we, us (*inclusive*)
mipela	me + fellow	we, us (*exclusive*)
ol	all	they, them

It is also possible to expand the pronouns to include the number of people being talked about:

mitupela	the two of us (excluding you)
mitripela	the three of us (excluding you)
yumitripela	the three of us (including you)
yutupela	the two of you
etc.	

PART I

ɞ ɞ ɞ ɞ ɞ ɞ ɞ ɞ ɞ ɞ

The Structure of English

Chapters 2 to 5 investigate the main dimensions of the anatomy, or structure, of the English language. We begin with the skeleton, grammar – a field that has aroused a great deal of controversy in recent years. What are the important characteristics of English grammar? Why do people complain about grammar so much? What is involved in studying usage – whether your own or other people's?

Much of the 'flesh' of the language comes from its enormous vocabulary. But how large is this vocabulary, and how can it be classified? What should you bear in mind when purchasing or consulting a dictionary? Chapter 3 looks at these questions, and also suggests a way of keeping track of the size of your own vocabulary.

Once we have words and grammar at our disposal, we can communicate, but we have a choice of medium – speaking or writing. Chapter 4 looks at speaking, outlining the pronunciation system of English. How many vowels and consonants are there, and what happens to them when we speak normal, fast conversation? The chapter introduces the thorny question of pronunciation errors, and ends by explaining the background to Received Pronunciation – the accent which many people think of as the best kind of English speech.

Chapter 5 raises the equally thorny issue of English spelling, generally condemned as chaotic. How regular is the writing system, in fact, and where does all the irregularity come from? There have been many proposals for spelling reform. Part I concludes by reviewing some of these, and reflecting on their chances of success.

2

ʕ ʕ ʕ ʕ ʕ ʕ ʕ ʕ ʕ ʕ

Grammar

BASIC ENGLISH COURSE
20 lessons
We teach you how to speak
so there's not much grammar.

I'm glad I was brought up to speak English – a much easier language than
Latin, German, and all those others with dozens of word endings.

English . . . has a grammar of great simplicity and flexibility.

The above advertisement appeared in a foreign Sunday paper not so
long ago. The second comment was made in a letter to a BBC

'Me mum sent a note in, Miss . . .'

Punch, 6 February 1985

programme on English. And the third appeared in a best-selling book
on the English language, published in 1986. Together, they illustrate
one of the most widespread fallacies about the language, especially in
its spoken form, that there's no grammar worth bothering about.

If only it were true. But you have only to ask foreigners who have
been struggling with the language for years, and they'll tell you the
opposite. 'I don't think I shall ever master all the rules of English
grammar,' said one. 'So many exceptions, so many tiny changes in
word order which make all the difference to what you're trying to
say,' said another, gloomily.

There are two reasons why people are contemptuous of English
grammar. First, there's the influence of Latin. For centuries, the
Latin language ruled the grammar-teaching world. People had to
know Latin to be accepted in educated society, and their knowledge of
grammar was based on how that language works. Here's the famous
verb that started millions of schoolchildren on their Latin-learning
road.

amo	I love	*amamus*	we love
amas	you love	*amatis*	you love
amat	he/she loves	*amant*	they love

When people started to analyse English grammar in the eighteenth
century, it seemed logical to look at the language using the terms and
distinctions which had proved so useful in studying Latin. English
had no word-endings, it seemed. Therefore, it had no 'grammar'.

But of course there is far more to grammar than word-endings.
Some languages (such as Chinese) have none at all. English has less
than a dozen types of regular ending (and a few irregular ones):

the plural *-s*	the girl → the girl*s*
the genitive *-'s* or *-s'*, marking such meanings as possession	the boy*'s* bike the boys*'* bikes
the past tense *-ed*	I walk → I walk*ed*
the past participle *-ed*	I walk → I have walk*ed*
the third person singular of the present tense, *-s*	I run → he run*s*
the verb ending which marks such meanings as duration, *-ing*	she laughs → she is laugh*ing*
the negative *-n't*	he is → he is*n't*
the comparative *-er*	big → bigg*er*

the superlative *-est*   big → bigg*est*
the shortened form of some verbs,   I'*ll* leave
   '*ll*, '*re*, etc.

Among the exceptions are certain nouns and adjectives, such as *mice*, *men*, *better* and *worst*, and about 300 irregular verbs, such as *gone*, *taken*, *saw*, and *ran*.

But these endings, whether regular or irregular, make up only a fraction of the grammar of modern English. The language makes very little use of word structure, or *morphology*, to express the meanings that Latin conveys in its word-endings. Most of English grammar is taken up with the rules governing the order in which words can appear: the field of *syntax*. Word order is crucial for English, as we can see from following examples, where the meaning of the sentence alters dramatically once the order varies:

> Dog bites postman *v.* Postman bites dog
> They are here *v.* Are they here?
> Only I kissed Joan *v.* I kissed only Joan
> Naturally, I got up *v.* I got up naturally (*not awkwardly*)
> Show me the last three pages (*of one book*) *v.* Show me the three last pages (*of   three books*)
> The man with a dog saw me *v.* The man saw me with a dog.

There are also many complex constructions, such as the use of *respectively*, which enables us to say several things at once in an economical way:

John, Mary, and Peter play tennis, baseball, and croquet respectively.

And there are thousands of rules forbidding us to put words in a certain order. Mother-tongue speakers never think twice about them, because they learned these rules as children. But the rules are there, none the less, making us use the first of the following alternatives, not the second (the asterisk shows that the sentence is unacceptable):

I walked to town	*I to town walked
Hardly had I left . . .	*Hardly I had left . . .
That's a fine old house	*That's an old fine house
John and I saw her	*I and John saw her
She switched it on	*She switched on it

Mother-tongue speakers instinctively know that the first is correct
and the second is not. But explaining why this is so to anyone who
asks (such as a foreign learner) is a specialist skill indeed.

GRAMMAR IN SPEECH AND WRITING

There is a second reason for the way people readily dismiss grammar:
the widespread feeling that only the written language is worth bothering about, and that spoken English has 'less' grammar because it
does not 'follow the rules' that are found in writing. A surprisingly
large number of people who have spoken English since they were
children are willing to admit that they 'don't speak English correctly',
or claim that 'foreigners speak better English than we do, because
they've learned the rules'. There is something seriously amiss here,
if mother-tongue speakers can be made to feel they are wrong, and
foreign learners are right. Certainly, foreigners are often mystified
by this reaction when they hear it.

There are indeed many differences between the way grammar is
used in writing English and the way it is used in speaking it. This is
only natural. When we are writing, we usually have time to make
notes, plan ahead, pause, reflect, change our mind, start again,
revise, proof-read, and generally polish the language until we have
reached a level which satisfies us. The reader sees only the finished
product.

But in everyday conversation (which is the kind of spoken language
we engage in most of the time) there is no time for such things to
happen. As we begin a conversation, or start to tell a story, we are
faced with listeners who react to what we are saying while we are
saying it. We do not have the time or opportunity to plan what we
want to say, and we have to allow for false starts, interruptions,
second thoughts, words on the tip of the tongue, and a host of other
disturbances which take place while we are in full flow.

Naturally, in such circumstances, we make use of all kinds of
grammatical features that wouldn't be necessary in writing – in particular, parenthetic phrases such as *you know*, *you see*, *I mean*, and
mind you. We make great use of *and* and *but* to join sentences together
– a feature of style which is often criticized when it appears in
writing, but which is extremely widespread in speech, as this extract

from a conversation shows (/ marks a break in the rhythm of the speech, – marks a pause):

it's not a select shopping centre by any means/ and there're lots of – council houses/ and flats/ and – erm – I mean I think it's fantastic/ because you can go up there/ and they're very nice-looking flats and everything/ it's – it's been fairly well designed/ – and you can go up there/ and and shop reasonably/ – but – at the same time/ just where we're living/ there's a sort of sprinkling/ of of little delicatessens/ and extravagant and extraordinarily expensive shops/ you see/ and very expensive cleaners etcetera/ – and I've been doing little surveys/ of the area/ and and looking/ you know . . .

This kind of speech looks weird in print, because it is not possible to show all the melody, stress, and tone of voice which made the speaker (a woman in her early twenties) sound perfectly natural in context. But it does show how spoken grammar differs from written. It would be possible to reduce the extract to a more compact, economical style, like the following (it uses 40 per cent fewer words), but the language immediately becomes more controlled, formal, and abrupt, and it simply would not sound right in everyday speech.

it's not a select shopping centre, by any means, but I think it's fantastic, because you can go up there and shop reasonably. There're lots of fairly well-designed council houses and very nice-looking flats. Just where we're living, there's a sprinkling of delicatessens and extravagant, extraordinarily expensive shops, cleaners, etcetera. I've been doing little surveys of the area, and looking . . .

It's important not to overestimate the differences between speech and writing, though. Probably over 95 per cent of the grammatical constructions in English appear in both spoken and written expression. All the examples on p. 21 could be used quite acceptably in either. And of course there are many styles of language use where the boundary between speech and writing almost disappears – as when people write material to be read aloud (as in radio plays and news broadcasts) or speak spontaneously so that what they say can be written down (as in dictation or teaching). The conclusion is clear: spoken English may be different, but it certainly does not lack grammatical structure.

KNOWING GRAMMAR AND 'KNOWING ABOUT' GRAMMAR

The advertisement at the beginning of this chapter carries a further implication: that when you learn a language, you don't need to know any grammatical terminology. That language school's teaching method, it would seem, is an 'oral' approach; their students will not be spending time learning English rules by heart and then trying to turn these rules into spontaneous speech (the 'Oh dear, how can I say anything if I can't remember my irregular verbs' problem). The hope is that, by giving the students lots of time to practise speaking, they will 'pick up' the right forms of expression, and gradually develop a sense of what the rules are – without anyone formally having to tell them.

She shall, will she?

The way grammatical usage is changing over *shall* and *will* is neatly captured in these 1985 newspaper headlines, both supposedly reporting the words of a member of the royal family, and appearing on the same day.

This method of language learning can work. Little children, after all, do it all the time. They follow a gradual process of trial and error, and never get bogged down in wondering what an irregular verb is. However, whether the same approach works for adults is currently controversial. Adults can often be helped by having a rule of grammar explained to them, rather than having to work it out for themselves. It's often a lot quicker than the trial and error technique, which can easily take a great deal of time. On the other hand, too much grammar work can kill any enthusiasm for language learning, as many people well remember from their school days.

The English language has suffered badly at the hands of the grammarians over the centuries. Many people have left school with the impression that English grammar is a dull, boring, pointless subject – simply because it was presented to them in a dull, boring and pointless way. They may even say that they don't know any grammar, or (as already noted) that they don't know the correct grammar. They feel insecure and defensive. Something is wrong when this happens.

The origins of the problem lie in the eighteenth century, when the first grammars of English were written. The grammarians shared the spirit of that age to establish order in the language, after what they saw as a chaotic period of expansion and experiment. Shakespeare and his contemporaries had added thousands of new words and usages to the language. The new dictionary-writers and grammarians felt it was their responsibility to sort out what had happened (see p. 206).

From the 1760s, grammarians such as Robert Lowth and Lindley Murray laid down rules which they thought should govern correct grammatical usage. This is the period when the rules were first formulated about such matters as saying *I shall* rather than *I will*, preferring *It is I* to *It is me*, avoiding a 'double negative' (*I don't have no interest in the matter*), never ending sentences with a preposition (*That's the man I was talking to*), and never splitting an infinitive (*I want to really try*). The early grammars were followed by others, and a tradition of correct usage came to be built up, which was then taught in public schools during the nineteenth century, and later in all schools. Many generations of schoolchildren learned how to analyse (or 'parse') a sentence into 'subject', 'predicate', and so on. They learned to label the different parts of speech (nouns, verbs, prepositions, conjunctions, etc.). And they learned about correct usage, as viewed by educated society, and tried to follow it in their own speech and writing. They were left in no doubt that failure to speak or write correctly would lead in the long term to social criticism and reduced career prospects – and in the short term to a more immediate form of suffering. As one correspondent to the BBC series *English Now* wrote:

The reason why the older generation feel so strongly about English grammar is that we were severely punished if we didn't obey the rules! One split infinitive, one whack; two split infinitives, two whacks; and so on.

But from the very beginning, people saw problems with this approach. Even in the eighteenth century, critics such as Joseph Priestley were arguing that it was impossible to reduce all the variation in a language to a single set of simple rules. It was pointed out that no language was perfectly neat and regular. There were always variations in usage which reflected variations in society, or individual patterns of emphasis. There would always be exceptions to the rules. And there were some very prestigious exceptions too: there are double negatives in Chaucer, Lord Macaulay split an infinitive on occasion, and one does not have to look far to find Shakespeare ending a sentence with a preposition:

> Who would these fardels bear,
> To grunt and sweat under a weary life,
> But that the dread of something after death,
> The undiscovered country, from whose bourn
> No traveller returns, puzzles the will,
> And makes us rather bear those ills we have
> Than fly to others that we know not of?
>
> *Hamlet*, III, i

The controversy continues to this day. People still argue over whether grammar should be approached from a *descriptive* or a *prescriptive* point of view. In the descriptive approach, the analyst gathers information about the way English is used, and tries to understand why such variation exists, and the different effects that come from choosing one construction rather than another. In the prescriptive approach, there is no such weighing of the evidence: one construction is considered to be a sign of educated speech or writing, and is recommended for use; the other is considered uneducated, and banned. These days, there are signs of a compromise position being worked out, as far as school teaching is concerned. Educators are

The top ten complaints about grammar

In a survey of letters sent in to the BBC radio series *English Now* in 1986, the following ten points of grammar were the ones about which listeners most often complained.

1. I shouldn't be used in *between you and I*. The pronoun should be *me* after a preposition, as in *Give it to me*.
   COMMENT This is true; but many people are unconsciously aware of the way grammars have criticized *me* in other constructions, recommending *It is I* or *He's bigger than I* as the correct form. They feel that *I* is somehow more polite, and as a result they begin to use it in places where it wouldn't normally go.

2. 'Split infinitives' should be avoided, as in *to boldly go* (often cited because of its use in *Star Trek*).
   COMMENT Grammars have long objected to the way an adverb can be used to separate *to* from the verb; but there are many cases where alternatives seem artificial, as in *I want you to really try*, where *really to try* and *to try really* are very awkward, and *I really want* means something different.

3. *Only* should be next to the word to which it relates; people shouldn't say *I only saw Fred* when they mean *I saw only Fred*.
   COMMENT The context usually makes it obvious which sense is intended. But it is wise to be careful in writing, where ambiguity can arise. Spoken usage is hardly ever ambiguous: *only* is always linked with the next word that carries a strong stress. Note the difference between *I only saw FRED* (and no one else) and *I only SAW Fred* (I didn't talk to him).

4. *None* should never be followed by a plural verb, as in *None of the cows are in the field*.
   COMMENT It is argued that *none* is a singular form, and should therefore take a singular verb. But usage has been influenced by the plural meaning of *none*, especially when followed by a plural noun: *none of the cows are ill* = '*they* are not ill'.

5. *Different[ly]* should be followed by *from* and not by *to* or *than*.
   COMMENT Grammarians were impressed by the meaning of the first syllable of this word in Latin: *dis–* = 'from'. But *to* has

come to be the more frequent British usage, perhaps because of the influence of *similar to, opposed to*, etc. *Than* is frequent in American English, and is often objected to in Britain for that reason.

6. A sentence shouldn't end with a preposition.

   COMMENT This rule was first introduced in the seventeenth century, but as we have seen (p. 26) it has been ignored, notably in recent years by Churchill, who found it something 'up with which he would not put'. In formal English, the rule tends to be followed; but in informal usage, final prepositions are normal. Compare the formal *That is the man to whom I was talking* and informal *That's the man I was talking to*.

7. People should say *I shall/you will/he will* when they are referring to future time, not *I will/you shall/he shall*.

   COMMENT There has been a tendency to replace *shall* by *will* for well over a century. It is now hardly ever used in American, Irish, or Scots English, and is becoming less common in other varieties. Usages such as *I'll have some coffee* and *I'll be thirty next week* are now in the majority.

8. *Hopefully* should not be used at the beginning of a sentence, as in *Hopefully, John will win his race*.

   COMMENT People argue that as it is the speaker, not John, who is being hopeful, a better construction would be *It is hoped that* . . . or *I hope that* . . . But *hopefully* is one of hundreds of adverbs that are used in this way: *frankly, naturally, fortunately*, etc. It is unclear why *hopefully* has come to be criticized, whereas the others have not.

9. *Whom* should be used, not *who*, in such sentences as *That's the man whom you saw*.

   COMMENT As the pronoun is being used as the object of the verb *saw*, this form is technically correct. But *whom* is felt to be very formal, and in informal speech people often replace it by *who*, or drop the pronoun altogether: *That's the man you saw*.

10. Double negatives, as in *He hasn't done nothing*, should be avoided.

    COMMENT This construction is no longer acceptable in standard English (though it was normal in Middle English). However, it is extremely common in non-standard speech throughout the world. Note that in the non-standard use the two negatives don't cancel each other out, and 'make a positive' (as two minus signs would in mathematics); they make a more emphatic negative. *He hasn't done nothing* does not mean 'He *has* done something'!

trying to get children to develop a sense of the variations which exist in English, at the same time pointing out the value of learning those styles which carry extra prestige within society.

But whichever approach is used, it is going to be necessary to *talk about* English grammar. Whether we take the view that all styles of English have their value, or wish to condemn all but the 'best' forms of standard English, or wish to develop a compromise, we will need some terms for talking about the sentence patterns which are at issue. This chapter has been no exception. I have used some familiar technical terms, such as 'word-ending', 'word order', 'sentence' and 'verb', as well as a few specialized terms, such as 'genitive' and 'infinitive'. A bit of basic terminology is essential to understand the English language, in just the same way that it is needed to understand chemistry, geography, or any other area of knowledge.

Everyone reading this book knows English grammar. They understand the sentence patterns I am using, and could use them in my place. But not everyone *knows about* grammar, so that they could analyse these sentence patterns into their parts, and give them such labels as *subject* and *object*, or *noun* and *preposition*. This is the knowledge which has to be learned specially, as an intellectual skill. Whether in school or beyond, the teacher's task is to devise ways of making this learning interesting and enjoyable, so that the language is enlivened by the study of grammar, and not strangled. It is a problem which has still not been entirely solved.

Grammar and You

All rules of grammar ultimately stem from the usage and preferences of the people who speak the language as a mother tongue. But what *is* your usage? What *are* your preferences? Are they the same as everyone else's?

Linguists have devised several ways of finding out how people use their language. One technique involves checking to see whether all the words of a certain type actually behave in the same way. Take adjectives, for instance. These are words like *big, small, red, happy*, and *interesting*. Their general role is plain enough: they all express an aspect or feature of something: *a big car, a small house*, and so on. But they do not all follow exactly the same grammatical rules. We can show this by working out how one of these words behaves grammatically, and then seeing whether the other words behave in the same way.

Happy will illustrate the point. If we look to see how this word can be used in English, we will come to such conclusions as these:

- It can be used between *the* and a noun: *the happy child.*
- It can be used after the forms of the verb *be*: *he is happy.*
- It can add the endings *–er* and *–est*: *happier, happiest.*
- It can be used with *more* and *most*: *She's more happy now than she was when she lived with Fred. It was a most happy time for all.*
- It can be preceded by such words as *very*: *the very happy child.*
- It can add *–ly*: *happily.*

Now let's see which other words work in exactly the same way. A simple way of doing this is to construct a table in which these rules are listed across the top, and the words we want to study are listed down one side. We ask the same questions of each word: Can it be used between *the* and a noun? Can it be used with *more* and *most*? And so on. If the answer is 'yes', we mark the place in the table with a plus sign. If the answer is 'no', we use a minus sign. And if we don't know, or aren't sure, we use a question mark. There is an adjective table below, with the first few lines filled in, along with some comments.

	Can it be used after *the*?	Can it be used after *be*?	Can it add *–er* or *–est*?	Can it take *more* or *most*?	Can it take *very*?	Can it add *–ly*?
happy	+	+	+	+	+	+
big	+	+	+	–	+	–
short	+	+	+	–	+	+[1]
asleep	–	+	–	–[2]	–[2]	–
interesting	+	+	–	+	+	+
red						
beautiful						
sad						
tall						
ill						
awake						
wooden						
Others?						

1. But notice that *shortly* has a new meaning: 'soon'. It does not mean 'in a short manner'.
2. *Asleep* and several other words beginning with *a-* cause problems. I have heard people say such things as *They're very asleep* and *Two more asleep children I've never seen!* But the usage isn't a normal one.

3

ぢ ぢ ぢ ぢ ぢ ぢ ぢ ぢ ぢ ぢ

Vocabulary

How many words are there in English? This apparently simple little question turns out to be surprisingly complicated. Estimates have been given ranging from half a million to over 2 million. It partly depends on what you count as English words, and partly on where you go looking for them.

Consider the problems if someone asked you to count the number of words in English. You would immediately find thousands of cases

'You wouldn't happen to have a dictionary would you?
They say there's an axolotl on the loose.'
Punch, 16 October 1985

where you would not be sure whether to count one word or two. In writing, it is often not clear whether something should be written as a single word, as two words, or hyphenated. Is it *washing machine* or *washing-machine*? *School children* or *schoolchildren*? *Flower pot*, *flower-pot* or *flowerpot*? Would you count all the items beginning with *foster* as new words: *foster brother*, *foster care*, *foster child*, *foster father*, *foster home*, etc.? Or would you treat them as combinations of old words: *foster + brother*, *care*, and so on? This is a big problem for the dictionary-makers, who often reach different conclusions about what should be done.

What would you do with *get at*, *get by*, *get in*, *get off*, *get over*, and the dozens of other cases where *get* is used with an additional word? Would you count *get* once, for all of these, or would you say that, because these items have different meanings (*get at*, for example, can mean 'nag'), they should be counted separately? In which case, what about *get it?*, *get your own back*, *get your act together*, and all the other 'idioms'? Would you say that these had to be counted separately too? Would you count *kick the bucket* (meaning 'die') as three familiar words or as a single idiom? It hardly seems sensible to count the words separately, for *kick* here has nothing to do with moving the foot, nor is *bucket* a container.

If you let the meaning influence you (as it should), then you will find your word count growing very rapidly indeed. But as soon as you do this, you will start to worry about other meanings, even in single words. Is there a single meaning for *high* in *high tea*, *high priest* and *high season*? Is the *lock* on a door the same basic meaning as the *lock* on a canal? Should *ring* (the shape) be kept separate from *ring* (the sound)? Are such cases 'the same word with different meanings' or 'different words'? These are the daily decisions that any word-counter (or dictionary-compiler) must make.

WHOSE ENGLISH ARE WE COUNTING?

Sooner or later, the question would arise about the *kind* of vocabulary to include in the count. There wouldn't be a difficulty if the words were part of standard English – used by educated people throughout the English-speaking world (see p. 261). Obviously these have to be counted. But what about the vast numbers of words which are not found everywhere – words which are restricted to a particular country (such as Canada, Britain, India, or Australia), or to a particular part of a country (such as Wales, Yorkshire or Liverpool)?

They will include words like *stroller* (push-chair) and *station* (stock farm) from Australia, *bach* (holiday cottage) and *pakeha* (white person) from New Zealand, *dorp* (village) and *indaba* (conference) from South Africa, *cwm* (valley) and *eisteddfod* (competitive arts festival) from Wales, *faucet* (tap) and *fall* (autumn) from North America, *fortnight* (two weeks) and *nappy* (baby wear) from Britain, *loch* (lake) and *wee* (small) from Scotland, *dunny* (money) and *duppy* (ghost) from Jamaica, *lakh* (a hundred thousand) and *crore* (ten million) from India, and many more.

Regional dialect words have every right to be included in an English vocabulary count. They are English words, after all – even if they are used only in a single locality. But no one knows how many there are. Several big dictionary projects exist, cataloguing the local words used in some of these areas, but in many parts of the world where English is a mother-tongue or second language (see p. 2) there has been little or no research. And the smaller the locality, the greater the problem. Everyone knows that 'local' words exist: 'we have our own word for such-and-such round here'. Local dialect societies sometimes print lists of them, and dialect surveys try to keep records of them. But surveys are lengthy and expensive enterprises, and not many have been completed. As a result, most regional vocabulary – especially that used in cities – is never recorded. There must be thousands of distinctive words inhabiting such areas as Brooklyn, the East End of London, San Francisco, Edinburgh and Liverpool, none of which has ever appeared in any dictionary.

The more colloquial varieties of English, and slang in particular, also tend to be given inadequate treatment. In dictionary-writing, the tradition has been to take material only from the written language, and this has led to the compilers concentrating on educated, standard forms. They commonly leave out non-standard expressions, such as everyday slang and obscenities, as well as the slang of specific social groups and areas, such as the army, sport, thieves, public school, banking, or medicine. In 1937 Eric Partridge devoted a whole dictionary to this world of 'slang and unconventional English'. Some of the words it contained were thought to be so shocking that

---

Dialect words

A small sample of local vocabulary from Liverpool – a dialect that
has come to be widely heard in recent years, in records, films,
television serials, and plays. Several of the words are also found
elsewhere (though not always with the same meaning).

airyated	upset, excited	la	lad (used to
bevvy	drink		address someone)
chippy	fish and chip shop	moggy	cat
cob	bad mood (as in	ollies	marbles
	He's got a cob on)	sarneys	sandwiches
diddyman	small man	scuffer	policeman
entry	back alley	spec	view (as in *I've*
gear	excellent, fine		*got a good spec*)
jam butty	bread and jam	wack	mister (used to
jigger	back alley		address someone)
judy	girl-friend	yocker	spit
kecks	trousers	youse	you (plural)

---

for several years many libraries banned it from their open shelves!

Keeping track of slang, though, is one of the most difficult tasks in vocabulary study, because it can be so shifting and short-lived. The life-span of a word or phrase may be only a few years – or even months. The expression might fall out of use in one social group, and reappear some time later in another. Who knows exactly how much use is still made today of such early jazz-world words as *groovy*, *hip*, *square*, *solid*, *cat*, and *have a ball*? Or how much use is made of the new slang terms derived from computers, such as *he's integrated* (= organized) or *she's high res* (= very alert, from 'high resolution')? Which words for 'being drunk' are now still current: *canned*, *blotto*, *squiffy*, *jagged*, *paralytic*, *smashed* . . . ? And how do we get at the vast special vocabulary which has now grown up in the drugs world? Word-lovers from time to time make collections, but the feeling always exists that the items listed are only the tip of a huge lexical iceberg.

SOME MARGINAL CASES

Estimating the vocabulary size of English is further complicated by the existence of thousands of uncertain cases – words which you wouldn't feel were part of the 'central' vocabulary of the language. On the other hand, you might well feel unhappy about leaving them out.

What would you do with all the abbreviations that exist, for example? A recent dictionary of abbreviated words lists over 400,000 entries. It includes old and familiar forms such as *flu*, *hi-fi*, *deb*, *FBI*, *UFO*, *NATO* and *BA*. There are large numbers of new technical terms, such as *VHS* (the video system), *AIDS*, and all the terms from computerspeak (*PC*, *RAM*, *ROM*, *BASIC*, *bit*) and space travel (*SRB* – solid rocket boosters, *OMS* – orbital manœuvring system, etc.). And there are thousands of coinages which have restricted regional currency, such as *RAC* (Royal Automobile Club), *AAA* (Automobile Association of America), or which reflect local organizations and attitudes – with varying levels of seriousness – such as *MADD* (Mothers Against Drunk Driving) and *DAMM* (Drinkers Against Mad Mothers).

Because these forms are dependent on 'bigger' words for their existence, you might well decide not to include them in your count. On the other hand, you could argue that they are often more important than the original words, and that the original words may not even be remembered or known (as many people find with such forms as *AIDS*). Personally, I would include them in my word count, but some dictionaries do not.

There are other marginal cases. What would you do with the names of people, places and things in the world? Should *London*, *Whitehall*, *Paris*, *Munich*, and *Spain* be included in your word count? You might think they should, especially knowing that many of these words are different in other languages (*München* and *España*, for example). However, it isn't usual to include them as part of the vocabulary of English, because the vast majority can appear in *any* language. Whichever language you speak, if you walk down Pall Mall, you can refer to where you are by using the words *Pall Mall* in your own language. The old music hall repartee relied on this point:

A: I say, I say, I say. I can speak French.
B: You can speak French? I didn't know that. Let me hear you speak French.
A: Paris, Marseilles, Nice, Calais, Jean-Paul Sartre . . .

The same applies to the names of people, animals, objects (such as trains and boats), and so on. Proper names aren't part of any one language: they are universal. However, it's important to note the usages where these words do take on special meanings, as in *Has Whitehall said anything about this?* Here, *Whitehall* means 'the Government'; it isn't just a place name. Dictionaries *would* usually include this kind of usage in their list. But it's not at all clear how many uses of this kind there are.

Fauna and flora present a further type of difficulty. Around a million species of insects have already been described, for example, which means that there must be around a million designations available to enable English-speaking specialists to talk about their subject. How much of this can be included in our word count? The largest dictionaries already include hundreds of thousands of technical and scientific terms, but none of them includes more than a fraction of the insect names – usually just the most important species. Add this total to that required for birds, fish, and other animals, and the theoretical size of the English vocabulary increases enormously.

TYPES OF VOCABULARY

It may not be possible to arrive at a satisfactory total for English vocabulary. The core vocabulary, as reflected in such dictionaries as the unabridged *Oxford English Dictionary* or *Webster's Third New International* seems to be something over half a million; but if we include some of the above categories, this total will increase by a factor of three or four. How is it all done? How does the language manage to construct so many words? How are new words formed?

There are really only a few ways of creating new words. Quite a large number are simply taken over from other languages; they are called 'borrowings', or 'loan-words' (slightly misleading expressions, when we consider that the language does not give them back!). A list of foreign words in English is given on p. 38 (it omits many details about the exact route these words took as they came into English – *tomato*, for example, did not come directly from the Central American language Nahuatl, but via Spanish). It's clear that an extraordinary range of languages is involved, with some (such as French, Latin, and Greek) being repeatedly used over the centuries. The reasons for this state of affairs are discussed in Part III.

Some sources of Modern English words

Afrikaans: trek, apartheid

American Indian languages: moccasin, wigwam, squaw

Anglo-Saxon: God, house, rain, sea, beer, sheep, gospel, rainbow, Sunday, crafty, wisdom, understand

Arabic: sultan, sheikh, hashish, harem, ghoul, algebra

Australian languages: dingo, wombat, boomerang, budgerigar

Chinese: ketchup, sampan, chow mein, kaolin, typhoon, yen (= desire)

Czech: robot

Dutch: frolic, cruise, slim

Eskimo: kayak, igloo, anorak

Finnish: sauna

French: aunt, debt, fruit, table, challenge, venison, medicine, justice, victory, sacrifice, prince, castle, dinner, grotesque, garage, moustache, unique, brochure, police, montage, voyeur

Gaelic: brogue, galore, leprechaun, banshee

German: waltz, hamster, zinc, plunder, poodle, paraffin, yodel, angst, strafe, snorkel

Greek: crisis, topic, stigma, coma, dogma, neurosis, pylon, therm, euphoria, schizophrenia

Hawaiian: ukulele, hula

Hebrew: shibboleth, kosher, kibbutz

Hindi: guru, pundit, sari, thug

Hungarian: goulash, paprika

Italian: sonnet, traffic, bandit, opera, balcony, soprano, lava, arcade, studio, scampi, timpani, ballot

Japanese: kimono, tycoon, judo

Latin: diocese, index, orbit, equator, compact, discuss, genius, circus, focus, ultimatum, alibi, aquarium

Malagasy: raffia

Malay: sarong, amok, gong

Nahuatl: tomato

Norwegian: ski, fjord, cosy

Old Norse: both, egg, knife, low, sky, take, they, want

Persian: sofa, shah, caravan, divan, bazaar, shawl

Portuguese: flamingo, buffalo, pagoda, veranda, marmalade

Quechuan: llama

Russian: rouble, czar, steppe, sputnik, intelligentsia

Sanskrit: yoga, swastika

Spanish: sherry, cannibal, banana, potato, cigar, rodeo, stampede, canyon, cafeteria, supremo, marijuana, junta

Swahili: safari, bwana

Swedish: ombudsman

Tahitian: tattoo

Tamil: catamaran

Tibetan: sherpa, yeti, yak

Tongan: taboo

Turkish: yoghurt, kiosk, fez, caftan, bosh, caviare

Welsh: crag, coracle, corgi

Yiddish: schemozzle, schmaltz

An even more important way of creating new words is to add prefixes and suffixes to old ones. There are over 100 common prefixes and suffixes in English, and they can be used singly or in various combinations. The prefixes include *anti-* (*antifreeze*), *co-* (*co-pilot*), *de-* (*defraud*), *ex-* (*ex-husband*), *non-* (*non-smoker*), *super-* (*supermarket*), *ultra-* (*ultra-modern*), and *un-* (*undecided*). Among the suffixes are -*able* (*drinkable*), -*ation* (*starvation*), -*eer* (*profiteer*), -*ful* (*glassful*), -*ish* (*childish*), -*let* (*booklet*), -*ness* (*goodness*) and -*ly* (*friendly*). Adding strings of prefixes and suffixes can produce such monster words as *indestructibility* and *antidisestablishmentarianism*.

A simple way of making new words is just to change the way they are used in a sentence, without adding any prefixes or suffixes. This process is known as *conversion*. Verbs can be converted from nouns, as when we say we're going to *tape a programme* or *butter some bread*. Nouns can be made from adjectives, as in *He's a natural* or *They're regulars*. Adjectives can be made from nouns, as in *a Liverpool accent*. Verbs can be made from prepositions, as in *to down tools*. And there are several other types.

Another important technique is to join two words together to make a different word, a *compound*, as in *blackbird*, *shopkeeper*, *stowaway*, *air-conditioning* and *frying-pan*. Note that the meaning of a compound isn't simply found by adding together the meaning of its parts: a *blackbird* isn't the same as a *black bird*, for instance. Also note, as we've already seen, that compounds aren't always written as single words. There are hundreds of thousands of compounds in English, especially in scientific fields.

There are several other ways in which new words can be formed, especially in the spoken language. We have already seen the importance of abbreviations – shortening a word (*phone*), using its initial letters (*NATO*), or blending two words (*brunch*, *breathalyser*). And there's also the curious process whereby new words can be made by repeating an element, or changing it very slightly, as in *goody-goody*, *ping-pong*, *criss-cross* and *mishmash*.

NEW WORDS FOR OLD

English vocabulary has a remarkable range, flexibility, and adaptability. Thanks to the periods of contact with foreign languages and its readiness to coin new words out of old elements, English seems to have far more words in its core vocabulary than other languages. For example, alongside *kingly* (from Anglo–Saxon) we find *royal* (from French) and *regal* (from Latin). There are many such sets of words, which add greatly to our opportunities to express subtle shades of meaning at various levels of style (see p. 176).

Of course, not everyone likes the rate at which English vocabulary continues to expand. There is often an antagonistic reaction to new words. Computer jargon has its adherents, but it also has its critics. Old rural dialect words may be admired, but the new words from urban dialects are often reviled. The latest slang is occasionally thought of as vivid and exciting, but more often it is condemned as imprecise and sloppy. The news that fresh varieties of English are developing around the world, bringing in large numbers of new words, is seen by some as a good thing, adding still further to the expressive potential of the language; but many people shake their heads, and mutter about the language going downhill. We shall address this question in Chapter 14.

People take vocabulary very personally, and will readily admit to having 'pet hates' about the way other people use words. Vocabulary – and especially change in vocabulary – is one of the most controversial issues in the field of language study. Some people are simply against language change on principle. Others, more sensibly, become worried only when they perceive a usage to be developing which seems to remove a useful distinction in meaning, or to add an ambiguity. They draw public attention to the way words of closely related appearance tend to be confused in popular use, such as *disinterested* and *uninterested*, *imply* and *infer*, or *militate* and *mitigate*. The need for precision is paramount in their minds.

It's difficult to say whether this kind of criticism can halt a change in meaning or use. The history of the language shows how thousands of words have altered their meaning over time, or added new meanings. The vocabulary now is not what it was in Shakespeare's day, and Shakespeare's vocabulary wasn't the same as Chaucer's. In Anglo-Saxon, *meat* meant 'food'; today, it means a certain type of food (apart from in such words as *mincemeat*). *Notorious* once meant 'widely known'; today it means 'widely and unfavourably known'. Similarly, *pretty* once meant 'ingenious' ('a pretty plot'), a *villain* was a farm labourer, *naughty* meant 'worth nothing', and a *publican* was a public servant.

People do not object to these changes in meaning today, or even notice them, because the new uses have been with us for a very long time. Objections are only made to words that are currently in the process of change. For instance, many people complain that they can no longer use *gay*, now that the meaning of 'homosexual' has been added to the previous meaning of 'joyful'. And they object to the over-use of words and phrases in place of more precise or economical alternatives, such as *nice*, *literally* (used as an intensifying word, as in *there were literally millions*), and *at this moment in time*. The worst judgement people can pass on an expression is to call it a cliché.

There is certainly a need to keep a careful eye on our use of words, and on the way other people use them. If what we say or write is unclear, ambiguous, or unintelligible, we do no service to ourselves or our listeners/readers. But critical monitoring of current usage is not the same as a blind opposition to all new words and meanings, such as objecting to all new verbs ending in *-ize* on principle (one of the commonest vocabulary complaints made by letter-writers to the BBC).

Do such objections do any good? It is difficult to know whether they can raise public consciousness sufficiently to influence the course of language change. The processes that govern change seem too complex and deeply rooted in society for the voices of a few individuals to have much effect. Certainly, the evidence seems to support the opposite view. For example, the objections which were being raised to new *-ize* verbs a few years ago have not stopped the acceptance of dozens of these verbs into the language.

A good way of illustrating this point is to look at the usage manuals which were around a generation ago, and compare them with those that are being published now. The first edition of Sir Ernest Gowers' *The Complete Plain Words* appeared in 1954. It included warnings about the use of *publicize*, *hospitalize*, *finalize*, *casualize* (employ casual labour) and *diarize* (enter into a diary). The first three of these have since come to be accepted, despite all the warnings. (Why the last two did not also win acceptance isn't at all clear.) In the third edition of Gowers' book, published in 1986, the objections to *publicize* and the others are no longer cited. Instead, new *-ize* words are mentioned as currently attracting opposition, such as *prioritize* and *routinize*.

What does the future hold for these new words? Will they still be used in a generation's time? No one can say. Linguists have excellent techniques for analysing vocabulary's past, but they have not yet discovered a means of predicting its future.

The etymological fallacy

When people object to the way a word has taken on a new meaning, they usually appeal to the word's history (or etymology) for support. The older meaning, it is said, is the 'correct' meaning. For example, the word *decimate* is nowadays widely used to mean 'destroy a lot of'. Those who know the Latin origins of the word, however, point out that originally the word meant 'destroy one tenth of' (*decem* being Latin for 'ten'). They therefore object to the modern usage, which they call 'loose' or 'careless', and insist that *decimate* be used 'properly'. (Ironically, this virtually bans the word from everyday use, for it is difficult indeed to imagine contexts where it proves necessary to destroy exactly one tenth of something – which is presumably why the word broadened its meaning in the first place!)

Reasoning of this kind is common. The 'real' meaning of *history* is 'investigation', because that is what the word meant in Greek. The 'real' meaning of *nice* is 'fastidious', because that is what it meant in Shakespeare's time (a sense still found in such phrases as *a nice distinction*). Always, an older meaning is preferred to the modern one.

Such reasoning is tempting, but we must guard against it. If it is true that the older a meaning, the 'truer' it is, we cannot (to take this last example) stop with Shakespeare. The word *nice* can be traced back to Old French, where it meant 'silly', and then back to Latin, where *nescius* meant 'ignorant'. We can even take the word further back in time, and guess at what it might have meant in the language from which Latin derived (Indo-European) – perhaps a meaning to do with 'cut'. So what is the correct meaning of *nice*, if we insist on looking to history? Is it 'fastidious', 'silly', 'ignorant'? Or must we conclude that we do not know what *nice* means, because its original use in Indo-European is obscure or lost?

The absurdity of the argument should be plain. If we argue from etymology, we shall never know what a word 'really' means. What a word may have meant at one point in its history is not relevant for later periods. It is fascinating to trace the changes in meaning which have taken place, but this should not lead us to condemn new senses, and to keep old senses artificially alive. Etymology is never a true guide to meaning. To believe the opposite is to engage in the 'etymological fallacy'.

How large is Your Vocabulary?

At two years old the average vocabulary is about three hundred words. By the age of five it is about five thousand. By twelve it is about 12,000. And there for most people it rests – at the same size as the repertoire employed by a popular daily newspaper . . . Graduates have an average vocabulary of about 23,000 words.

Jane Bouttell, *Guardian*, 12 August 1986

Shakespeare had one of the largest vocabularies of any English writer, some 30,000 words. (Estimates of an educated person's vocabulary today vary, but it is probably about half this, 15,000.)

Robert McCrum, *et al.*, *The Story of English*, 1986, p. 102

There seems to be no more agreement about the size of an adult's vocabulary than there is about the total number of words in English. Estimates do indeed vary. I have heard people talk of the 'educated' total as being in excess of 50,000, even 100,000 words. Part of the problem, I imagine, is what is meant by 'educated'.

How can we find out the truth of the matter? We might tape-record everything we said and heard for a month, or a year, and keep a record of everything we read and wrote. Then we could tabulate all the words, mark which ones we understood and which we failed to understand, and count up. But life is too short.

An alternative, which can be carried out in a few hours, gives a fairly good idea. You take a medium-sized dictionary – one which contains about 100,000 entries – and test your knowledge of a sample of the words it contains. A sample of about 2 per cent of the whole, taken from various sections of the alphabet, gives a reasonable result. In other words, if such a dictionary were 2,000 pages long, you would have a sample of forty pages.

Part of one person's vocabulary estimates, using the headwords of the *Longman Dictionary of the English Language* (90,000 + headwords).

	KNOWN			USED		
	Well	Vaguely	No	Often	Occasionally	Never
cablese		✓				✓
cable stitch	✓			✓		
cable television	✓				✓	
cablevision		✓				✓
cableway			✓			✓
cabman		✓				✓
cabob			✓			✓
Caboc			✓			✓
cabochon (noun)			✓			✓
cabochon (adverb)			✓			✓
caboodle	✓				✓	
caboose		✓				✓
cabotage			✓			✓
cab-rank	✓			✓		
cabriole			✓			✓
cabriolet			✓			✓
cabstand	✓					✓
cacanny (noun)			✓			✓
cacanny (verb)			✓			✓
cacao		✓			✓	
cacao bean		✓			✓	
cacao butter			✓			✓
cachalot			✓			✓
cache (noun)	✓				✓	
cache (verb)			✓			✓
cachectic			✓			✓
cache-sexe			✓			✓
cachet	✓				✓	
cachexia			✓			✓
cachinnate			✓			✓
cachinnation			✓			✓
cachou	✓				✓	
cachucha			✓			✓
cacique			✓			✓

It's wise to break this sample down into a series of selections, say of five pages each, from different parts of the dictionary. It wouldn't be sensible to take all forty pages from the letter U, for instance, as a large number of these words would begin with *un-*, and this would hardly be typical. On the other hand, prefixes are an important aspect of English word formation (see p. 39), so we mustn't exclude them entirely. Similarly, it would be silly to include a section containing a large number of scientific words (such as the section containing *electro-*), or rare words (such as those beginning with X).

One possible sample, which tries to balance various factors of this kind, takes sections of five complete pages from each of the following parts of the dictionary: C-, EX-, J-, O-, PL-, SC-, TO-, and UN-. Begin with the first full page in each case – in other words, don't include the very first page of the C section, if the heading takes up a large part of the page; ignore the first few EX- entries, if they start towards the bottom of a page; and so on.

Draw up a table of words like the one on p. 45. On the left-hand side write in the headwords from the dictionary, as they appear. Do not include any *parts* of words which the dictionary might list, such as *cac-* or *-caine*, but *do* include words with affixes, such as *cadetship* alongside *cadet*, even if the former is listed only as *-ship* within the entry on *cadet*. In short, include all items in bold face within an entry. Include phrases or idioms (e.g. *call the tune*). Ignore alternative spellings (e.g. *caeserian/caesarian*).

The table has two columns: the first asks you to say whether you think you know the word, from having heard or seen it used; the second whether you think you actually use it yourself in your speech or writing. This is the difference between *passive* and *active* vocabulary. Within each column, there are three judgements to be made. For passive vocabulary, you ask, 'Do I know the word well, vaguely, or not at all?' For active vocabulary, you ask, 'Do I use the word often, occasionally, or not at all?' Place a tick in the appropriate column. If you are uncertain, use the final column. You may need to look at the definition or examples given next to the word, before you can decide. Ignore the number of meanings the word has: if you know or use the word in *any* of its meanings, that will do. (Deciding how many *meanings* of a word you know or use would be another, much vaster, project!)

When you've finished, add up the ticks in each column, and multiply the total by fifty (if the sample was 2 per cent of the whole). The total in the first column is probably an underestimate of your vocabulary size. And if you take the first two columns together, the total will probably be an overestimate.

This procedure of course doesn't allow for people who happen to know a large number of non-standard words that may not be in the dictionary (such as local dialect words). If you are such a person, the figures will have to be adjusted again – but that will be pure guesswork.

Here are the estimates for the first two columns, as filled in by a female office secretary in her fifties:

Words known		*Words used*	
Well	30,050	Often	16,300
Vaguely	8,250	Occasionally	15,200
	38,300		31,500

The results are interesting. Note that passive vocabulary is much larger than active. This will always be the case. Note also that it's easier to make up your mind about the words you definitely know than the words you frequently use.

Even allowing for wishful thinking, sampling bias, and other such factors, it would seem that some of the widely quoted estimates of our vocabulary size are a long way from reality.

Which dictionary?

Plotting the words you know presupposes that you have a good dictionary at home. But what counts as a good dictionary? Here are twelve criteria to bear in mind if you are buying a new one, or evaluating an old one.

1. *Does it have the words you want to look up?* Keep a note of some of the words which have puzzled you in recent weeks, and use them as a test. Don't assume that the number of items mentioned on the cover is a guide to content. Dictionaries count their words in different ways, and a book

containing 50,000 'words' may actually contain less information than one containing 40,000 'entries'. The first might count *perfect*, *perfectible* and *perfectibility* as three separate items; the second might count them all under the one heading *perfect* (*-ible*, *-ibility*).

2. *Is it up-to-date?* Given the speed at which English vocabulary is expanding (see p. 34), any dictionary which hasn't been revised in the past five years is likely to contain omissions of importance. Keep a note of a few new words you have come across (e.g. *yuppy*, *yomp*), and see whether they are included.

3. *Does it have good international coverage?* Use some of the words on p. 34 to see whether American, Australian, and other varieties of English are included. Check that the dictionary tells you which area the word is used in (e.g. that *nappy* is British). Look at the list of abbreviations at the front of the book to see which geographical labels are given.

4. *Can you find the word or phrase you want?* Try looking up some words with alternative spellings (e.g. *esophagus* and *oesophagus*) and see whether both are included. Or idioms, such as *kick the bucket*. Check the preface to the dictionary to see what guidance is given.

5. *Are the entries clearly laid out?* Look at a long entry, such as *get* or *take*, and see how easy it is to find your way about in it. Are different senses, examples, and labels clearly distinguished?

6. *Are the definitions clear?* Do you need the dictionary to look up the words used in the definition (e.g. *dog* as 'carnivorous quadruped . . .')? Are related senses grouped together in a clear way? Is there any sign of 'vicious circularity' – defining X as Y, and Y as X? In particular, do the entries contain examples? Very often a definition is unclear without an accompanying real-life example (a *citation*) of how the word is used.

7. *Does it contain lists of related words?* Some dictionaries group words of similar or different meaning together, and discuss the differences between them, e.g. *clever*, *adroit*, *cunning* and *ingenious*. Does it at least give a cross-reference to words of related meaning?

8. *Does it give guidance about usage?* Check some well-known problems and see what the dictionary says about them, such as *disinterested*, *will/shall* and *hopefully*. Is there a large number of labels telling you about the stylistic level of the word, e.g. *formal*, *derogatory*, *archaic*, and *technical*? Is any information given about grammatical usage, apart from labelling the part of speech – noun, verb, etc. – a word belongs to?

9. *What information does it give about pronunciation?* Does it give alternative pronunciations, where these exist (as with *controversy*)? Is a clear system used for showing how words are pronounced? Is the stress-pattern of the word clearly shown?

10. *Does it contain information about where a word comes from (etymology)?* Does the dictionary give only a recent source (e.g. *tomato* Spanish), an original source (e.g. *tomato* Nahuatl), or trace the historical path the word has taken?

11. *Does it contain encyclopedic information?* Some dictionaries contain information about people, places and events. Some have pictures of objects otherwise difficult to explain (such as flags, birds, parts of a car). Some add separate sections giving special data, such as abbreviations, or tables of weights and measures.

12. *Will it last?* Will the binding allow it to be opened out flat? Is the paper of a good quality?

4

££££££££££

Pronunciation

How fast do you talk? One way to find out is to tape-record a piece of conversation, locate a reasonably fluent passage, and count how much is said in, say, thirty seconds or a minute. If you can't find a passage that isn't full of pauses and hesitation noises, then try reading aloud. Start at the top of a page, and time yourself reading aloud as naturally as you can for exactly one minute. Then count up.

'Quick, Raymond – is it Iranian as in *barn*,
or is it Iranian as in *rain*?'

But count what? What's the best way of calculating how much is said? The obvious method would be to count the number of *words* in the passage, but in fact this doesn't give a very helpful result. After all, if you're using many long words, you'll end up with a lower 'score' than if the passage consisted mainly of short words. A better technique is to count the number of syllables, or 'beats'. Some words contain just one syllable (*the*, *cat*); some have two (*po-lice*, *en-joy*); and some have three (*e-le-phant*, *di-vi-sive*) or more (*de-ve-lop-ment*, *in-con-se-quen-tial*).

In everyday conversation, people speak at about five or six syllables a second – around 300 a minute. This is an average, of course. Some people are naturally fast, and others naturally slow, in their manner of speech. And speed varies greatly depending on the context. When reading aloud, the average is much lower – around 250 syllables per minute (spm). Reading the news on radio or television may produce even slower speeds, of around 200 spm. By contrast, in the middle of an exciting story, in intimate surroundings, a speaker can easily reach speeds of 500 spm – though not usually for more than a few seconds at a time. Foreigners may think English people speak quickly – sometimes they do!

To understand what happens in English pronunciation, we have to remember the speed at which speech normally takes place. If we don't, we will end up with an artificial or misleading picture of what the language is like. To take just two examples. Many people think that it is essential to pronounce every sound in a word – to 'follow the spelling'. They then get very critical of public speakers who leave sounds out, or who put extra sounds in. Or again, they think that speech is simply a matter of stringing together a series of vowels and consonants – that all we'd have to do, if we were teaching English to foreigners, would be teach them how to pronounce each sound separately, and perfect pronunciation would come as soon as the sounds were put together. Both these views, as we'll see, are some distance from reality.

THE SEGMENTS OF PRONUNCIATION

We are used to seeing the written language as a sequence of letters, separated by different amounts of space. This is how we were taught to write. We formed our letters one at a time, and then slowly and effortfully brought them together in 'joined-up' writing. We learned to call some of these letters 'vowels' (*a*, *e*, *i*, *o*, and *u*) and the others 'consonants'.

Although we all learned to listen and speak long before we could read and write, it is one of life's ironies that we don't learn *about* spoken language until long after we have learned to handle written language. As a result, it is inevitable that we think of speech in the same frame of reference as we do writing. We even use the same terms, and it can come as something of a shock to realize that these terms don't have the same meaning.

A good example of this problem is the way we have to re-think the idea that 'there are five vowels' when we begin to discuss speech. There are in fact as many as twenty vowel sounds in most English accents. The set of vowels used in the most prestigious accent of England, 'Received Pronunciation' (see p. 62), is given below. Because there aren't enough written vowel symbols to go round, it's necessary to develop a special system of transcription (a *phonetic transcription*) to identify each one. The symbols used in one such system are given alongside each vowel. (Note how many different spellings the vowels have – a problem we discuss in Chapter 5.)

The difference between spoken and written consonants is not quite so dramatic. There are 21 consonant letters in the written alphabet,

---

The vowel system of Received Pronunciation

The transcription is the one used by A. C. Gimson in *An Introduction to the Pronunciation of English* (London, 1980).

/iː/	as in *sea, feet, me, field*	/ɜː/	as in *bird, her, turn*
/ɪ/	as in *him, village, women*	/ə/	as in *butter, sofa, about*
/e/	as in *get, head, Thames*	/eɪ/	as in *ape, waist, they*
/æ/	as in *sat, hand, plait*	/aɪ/	as in *time, cry, die, high*
/ʌ/	as in *sun, son, blood, does*	/ɔɪ/	as in *boy, noise, voice*
/ɑː/	as in *father, car, calm*	/əʊ/	as in *so, road, toe, know*
/ɒ/	as in *dog, swan, cough*	/aʊ/	as in *out, how, house*
/ɔː/	as in *cord, saw, all, more*	/ɪə/	as in *deer, here, fierce*
/ʊ/	as in *put, wolf, good*	/ɛə/	as in *care, air, bear*
/uː/	as in *soon, do, soup, shoe*	/ʊə/	as in *poor, sure, tour*

The consonant system of Received Pronunciation

/p/	as in *pie*	/s/	as in *so*
/b/	as in *by*	/z/	as in *zoo*
/t/	as in *tie*	/ʃ/	as in *shoe*
/d/	as in *die*	/ʒ/	as in *beige*
/k/	as in *coo*	/h/	as in *hi*
/g/	as in *go*	/m/	as in *my*
/ʧ/	as in *chew*	/n/	as in *no*
/ʤ/	as in *jaw*	/ŋ/	as in *sing*
/f/	as in *fee*	/l/	as in *lie*
/v/	as in *view*	/r/	as in *row*
/θ/	as in *thin*	/w/	as in *way*
/ð/	as in *the*	/j/	as in *you*

Note that consonants may also appear in 'clusters', such as *stone*, *cups* and *try*. Up to three consonants may be used together at the beginning of a spoken word in English (as in *string*). Up to four consonants may be used together at the end, though not always very comfortably (as in *twelfths*/twelfθs/and *glimpsed*/glɪmpst/).

and there are 24 consonant sounds in Received Pronunciation (see above). Several of these sounds would be spelled with two letters in writing. It's important to appreciate that this is only a spelling convention: the first sound in the word *thin* is spelled with two letters, but it is still only *one* sound, made by the tip of the tongue between the teeth. The question 'How many consonants are there at the beginning of *thin*?' has two answers, therefore: 'Two, in writing', 'One, in speech'.

But vowels and consonants have one thing in common: they provide us with the basic building blocks, or *segments*, of speech, as they do of writing. By changing these segments, we alter the shape of words, and thus their meaning. Ringing the changes produces *man*, *map*, *mat*, *met*, *let*, *lit*, *slit*, *spit*, and so on. By changing one of the segments, we can change the meaning of a word. Sounds which can do this are called *phonemes* in linguistic studies.

This kind of approach enables us to take any sentence and analyse it into a sequence of vowel and consonant segments. Here's an example, with the transcription showing how the sentence would be said 'word at a time':

I   should be   surprised   if John and   Mary were late.

aɪ ʃʊd   biː sɜː praɪzd ɪf ʤɒn ænd mɛərɪ wɜː leɪt

It appears from a transcription like this that speech is made up of a sequence of single sounds, and that the words are separated by tiny pauses. Many people do think of speech in this way, as if it were 'writing read aloud'. Once again, this is the result of being brainwashed by years of thinking of language as *written* language. In reality, it isn't at all like this. There is no tiny pause between each word. And we do not make first one sound with our vocal organs, then move on to the next, then the next, and so on.

The essential thing to appreciate about pronunciation is that sounds inevitably run together. A better impression of how speech works, in fact, would be to print the transcription like this:

aɪʃʊbɪspraɪzdɪfʤɒnəmɛərɪwəleɪt

This much more readily conveys the speed at which the sentence would be said, though it is much more difficult to read.

However, if you compare this transcription with the one above, you'll notice certain differences. The /d/ of *should* has disappeared. The vowel sound of *be* has changed. The first vowel of *surprised* has disappeared. The pronunciation of *and* has totally altered. And the vowel in *were* has been replaced. What is going on?

These differences aren't random. Changes in pronunciation are inevitable when we start to speed up our speech, and run words together. As we begin to speak a word, we use our vocal organs to make the first sound, but already our brain is planning how to make the second sound, and the third. This planning may be so advanced, in fact, that the brain may already have sent signals to the vocal organs telling them to get ready for these later sounds.

So, in the above sentence, the lips are preparing for the /b/ sound of *be* long before the tongue has finished pronouncing the /d/ sound at the end of *should*. The faster we speak, the less time there is for the tongue to do anything at all. And there comes a certain point when we simply do not try to keep the pronunciation separate. We allow our /d/ to come out as a /b/, or we just drop it altogether. In phonetics textbooks, when one sound is influenced by another in this way, it is called *assimilation*. When the sound is dropped completely, it is called *elision*.

There's another example of assimilation and elision later in the same sentence. When *and* is used before an /m/ sound, at normal conversational speed, the /d/ is dropped. (*And* is often spelled *'n* or *n'* in writing that tries to reflect the nature of informal speech.) The /n/ sound is also affected by the following /m/, and blends with it, to produce a single /m/.

You can practise the effects of assimilation and elision very easily. Try saying the above sentence slowly, with every sound produced

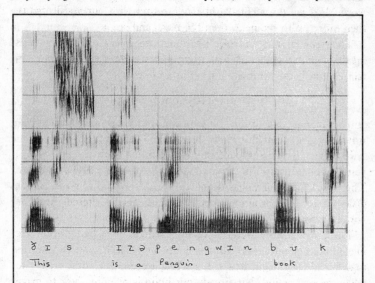

A spectrograph is a machine which turns sound waves into a pattern of marks on paper. The above pattern is what emerged when I recorded the sentence 'This is a Penguin book' on a spectrograph. The vowels and consonants can be identified, as shown by the symbols. But note that the gaps between the symbols aren't reflected by a similar pattern of gaps on the paper. The sound waves run continuously from one sound to the next, showing that the vocal organs are continuously in use.

clearly and distinctly. Now say it faster, but trying to keep all the sounds in. Now faster still . . . There will come a point when it proves impossible to 'get your tongue round all the sounds'. Something has to give. You will automatically start to assimilate and elide.

Or again, you can show the way the brain anticipates later sounds by watching what happens to your lips when you say certain words in front of a mirror. Take the two words *she* and *shoe*. First, practise the sounds separately. Say the *sh* consonant by itself – as if you were telling someone to be quiet. Note how you hold your lips. Then say the vowel of each word, still looking at the lips: first the /iː/ of *she*, then the /uː/ of *shoe*. Notice how the lips become very rounded for /uː/. Now say the whole word *shoe*, and watch what happens to the lips as you start to say the *sh*. They will start to become rounded in shape right away. This doesn't happen when you say the whole word *she*. Say the two one after the other: *she* – *shoe* – *she* – *shoe*. One *sh* is lip-rounded, the other is not.

It should be clear what is happening. The brain 'knows' that a vowel is due later in the word, and that it has to be pronounced with the lips rounded, so it sends instructions to the lips to get ready, right at the beginning of the word. As a result the boundary between the two sounds is extremely difficult to draw.

This kind of thing is happening all the time in speech. The most dramatic effects take place when we speak very quickly, but even in fairly slow speech it is impossible to eliminate them. Try saying *shoe* as slowly as you can, and you will still notice the 'pull' on the lips as the /uː/ sound approaches.

Here are some other sequences where the last sound of the first word is affected by the first sound of the second:

> *that boy* the /t/ sound changes into a /p/
> *that girl* the /t/ sound changes into a /k/
> *this shop* the /s/ sound changes into a /ʃ/

In such sequences as *next day*, *last chance*, *left turn*, and *kept quiet*, the /t/ at the end of the first word is dropped. We actually pronounce *lef' turn*, and it needs quite an effort of will to say the sequence with the first /t/ in. The same thing happens at the end of a word like *cyclists*. The *t* here is hardly ever pronounced in conversational speech.

Sometimes, the two sounds influence each other, so that they *both* change. This happens in such sequences as *would you*, where the /d/ of *would* and the /j/ of *you* combine to produce /ʤ/ (as in the first sound of *jaw*). Similarly, in *what you* (as in *I don't know what you see in her*), the two consonants combine to produce /tʃ/ (as in *chew*). Informal speech *What you doing?* is often written so as to show this blend, using *wotcha* or *wotcher*.

And lastly, an example of a sound being added. In Received Pronunciation, the *r* spelling at the end of a word is not sounded, when the word is said on its own: *four*, *mother*, *care*. But when it is followed by a vowel, at normal speed, the /r/ *is* pronounced: *four o'clock*. This is called a 'linking *r*'. By making this link, speakers find it easier to pronounce the words in a smooth sequence.

PRONUNCIATION WORRIES

It is of course possible, on special occasions, and with special training, to speak English in a way which avoids making most of the effects noted above. Actors declaiming the poetic lines of Shakespeare would generally avoid them (though they would be present in the prose passages representing everyday speech). And generally actors try to pronounce words clearly, paying special attention to their endings, and without rushing weak syllables. In this way, the words can be heard more clearly at the back of the theatre. But their speech is much slower than normal conversation as a result. In three renditions of Hamlet's 'To be, or not to be' speech by different actors, the speeds ranged from 130 to 190 spm – on average, half the speed of normal conversation.

The same point applies to other professional voice users, such as news broadcasters, radio announcers, priests, judges, and politicians. These people all have to speak in abnormal conditions – from a pulpit, in front of a crowd, into a microphone. In most cases, the listeners cannot see the speaker's face clearly enough (or see it at all, in the case of radio) to enable them to get clues from the movement of the lips, or from the facial expression, as to what is being said. To be sure that their speech stands the best chance of being understood by all, then, professional speakers know that they must speak relatively slowly and distinctly. If they do not, they risk criticism of being unintelligible, or of being too informal, casual, or 'sloppy'.

Enter the radio listeners, for the most common of all complaints to the BBC concerns the topic of pronunciation. And sloppy speech is the charge most often cited. The irony, of course, is that in almost every case the words called sloppy are in fact perfectly normal pronunciations in everyday speech, and everyone uses them. They include such forms as *Feb'ry* for *February*, *lib'ry* for *library*, *Antar'tic* for *Antarctic*, *as'matic* for *asthmatic*, *twel'ths* for *twelfths*, *patien's* for *patients*, *reco'nize* for *recognize*, and so on. It's very difficult in fact to say some of these words in their 'full' form – try pronouncing the second *t* in *patients*, for example. But many listeners, it seems, expect such precise articulation over the air, and are ready to demand it in writing, to the tune of thousands of letters each year.

Most listeners give just one reason for their complaint: a letter is there in the spelling, and so it should be pronounced. This is another example of the widespread belief, mentioned above, that speech is a poor relation of writing. We always need to remind ourselves that speech came first, in the history of our species, and that we all learn to speak before we learn to write. To be worried about our pronunciation because it does not match the spelling is a strange reversal of priorities. We also need to remember that pronunciation patterns have changed radically since the days when the spelling system was laid down. English spelling hasn't been a good guide to pronunciation for hundreds of years (see Chapter 5).

But despite all this, many people do get very angry when sounds are left out that they think ought to be there, or sounds are put in which they think ought not to be. Probably the most famous case of this last point is the use of an 'intrusive *r*' by speakers of Received Pronunciation: the insertion of an /r/ between vowels, when there is no *r* in the spelling. The most well-known instance, because of its frequency in the news, is *law and order* – widely known as 'Laura Norder'.

One listener sent in a collection of over 100 intrusive *r*s which he had heard in one day's listening. He included examples like *Shah (r) of Persia*, *draw(r)ing*, and *awe(r)-inspiring*. These are the noticeable ones, because the /r/ stands out clearly after the *ah/aw* vowels, which are said with the mouth quite widely open. It's much more difficult to hear this kind of /r/ when it occurs after the less sonorous /ə/ vowel

– the vowel that we use at the end of words like *sofa* or *Persia*. Unless Received Pronunciation speakers are taking extreme care, and speaking very self-consciously, they automatically put an /r/ into such phrases as *Africa(r) and Asia*, *an area(r) of disagreement*, and *drama(r) and music*. I have a tape recording of a critic vociferously condemning the intrusive *r* in *law and order*, in the course of which he said 'the idea of an intrusive *r* is obnoxious', putting in an /r/ at the end of *idea*!

Where does the intrusive *r* come from? It's the result of these speakers unconsciously extending a pattern already present in their accent, as found in the linking *r* sequence described above. It is important to notice that, although there are thousands of English words which end in the letter *r*, only four kinds of vowel are involved: /ɔː/, as in *four*, /ɑː/ as in *car*, /ɜː/ as in *fur*, and /ə/ as in *mother*. What has happened is that, over the years, the linking /r/ has been extended to *all* words ending in one of these four vowels, when they're followed by another vowel. The effect is most noticeable in words ending in /ɔː/, as in *law and order*, because there are in fact not very many such words in the language, so the usage tends to stand out.

Of course, explaining why a pronunciation has developed doesn't explain why some people have come to hate it. It's the same with other areas of usage. Why do some people hate *hopefully* (see p. 29)? The reason is likely to be something to do with the way one social group, at some time in the past, adopted a usage in order to keep themselves apart from another social group which did not. In particular, an accent comes to be used like a badge, showing a person's social identity. At any one time, there are several pronunciation patterns which are 'loaded' in this way. Current examples include 'dropping the *h*' ('*ospital* for *hospital*) and 'dropping the *g*' (*walkin'* for *walking*). These days such forms are considered to be uneducated – though a century ago, they were often to be found in cultured speech (as in the upper-class use of *huntin'*, *shootin' and fishin'*).

All of this presents radio managers with a problem, of course. Although only a minority of listeners are antagonized by such matters, none the less they are antagonized – and this is not what radio broadcasting is meant to be about. Announcers and presenters who are sensitive to these issues therefore often go out of their way to avoid using a pronunciation which they know will upset people. They

Controversies of the 1980s

The following list includes many of the words which have
alternative pronunciations in current English. The asterisk
indicates the pronunciation recommended in the 1981 BBC
guide compiled by Robert Burchfield.

adversary	stress on *1st or 2nd syllable
apartheid	vowel in 3rd syllable as in *height* or *hate
apparatus	vowel in 3rd syllable as in *car* or **fate*
applicable	stress on *1st or 2nd syllable
ate	vowel as in *set* or *late*
centenary	vowel in 2nd syllable as in *ten* or **teen*
centrifugal	stress on *2nd or 3rd syllable
comparable	stress on *1st or 2nd syllable
contribute	stress on 1st or *2nd syllable
controversy	stress on *1st or 2nd syllable
deity	vowel in 1st syllable as in *say* or **see*
derisive	s in 2nd syllable as in **rice* or *rise*
dilemma	vowel in 1st syllable as in **did* or *die*
diphtheria	ph as */f/ or /p/
dispute	stress on 1st or *2nd syllable
economic	vowel in 1st syllable as in *met* or *me* (both accepted)
envelope	vowel in 1st syllable as in **den* or *don*
furore	said as *3 syllables or 2
homosexual	vowel in 1st syllable as in **hot* or *home*
inherent	vowel in 2nd syllable as in **see* or *set*
kilometre	stress on *1st or 2nd syllable
longitude	ng as in **range* or *long*
medicine	said as *2 syllables or 3
migraine	vowel in 1st syllable as in **me* or *my*
pejorative	stress on 1st or *2nd syllable
plastic	vowel in 1st syllable as in **cat* or *car*
primarily	stress on *1st or 2nd syllable
privacy	vowel in 1st syllable as in **sit* or *sigh*
sheikh	vowel as in *see* or **say*
Soviet	vowel in 1st syllable as in **so* or *cot*
status	vowel in 1st syllable as in *sat* or **state*
subsidence	vowel in 2nd syllable as in *Sid* or **side*
trait	final t *silent or sounded

may go through their scripts and underline problem cases. Far more than the intrusive *r* is involved, of course. The problems include changes in stress (e.g. *dispute* vs *dispute*) and the pronunciation of individual words (e.g. saying *recognize* with or without the *g*). A selection of issues is given on p. 60. Foreign words pose special problems, as do the names of people and places. A Pronunciation Unit has long been established at the BBC to help answer queries about such matters. During the 1986 World Cup matches, the Unit had to issue guidelines to its commentators about the players, referees, linesmen, managers, and others involved – it took twenty-seven pages.

The problem becomes particularly acute if a radio channel decides to adopt a policy of friendliness or informality in response to listener demand. To make speech come across in a normally informal way, it is necessary to speed it up, and to introduce assimilations and elisions. If these are not introduced, either because they lessen the clarity of what is said or because they attract listener criticism, the speech will inevitably sound formal, clipped, and controlled. But listeners cannot have it both ways. If they want their announcers to sound friendly, they must expect a chatty style, with all the consequences that has for pronunciation.

As long as society contains divisions, there will always be differences in pronunciation, and, as a consequence, arguments about which form is best and which accent is most acceptable. The arguments can be healthy and informative, or nasty and intolerant. They are usually the latter. BBC announcers with accents other than Received Pronunciation regularly receive hate mail. And when I present *English Now* on Radio 4, my own accent – a mixture of Wales, Liverpool, and southern England (see p. 86) – is often criticized. The letter-writers usually ask for the removal, forthwith, of the offending parties.

Getting the sack because of your speech isn't unknown. I know of two cases – one in an estate agent's, the other in a hairdresser's – where assistants have had to leave because their accents were felt to be inappropriate. And in 1970 there was a much-publicized case of a blacksmith who committed suicide because he could not cope with the ridicule levelled at his accent when he moved from Yorkshire to the South of England. Remembering such stories, a tiny plea for tolerance would seem a reasonable way to end this section.

Received Pronunciation

In England, there is one accent that has come to stand out above all others, conveying associations of respectable social standing and a good education. This 'prestige' accent is known as Received Pronunciation, or RP. It is often associated with the south-east of England, where most RP-speakers live or work, but in fact it can be found anywhere in the country. Accents usually tell us where in the country a person is from; RP tells us only about a speaker's social or educational background.

The ancestral form of RP developed in the late Middle Ages, in London and the south-east, as the accent of the court and the upper classes. It was well established over 400 years ago. The Elizabethan courtier George Puttenham, writing in 1589, thought that the English of 'northern men, whether they be noblemen or gentlemen . . . is not so courtly or so current as our Southern English is'. Some courtiers did hold on to their local speech – Walter Raleigh kept his Devonshire accent, for instance. But most people anxious for social advancement would move to London and adopt the accent they found there. As a result, the accent soon came to symbolize a person's high position in society.

During the nineteenth century, RP became the accent of the public schools, such as Eton, Harrow, and Winchester, and was soon the main sign that a speaker had received a good education. It spread rapidly throughout the Civil Service of the British Empire and the armed forces, and became the voice of authority and power.

Because RP had few regional overtones and was more widely understood than any regional accent, it came to be adopted by the BBC when radio broadcasting began in the 1920s. During the Second World War, the accent became associated in many people's minds as

he voice of freedom. The terms RP and BBC English became
nymous.

e days, with the breakdown of rigid divisions between social
l the development of the mass media, RP is no longer the
social élite. It is now best described as an 'educated'
ps 'accents' would be more precise, for there are
ays have been) several varieties. The most widely
enerally heard on the BBC. But in addition
ioned and trend-setting forms of RP. The
ften described as 'far back', or 'frightfully,
Ranger' accent of the 1980s. The more
d mainly in older speakers – what is
her 'plummy' tone of voice. You'll hear
it i.   lays or announcements from the 1920s
and i

Early BBC recordings show the remarkable extent to which RP
has altered over just a few decades, and they make the point that no
accent is immune to change, not even the 'best'. In addition, RP is no
longer as widely used as it was fifty years ago. Only about 3 per cent
of British people speak it in a pure form now. Most other educated
people have developed an accent which is a mixture of RP and
various regional characteristics – 'modified' RP, some call it, or
perhaps we should talk about modified RPs, as in each case the kind
of modification stems from a person's regional background, and this
varies greatly.

Regionally modified speech (see Chapter 7) seems ready to make a
come-back in educated British society. In late Victorian times, regional
accents were heavily stigmatized, and this attitude is still to be found,
as we have seen (p. 61). But times are changing. Several contemporary
politicians make a virtue out of their regional background, and the
BBC employs several announcers with regionally modified accents.
Nor is it uncommon, these days, to find educated people expressing
hostility towards RP, both within and outside Britain, because of its
traditional association with conservative values.

None the less, RP continues to be the most widely used accent in
the Court, Parliament, the Church of England, the legal profession,
and in other national institutions. It has received more linguistic
research than any other accent. It is still the only accent taught to

Some voices from the past

It is curious how fashion changes pronunciation. In my youth everybody said 'Lonnon' not 'London' . . . The now fashionable pronunciation of several words is to me at least very offensive: *CONtemplate* is bad enough; but *BALcony* makes me sick.

Samuel Rogers, *Recollections of the Table-talk of Samuel Rogers* (1855)

These were new stress patterns in Rogers' day; earlier, the words were pronounced *conTEMplate* and *balCOny*.

I have lived to see great changes in this respect. I have known the mute 'h' to become audible, and the audible 'h' to become mute. I was taught to pronounce the words *humble, hospital, herbs, honest* without an 'h', and can't get out of my old fashion without a struggle. Nevertheless people now talk of *humble, hospital, herb*, and I have heard people talk of *a honest* man.

Samuel Lysons, *Our Vulgar Tongue* (1868)

Grannie used to talk of *chaney* (china), *laylocks* (lilac) and *goold* (gold); of the *Prooshians* and the *Rooshians*; of things being 'plaguey dear' and 'plaguey bad'. In my childhood, however, half my elders used such expressions, which now seem to be almost extinct. '*Obleege* me by passing the *cowcumber*' Uncle Julius always used to say.

Augustus Hare, *The Story of My Life* (1896)

[George IV, telling what happened when he offered snuff to the actor, Kemble]: 'If you will take a pinch . . . you will much obleege me.' Kemble paused for a moment, and, dipping his fingers and thumb into the box, replied, 'I accept your Royal Highness's offer with gratitude; but, if you can extend your royal jaws so wide, pray, another time, say oblige.' And I did so, ever after, I assure you.

Mrs Matthews, *Memoirs of Charles Matthews, Comedian* (1839) foreigners who wish to learn a British model, and it is thus widely used abroad. In fact, today there are far more foreign speakers of R P in other countries than mother-tongue users in Britain.

5

ᵍ ᵍ ᵍ ᵍ ᵍ ᵍ ᵍ ᵍ ᵍ ᵍ

Spelling

Though the rough cough and hiccough plough me through, I ought to cross
the lough.

> Beware of heard, a dreadful word,
> That looks like beard and sounds like bird,
> And dead: it's said like bed, not bead,
> For Goodness' sake, don't call it deed!
> Watch out for meat and great and threat,
> They rhyme with suite and straight and debt.

Anon

Punch, 15 September 1982

'Chaotic', 'unpredictable', 'disorganized', 'a mess' – these are just a few of the more repeatable expressions used to describe English spelling. And with examples such as the above to use as evidence, the descriptions seem quite apt.

On the other hand, I could have begun this chapter with a quotation from a different kind of poem, such as this one from Dr Seuss's *The Cat in a Hat* (1957):

> I can hold up the cup
> And the milk and the cake!
> I can hold up these books!
> And the fish on a rake!
>
> I can hold the toy ship
> And a little toy man!
> And look! With my tail
> I can hold a red fan!

Most of the words in this extract are spelled in a perfectly regular way. Look at how the /i/ sound is routinely *i* in *milk*, *fish*, *ship* and *little*; or the /a/ sound is *a* in *and, can, man*, and *fan*. There's little sign of chaos here.

There seems to be both regularity and irregularity in English spelling. It isn't *totally* chaotic. But the question remains: just how chaotic *is* it?

It isn't easy to arrive at a definite figure – to say that X per cent of English words are irregular in their spelling. For a start, it isn't obvious just how many words there are (see Chapter 3), or whether all words should be considered. If we include all the proper names (of people and places), the irregularity percentage will be enormous, for there are thousands of idiosyncratic name spellings (most noticeable in such famous cases as *Featherstonehaugh*, pronounced 'Fanshaw'). People who find their name being regularly mis-spelled, or who find it necessary to spell out where they live each time they give their address over the phone, are thoroughly familiar with this point. On the other hand, if we include the thousands of lengthy scientific or technical terms in English (such as the full name of DDT – *dichlorodiphenyltrichloroethane*), we will find that the vast majority of the syllables are spelled according to quite regular rules, as we sense when we 'sound out' these long words to ourselves, syllable by syllable. The irregularity percentage will then be tiny.

Even if we restrict the question to 'everyday' vocabulary, there is still a problem: namely, how do we deal with related words? If we say that *friend* is irregular, then do we say that *friends* is *another* irregular word, or is it the *same* word with an *-s* ending? The same point would apply to *their* and *theirs*, *do* and *does* and many more. If we go the first way, we dramatically increase the total of irregular words in the language; if we go the second way, we keep the total down.

We can make this point in a more general way by considering the present paragraph. It consists of forty-five words. Now, let us focus on just one of the irregularly spelled words it contains, *the*. What percentage of the paragraph is made up of *the*?

There are two answers to this question. If we count every single instance (or 'token') of *the*, we obtain a total of five – 11 per cent of all words in the paragraph. However, if we look at the number of *different* words (word 'types'), counting each word only once, regardless of how many times it is used, then we get a quite different figure. There are thirty-five different words in the paragraph. From this point of view, *the* is just one of the thirty-five – about 3 per cent.

Some irregular English spellings

although	could	key	said
among	course	lamb	salt
answer	debt	listen	says
are	do	move	shoe
aunt	does	none	shoulder
autumn	done	of	some
blood	dough	once	sugar
build	eye	one	talk
castle	friend	only	two
clerk	gone	own	was
climb	great	people	water
colour	have	pretty	were
comb	hour	quay	where
come	island	receive	who
cough	journey	rough	you

Hence if we were to count all the irregular words in a large sample of English writing, the results would vary enormously, depending on whether we were counting word types or word tokens. If we calculated the irregularity based on word types, the percentage would be very much smaller than any count based on word tokens.

A failure to appreciate this distinction between types and tokens lies behind the view that English spelling is mad. There are only about 400 everyday words in English whose spelling is wholly irregular – that is, there are relatively few irregular word types (some are given in the panel on p. 68). The trouble is that many of these words are amongst the most frequently used words in the language; they are thus constantly before our eyes as word tokens. As a result, English spelling gives the impression of being more irregular than it really is.

This is both bad news and good news for the child learning to spell, of course. A child who could not spell *the* correctly would automatically have errors totalling 11 per cent in the above paragraph (ignoring what would happen to the other words). Failing to know just this *one* word would produce a large number of errors. On the other hand, once the child learned to spell *the*, the number of errors would fall immediately by 11 per cent. Learning this one word would produce a noticeable general improvement. Not that *the* is a very realistic example, as few children have trouble with this particular word, but the principle involved applies to all words, including those which *are* well-known problems (such as *their*, *does*, *friend*, *once*, and *was*).

Don't be surprised, then, to hear very different figures cited in answer to the question, 'How irregular is English spelling?' Everything depends on what is counted, and how. Also, some people who argue this issue have an axe to grind. For instance, they may have an interest in promoting a particular system of spelling reform (see p. 79), and therefore they will wish to stress the irregularity in the language. However, the main conclusion from the studies which have been carried out is that we must not exaggerate the problem. English is much more regular in spelling than the traditional criticisms would have us believe. A major American study, published in the early 1970s, carried out a computer analysis of 17,000 words and showed that no less than 84 per cent of the words were spelled according to a regular pattern, and that only 3 per cent were so unpredictable that they would have to be learned by heart. Several other projects have reported comparable results of 75 per cent regularity or more. Accordingly, the suggestion that English spelling is fundamentally chaotic seems to be nonsense.

If this is so, then why all the fuss? Why are there so many people who have unhappy memories of 'learning to spell'? Why are there thousands of children right now having to spend hours practising their spellings, at home or in school? Why are there so many who, having devoted so much time and energy to the task, are still unable to spell with confidence? According to some estimates, as many as 2 per cent of the population have a major, persistent handicap in spelling.

The answer is simple. Children are rarely taught *how* to spell. They are told they must learn spellings off by heart, of course, and they are rigorously tested in them. But to learn something by heart doesn't explain what it is you have learned. In order to *understand* the spelling system of English, children need to be given reasons for why the spellings are as they are, and told about how these spellings relate to the way they pronounce the words. But the children are rarely taught about these principles. Spelling becomes a massive, boring memory task – ten words a night, for ever, it seems. As a result, they never develop a sense of the system which is present, so that when they encounter new words, they have to resort to guesswork.

Teachers often express surprise that a child who has been quick to learn to read should be a poor speller. They assume that reading, once taught, automatically means that spelling will be 'caught'. But there is no correlation between reading ability and spelling ability. Totally different skills are involved. Spelling involves a set of active, productive, conscious processes that are not required for reading. To take just one contrast: it is possible to read very selectively, by spotting just some of the letters or words in a piece of writing, and 'guessing' the rest (as we do when we 'skim' a newspaper story). You can't spell in this way. Spellers have got to get it *all* right, letter by letter.

Also, more things can go wrong when you try to spell than when you try to read. Take the word *meep*. Faced with this word on the page (whatever it might mean), there is really only one possible way

A page from Group 3 of Schonell's *The Essential Spelling List* (1932), which continues to be widely used in schools today. The words selected are those that the author had found to be commonly used in children's writing. They were useful words, as can be seen from the way the list brings together words related in grammar or meaning (e.g. *goose/geese*). But it is not possible to see the spelling *system* when working through words like this. Regular and irregular spellings are put side by side (e.g. *patch/-watch*) with little apparent order.

match	June	picking
catch	July	picked
patch	September	learned
watch	November	reached

fetch	ditch	snatch	everyone

care	infant	tender
careless	darling	gentle
useless	cradle	weak
useful	young	dull

purse	nurse	fur	beak

hammer	too	lunch
bench	tool	buy
blade	stool	beef
wire	fool	cloth

blood	goose	geese	cheese

change	break	brighter
changed	broke	brightest
taken	broken	safer
eaten	stole	safest

cooler	deeper	finer	miner

hiding	skate	chief
shining	skating	thief
smiling	darkness	grief
hoping	illness	burnt

should	cheer	quickly	nearly

of pronouncing it. The task of reading it aloud is easy. But if you heard this word pronounced, without ever having seen it, and were then asked how to spell it, you would be faced with at least three alternatives: is it *meep*, *mepe*, or *meap*? The task facing you as a speller is far greater than that facing you as a reader. (However, the situation is helped by the way that some spelling patterns are much more common than others – in RP the same vowel sound turns up in *cot* and *wash*, but the *o* spelling accounts for 95 per cent of the cases.)

The study of the errors children make when they are learning to spell (errors like *our* for *hour*, or *sed* for *said*) shows that spelling is not just a visual matter, but a matter of relating letters to sounds. The children spell the word as they hear it in their heads – a very sensible tactic, which would have worked well enough if things hadn't gone awry in the history of English (see p. 74). We don't learn to spell by studying the 'shape' of the word, and remembering that. Children who try to spell by remembering visual shapes soon get into deep water. Lucy, for example, aged twelve would happily spell *fruit* as *furit*, *firut*, and the like. *Women* became *wemon*, *bodies* became *boides*. She 'knew' which letters should be there, from her visual memory, but they didn't always turn up in the right order. As soon as she was taught to 'sound the word out' as she spelled, this problem began to diminish.

However, learning about the predictable links between spelling and pronunciation, the principles on which the spelling system is based – in short, the 'spelling rules' – is far from commonplace. Most traditional spelling rules are based on the written language only. Consider these two examples: 'to form the plural of nouns ending in y, change *y* to *i* and add *es*' (*cry* – *cries*), and '*i* goes before *e* except after *c*' (quite a useful reminder, though there are a few exceptions – *weird*, *neighbour*, etc.). In such cases, we don't need to know anything about the sounds conveyed by the letters: the rules work on the letters alone. Rules of this kind are useful, as far as they go. The trouble is, of course, that they don't go very far. They need to be supplemented by more basic rules which tell the learners to relate what they *see* to what they *hear*. Ironically, it is these rules which are usually not taught, but left for children to 'pick up' as best they can. Not surprisingly, most children don't.

As an example of how sounds and spellings relate, let's look at the question of whether to use one consonant letter or two, when adding *-ing* to a verb that ends in a consonant, such as *hop* and *sit*. This is a very common spelling confusion, with children often writing *hoping* for *hopping*, or vice versa. But the basic rule is simple, as long as the link between pronunciation and spelling is pointed out. First it is essential to hear the difference between vowels which are very short in length, as in *sit, set, sat, cot, cut, full*, and those which are much longer, as in *me, car, say, go*, etc. (see p. 52). It then emerges that the consonant sound is spelled with a double letter if the verb contains one of the short vowels, and it is kept single if the verb contains a long vowel.

Short		Long	
hop	hopping	hope	hoping
can	canning	cane	caning
sham	shamming	shame	shaming
bet	betting	beat	beating
man	manning	mean	meaning

Thus, if you had never come across the verb *sabing* before, you would know that it must come from 'to sabe'; *sabbing*, by contrast, would have to come from 'to sab'. This is what a good spelling rule does: it tells you not just about the words you already know, but about those you haven't yet learned, or which haven't even been invented yet.

The rule relates many words other than verbs:

latter	later
comma	coma
red	redder
bitter	biter
dinner	diner
broad	broader

This isn't the whole story, of course. All the above verbs are words of one syllable. When longer words are brought in, we have to hear whether the preceding syllable is *stressed* or not. If it is, there is usually doubling; if it isn't, there isn't.

occur	occurring	enter	entering
patrol	patrolling	visit	visiting
permit	permitting	develop	developing

These rules account for thousands of words. By contrast, there are relatively few exceptions (several of which can be learned as 'rules within rules'). Here are some of them:

● If the verb already ends in a double consonant, it keeps it, even if it has a long vowel sound, e.g. *purr/purring*, *err/erring*.
● Verbs with a short vowel sound spelled with two vowel letters don't double the consonant, e.g. *dread/dreading*.
● Verbs ending in *l*, *m*, *g*, and (sometimes) *p* tend to double the consonant anyway, e.g. *cancelling*, *programming*, *humbugging*, *kidnapping*. Usage varies between British and American English. Doubling is normal in British English, for such words as *travelling* and *worshipping*. US English prefers the single consonant letter: *traveling* and *worshiping*.
● With a very few verbs ending in -*s*, both forms are possible, e.g. *focusing/focussing*, *biasing/biassing*.
● With verbs ending in a vowel followed by *c*, the doubling of *c* is spelled *ck*, e.g. *panic/panicking*.

This is just one example of the kind of relationship which exists between sounds and spellings in English. Working through such cases shows that there is a system – there are several rules, even though there are exceptions. But why are there so many rules? And where do the exceptions come from? Questions such as these require historical answers.

WHERE DO THE IRREGULARITIES COME FROM?

The English spelling system is the result of a process of development that has been going on for over 1,000 years. The complications we are left with today are the result of the major linguistic and social events which took place during this time.

● Some of the complications arose at the outset, when Old English was first written down by the Roman missionaries (see p. 153), using the 23-letter Latin alphabet – the same as our modern alphabet, except that there was no distinction between I and J or U and V, and there was no W (these were added in the Middle English period) – but there were simply not enough letters to cope with Old English, which contained nearly forty vowels and consonants. The missionaries used extra symbols from the local runic alphabet to write sounds that were noticeably different from Latin (such as the *th* sound). But despite this, it still proved necessary to use some letters (such as *c* and *g*) for more than one sound, and to represent some sounds by combinations of letters (such as *sc* – the equivalent of present-day *sh*).

● After the Norman Conquest, the French scribes brought their own ideas about spelling to bear on the language. Several Old English spellings were replaced. The French introduced *qu*, where Old English had used *cw* (e.g. *queen*). They brought in *gh* (instead of *h*) in such words as *night* and *enough*, and *ch* (instead of *c*) in such words as *church*. They used *ou* for *u* (e.g. *house*). They began to use *c* before *e* or *i* in such words as *circle* and *cell*. Because the letter *u* was written in a very similar way to *v*, *n*, and *m*, words containing a sequence of these letters were difficult to read; they therefore often replaced the *u* with an *o*, in such cases as *come*, *love*, *one*, and *son*. By the beginning of the fifteenth century, English spelling was a mixture of two systems – Old English and French.

● The introduction of printing in 1476 brought further consequences. In the early fifteenth century, there were many ways of spelling words, reflecting regional variations in pronunciation. William Caxton had to choose one system as a standard to follow in his printing house (see p. 190). He chose the system which reflected the speech of the London area. As a result, the spelling of many words became stable for the first time, and the notion of a 'correct' spelling began to grow.

However, although spelling stayed relatively stable, pronunciation did not. During the fifteenth century, the sounds of London speech were undergoing the greatest change in its history. Six of the vowels of Middle English altered completely. To take just one such change: in Chaucer's time, the word *name* was pronounced with an /ɑː/ vowel sound like that of *calm*, which is why it is spelled with an *a* vowel now. It was the fifteenth-century 'vowel shift' which changed the pronunciation to its modern form (see p. 183). Before the advent of printing, the scribes would have heard this new pronunciation, and changed the spelling to suit. *Name* would have come to be spelled *neim* or *naym*, or some such. But after the advent of printing, changes of this kind were no longer acceptable. The consequence is that our

modern spelling in many respects reflects the way words were pronounced in Chaucer's time.

The same kind of reasoning explains many of the 'silent letters' of
modern English spelling. The *k* of such words as *knee*, *know*, and
knight was pronounced in Old English, but it ceased to be sounded
during the fifteenth century. The *e* at the end of such words as *name*
and *stone* was also pronounced – the sound was similiar to the last
vowel of *sofa* – but it became silent during this period. The spelling,
however, continued to reflect the older sounds.

Spell the modern way?

One of the most noticeable present-day trends is the use of deviant
spelling as part of a trade-name or advertising campaign. The
motivation for the distinctive trade-mark is to provide an un-
ambiguous, identifiable product name, which won't be confused
with a 'common' word in the language. In the case of slogans, the
aim is memorability. It remains an open question whether the
proliferation of such forms causes any problems for children
trying to make sense of the bewildering array of spellings
they see around them.

Miami for the chosen phew	Heinz Buildz Kidz
(*advertising holidays*)	Loc-tite
EZ Lern (*US driving school*)	No-glu
Fetherwate	Resistoyl
Hyway Inn	Rol-it-on
Kilzum (*insect spray*)	Wundertowl
Kwiksave	

● In the sixteenth century, there was a fashion among learned writers
to show the history (or *etymology*) of a word in its spelling, and
several of these new spellings became standard. This is where the
silent *b* in *debt* comes from, for instance. The word had no *b* sound in
Middle English. The *b* was added by people who wished to remind
everyone that the word comes from *debitum* in Latin. Similarly, a *b*
was added to *doubt* (from *dubitare*) and a *g* to *reign* (from *regno*). In
addition, there was a concern to 'tidy up' the spelling – for example,

leading people to think that, because there was a *gh* in *night* and *light*, there should be one in *delight* and *tight* also.

● In the late sixteenth and early seventeenth centuries, a new wave of loan words arrived in English from such languages as French, Latin, Greek, Spanish, Italian, and Portuguese (see p. 174). They brought with them a host of un-English-looking spellings – words which ended in strange combinations of vowels and consonants, such as *bizarre*, *brusque*, *canoe*, *cocoa*, *gazette*, *moustache*, and *intrigue*. Some of the strangest spellings in the language stem from this period.

Because of the complex history of the English language, which we discuss in Part III, English spelling is a curious mixture of different influences. It is surprising, indeed, that with such a chequered history so much regularity should have been retained. But the changes took place over a lengthy time scale, and many of the spellings were tried out for long periods (often accompanied by considerable debate, especially in the sixteenth century) before they were finally adopted. The result is a system which, despite its weaknesses, has proved to be sufficiently functional that it has so far resisted all proposals for its fundamental reform.

A dozen confusibles

There are many pairs of words in English which sound the same (or nearly the same) but which are spelled differently. Some of the items which are most commonly confused are listed below. The context will make it clear which sense is intended. The correct spellings are indicated at the end of the list, using the convention *A* (for the first alternative) or *B* (for the second).

1. Did they all accept/except?
2. Everyone accept/except John left.
3. Did we prophecy/prophesy the right result?
4. It was a rotten prophecy/prophesy.
5. Has he made any allusions/illusions to the problem?
6. He's under no allusions/illusions about its difficulty.
7. I want to amend/emend what I wrote.
8. I want to amend/emend my ways.

9. She was born/borne through the crowds.
10. She was born/borne in 1568.
11. That will complement/compliment your shirt nicely.
12. Thank you for your complement/compliment.
13. Someone's complained to the council/counsel.
14. You should take some council/counsel about that.
15. You need a new licence/license for that hamster.
16. I'll licence/license it next week.
17. Look at that fantastic lightning/lightening.
18. I think the sky's lightning/lightening now.
19. I need some more stationary/stationery.
20. That car's stationary/stationery.
21. I'm the principle/principal speaker.
22. I'm going to stick to my principles/principals.
23. I'm going to do some sowing/sewing in the sitting room.
24. I'm going to do some sowing/sewing in the long field.

1. A; 2. B; 3. B; 4. A; 5. A; 6. B; 7. B; 8. A; 9. B; 10. A; 11. A; 12. B; 13. A;
14. B; 15. A (in UK), B (in USA); 16. B; 17. A; 18. B; 19. B; 20. A; 21. B;
22. A; 23. B; 24. A

Spelling Reform

Despite the existence of a great deal of regularity in English spelling, everyone would agree that a lot of time and money would be saved if the system could be improved by eliminating all the irregularities. Proposals for spelling reform can be traced back to the sixteenth century, but the main movements in favour of reform developed in both America and Britain in the nineteenth century. The Spelling Reform Association was founded in the USA in 1876, and the British Simplified Spelling Society in 1908. Since then, there have been many proposals made and systems devised, some in minute detail.

The arguments in favour of spelling reform are easy to state. Children and foreign learners of English would save much time and emotional effort in learning to read and write. People using the language would save time and money, because they would be able to write English more rapidly, and with fewer letters – as many as 15 per cent fewer, according to some estimates. Over the years, the saving in terms of paper, ink, storage, and so on would be very great.

The arguments against spelling reform are just as easy to state. How could a programme of spelling reform be introduced in a practical or realistic way? How does one persuade people who have learned the old system to adopt a new one? How does one avoid any major break in continuity between old and new spellings? How does one avoid the problems of representing different regional accents in the spelling – for example, accents which pronounce an *r* after vowels, and those which do not (see p. 87)?

So far, the disadvantages have proved overwhelming. The nearest the Simplified Spelling Society came to success was in 1949, when their publication, called 'Nue Spelling', was presented to Parliament. The bill was defeated, but only by eighty-seven votes to eighty-four!

In 1953, another bill in fact passed its first stage, but was later withdrawn.

One of the biggest problems facing the spelling reform movement is the lack of any universal agreement as to what the best alternative system might be. Over the years, hundreds of proposals have been made, differing from each other in all kinds of ways. Some systems, such as Nue Spelling, stay with familiar letters, and try to use them in a regular way. Others go in for a number of invented symbols, which supplement the letters already in use. The initial teaching alphabet devised by James Pitman in 1959 is of this kind, although it wasn't a proposal for the permanent reform of English spelling, but a system intended to help children when they were learning to read. In addition, there are a few systems which present a totally radical solution – a fresh start in which all old letters are eliminated and brand new symbols introduced. George Bernard Shaw's Proposed British Alphabet ('Shavian') falls within this last category.

Despite more than a century of effort, the spelling reform movement has made little progress. The case is still regularly argued, but the arguments largely fall on deaf ears.

The beginning of Lincoln's Gettysburg Address, in Nue Spelling

Forskor and seven yeerz agoe our faadherz braut forth on dhis kontinent a nue naeshon, konseevd in liberti, and dedikaeted to the propozishon dhat aul men ar kreeaeted eekwal. Nou we ar en.gaejd in a graet sivil wor, testing whedher dhat naeshon, or eni naeshon soe konseevd and soe dedikaeted, kan long enduer. We ar met on a graet batlfeeld ov dhat wor.

And a less radical system, 'Regularized English'

Regularized Inglish iz a system ov spelling which lays down definit rules ov pronunciation which wood make it eazier for aull children to lern to read and write. In aull probability it wood lead to a saving ov at least wun year's wurk for aull schoolchildren. It wood aulso contribute very largely towaurdz abolition ov the existing amount ov illiteracy and backwardness in reading.

Shaw's proposed British alphabet

Shaw left instructions in his will that an alphabet of at least forty letters should be published, which would enable English to be written in a regular way. After a competition, a design by Kingsley Read was adjudged the winner. The following extract from Lincoln's address ('But in a larger sense . . .') illustrates the alphabet in use. A key to the symbols is given below.

From Lincoln's speech at Gettysburg

The Shaw Alphabet Reading Key

The letters are classified as Tall, Deep, Short, and Compound.
Beneath each letter is its full name : its *sound* is shown in **bold** type.

Tall :	peep	tot	kick	fee	thigh	so	sure	church	yea	hung
Deep :	bib	dead	gag	vow	they	zoo	meaSure	judge	woe	ha-ha
Short :	loll	mime	if	egg	ash	ado	on	wool	out	ah
	roar	nun	eat	age	ice	up	oak	ooze	oil	awe
Compound :	are	or	air	err	array	ear	Ian	yew		

The four most frequent words are represented by single letters : the ۹, of ʃ, and ٦, to ۱.
Proper names may be distinguished by a preceding ' Namer ' dot : e.g. ·)O/, Rome.
Punctuation and numerals are unchanged.

PART II

ℰ ℰ ℰ ℰ ℰ

The Uses of English

The uses of a language are as varied as life itself. It would make this guide considerably overweight to deal with the thousands of ways in which people all over the world alter aspects of English structure in their professional and daily lives. Part II therefore does not attempt to be comprehensive, but rather isolates several general themes which are at the heart of the matter.

Chapter 6 deals with some very general ways in which English can vary. There is geographical and social variation, in the form of distinctive accents and dialects. There are the many differences between spoken and written language, whose importance is usually underestimated. And there are the varieties associated with different occupations and activities. We look in some detail at two of these varieties, and illustrate several more.

English at work in Chapter 6 contrasts with English at play in Chapter 7. There are many ways in which we play with the language – jokes, riddles, verbal contests, comic alphabets, and word games, to name but a few. These are described and illustrated, and the chapter concludes with a survey of the symbolic meaning of sounds in the language.

English can be used to identify regional or social groups, but it can also be a sign of individuality. Chapter 8 therefore looks at some of the ways in which a person's own style can be identified. The field of authorship research takes us into the domain of literature (who wrote Shakespeare's plays?) and forensic science. And the range of 'deviant' forms of English makes us consider the way sounds, spellings, grammar, and vocabulary are used distinctively in poetry. Part II then concludes with some general observations on the possible existence of statistical laws in the language.

6

🌿 🌿 🌿 🌿 🌿 🌿 🌿 🌿 🌿 🌿

Language Variety

Experts on English these days are fond of the unexpected plural: we find books and articles talking about 'the English languages' or 'the new Englishes'. What they are emphasizing is the remarkable variety which can be observed in the way sounds, spellings, grammar, and vocabulary are used within the English-speaking world. There have been hints of this in the first part of the book, but there the focus

'Tell me, do I detect a trace of northern mid-Atlantic accent in that Home Counties mid-Atlantic accent?'

Punch, 2 January 1985

was on the common core of the language – on the facts and factors which need to be taken into account regardless of the kind of English we choose to study. Now we must reverse the viewpoint, and look at the way the structure of the language changes depending on which people are using it, where they are, and what they are doing.

ACCENTS AND DIALECTS

The variations that are most often noticed and commented upon are those arising out of our geographical background. This is mainly a matter of regional *accent* – a way of pronouncing the words and sentences of the language that identifies the speaker's geographical origin. Everyone has an accent. The identification is often a very general one: 'American', 'Australian', 'British', 'Irish', 'Welsh', 'north-country', 'west-country', 'east-coast'. But just as often it is quite specific, referring to individual counties, cities, or smaller localities: 'Yorkshire', 'Lancashire', 'Liverpool', 'New York', 'Brooklyn'. Within a country, an accent may become so much an educated standard that it conveys little or no regional information. This is what has happened in the case of Received Pronunciation (see p. 62). You can't tell where R P speakers are from; all you can say is that they have received a certain kind of education. But on the world stage, R P speakers are not accent-less: they are very definitely British.

Some people are very good at identifying accents. There have been radio shows in which experts have tried to identify the regional background of members of the audience, just from their voices. In *Pygmalion*, George Bernard Shaw has Henry Higgins claiming: '*I* can place any man within six miles. I can place him within two miles in London. Sometimes within two streets.' Higgins wouldn't have so much success now. These days, it is much less usual for people to live their whole lives in one place, and 'mixed' accents have become more widespread. I am a typical example. After twelve years in North Wales, ten years in Liverpool, twenty years in Berkshire, and a subsequent period back in Wales, my own accent is perhaps most charitably described as a hybrid – or mess, if you prefer. It shows features associated with these different areas; and it is not entirely consistent.

Three British accent boundaries

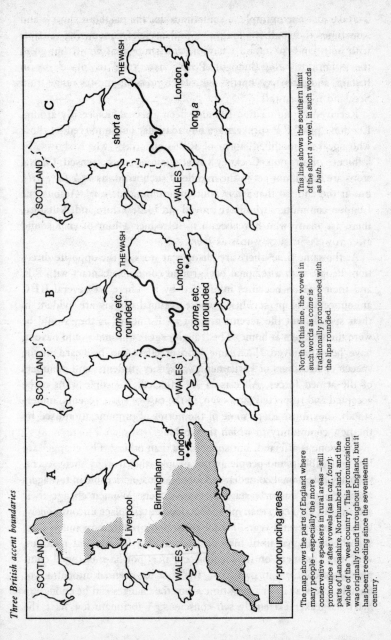

The map shows the parts of England where many people – especially the more conservative speakers in rural areas – still pronounce *r* after vowels (as in *car, four*): parts of Lancashire, Northumberland, and the whole of the 'west country'. This pronunciation was originally found throughout England, but it has been receding since the seventeenth century.

North of this line, the vowel in such words as *come* is traditionally pronounced with the lips rounded.

This line shows the southern limit of the short *a* vowel, in such words as *bath*.

To take just one example, I sometimes use the northern short *a* and sometimes the southern long *a*. I find myself pronouncing *example* with both kinds of *a*, and I have a *bath* (short *a*) at home, but go to the swimming *baths* (long *a*). People have tried to 'place' me in Britain, and often say 'north', but, when pressed, guesses range from Scotland to Cornwall.

Received Pronunciation has also been affected. Especially around London, 'pure' RP speakers are nowadays far outnumbered by those who speak a 'modified' form of RP – an accent which shows the influence of a region. Cockney vowel qualities can be sensed. Glottal stops are heard, not yet in the middle of such words as *bo'le* for *bottle*, but at the end, so that *smart* is often pronounced *smar'*. Among the London commuters who have moved out to Berkshire and Wiltshire, there are many who have begun to introduce a hint of an *r* sound after vowels, in such words as *four*.

At the same time, there are changes at work in the opposite direction. People with a regional background come into contact with RP, and their speech becomes influenced by it. There are several BBC announcers and personalities whose regional origins are evident in their speech, but the accents are not as distinctive as they would be were the speakers at home. The 'rough edges', as some would have it, have been removed. The same kind of effect can be heard in the speech of Members of Parliament, university students, and members of the armed forces. All classes are affected. If people want to be accepted and respected (and even, in the case of some accents, understood), they must adopt some of the norms of pronunciation used by the new community to which they belong.

Everyone is affected, but some more than others. The changes are less noticeable in old people and in people who 'live' by their accent, such as professional comedians. They are most noticeable in teenagers and people at an early stage in their careers. Women change their accents more quickly than men. The changes take place unconsciously, usually over several years. People often don't realize how much their speech has altered until they go back to visit friends and relatives, who may comment on it. Their accent may not have changed completely, of course – in particular, traces of the original intonation, or melody, can stay a very long time – but the changes can be enough to make a speaker extremely self-conscious. A fortunate few have the ability to be 'bilingual', switching back into their original accent without difficulty.

Who drops their aitches?

Several sociolinguistic studies in recent years have been devoted to plotting the way a sound change moves through a community. They show that, in addition to age and sex, social class is also an important factor. The figures below indicate what proportion of people in two English cities 'drop their *hs*' at the beginning of such words as *head*. The speakers were divided into five social classes, based on their income, occupation, and type of education. In both cities, there is a steady increase in the amount of *h*-dropping as you go down this social scale. The proportion is always greater in Bradford, suggesting that *h*-dropping has been a feature of that city for a longer period of time. But note that, in both cities, not all the working class people drop the *h*, and not all the middle-class people keep it.

	Bradford (%)	Norwich (%)
Middle middle class	12	6
Lower middle class	28	14
Upper working class	67	40
Middle working class	89	60
Lower working class	93	60

Many of these points emerge again when we take up the notion of *dialect*, which is a much broader concept than that of accent. Accents are restricted to matters of pronunciation, whereas dialects include variations in grammar, vocabulary, and spelling. If we heard one person say *He be ready* and another say *He is ready*, we would say they were using different dialects, because this is a difference of grammar. Similarly, if one person said *pavement* where another said *sidewalk*, this too would be considered dialectal, because it is a matter of vocabulary. And the use of *color* instead of *colour* illustrates a dialectal difference in spelling.

Just as everyone has an accent, so everyone speaks a dialect. This point sometimes comes as a surprise to people who have been brought up to think of 'dialects' as belonging only to country yokels. But rural dialects make up only some of the regionally distinctive varieties of English. Urban dialects exist too – indeed, they are on the increase as cities grow. (It is often said that dialects are dying out, but this is true only of some rural dialects.) And there are also national dialects of English – words and (to a lesser extent) grammatical constructions that identify which part of the international English-speaking world you are from. If you have lived all your life in the USA, your vocabulary, grammar, and spelling will signal to any outsider that you are American. Similarly, there are words and structures which are distinctively British, Australian, Indian, South African, and so on (see Chapter 12). Dialect signals are an inevitable part of speech.

Having said this, it is important not to overstate the extent to which dialect features are used, especially in the written language. The local newspapers of New York, London, Sydney, or Toronto contain very few words that are not also used or recognized in English-speaking countries everywhere. And from the transcript of an international debate on television between an American and a Briton you would only occasionally be able to distinguish between them on dialect grounds. There may be several thousand dialect words in a

---

The survey of English dialects

Between 1950 and 1961 a large-scale dialect survey was undertaken in 313 localities throughout England by Harold Orton and Eugene Dieth. The localities were usually not more than fifteen miles apart, and generally consisted of villages with a fairly stable population. The informants were natives of the locality, mainly male agricultural workers over sixty years of age. Around 1,300 questions were used, on such themes as farming, animals, housekeeping, weather, and social activities; over 404,000 items of information were recorded. Between 1962 and 1971, the basic material of the survey was published in several volumes. The map opposite shows the kind of information the survey provided – the different words for *newt* and their locations.

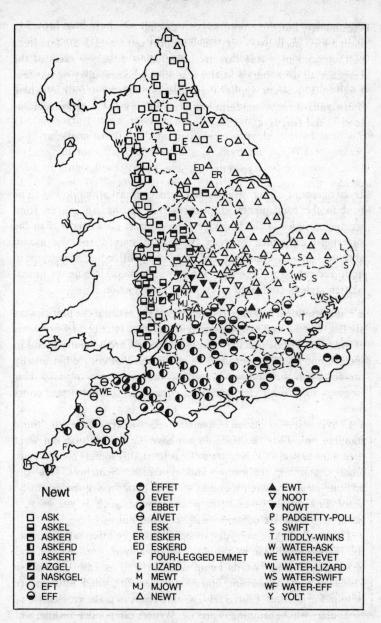

Newt

	◐ EFFET	▲ EWT
	◑ EVET	▽ NOOT
	◒ EBBET	▼ NOWT
□ ASK	⊖ AIVET	P PADGETTY-POLL
▤ ASKEL	E ESK	S SWIFT
▥ ASKER	ER ESKER	T TIDDLY-WINKS
◨ ASKERD	ED ESKERD	W WATER-ASK
◧ ASKERT	F FOUR-LEGGED EMMET	WE WATER-EVET
◩ AZGEL	L LIZARD	WL WATER-LIZARD
◪ NASKGEL	M MEWT	WS WATER-SWIFT
○ EFT	MJ MJOWT	WF WATER-EFF
● EFF	△ NEWT	Y YOLT

community, but these tend to be restricted to informal speech or to literature. This is also a very small number compared to the hundreds of thousands of words that are accepted by educated users of the language all over the world and comprise the vocabulary of *standard* English. This point applies even more strongly to grammar, where non-standard variations form but a tiny minority of the constructions used in the language.

SPEECH AND WRITING

In any account of the varieties of English, special attention has to be paid to the fundamental differences that distinguish spoken from written varieties of the language. The contrast goes deeper than the superficial difference between the use of sounds and the use of graphic symbols. Grammar and vocabulary differ too, sometimes in quite radical ways. The contrast is most noticeable when a formal written style is compared to everyday conversation.

● Conversational language is often inexplicit, because the participants are face-to-face, and can rely on the situation to clear up any problems of meaning. Phrases such as *that one over there* are regularly found in speech, but would be out of place in writing. Writers are not usually present when their output is read, so they must aim to make their language sufficiently clear and precise that it can be interpreted on its own.

● Conversation is usually spontaneous; speakers have to 'think standing up'. They therefore do not have the time to plan out what they want to say, and their grammar is inevitably loosely constructed, often containing rephrasing and repetition. Sentences lack the intricate structure often found in writing. Lengthy sequences can be heard, linked only by *and* (see p. 23). Phrases such as *you know*, *I mean*, or *you see* are common in speech, but not in writing.

● The vocabulary of everyday speech tends to be informal, domestic, and more limited than in writing. There is a much greater likelihood of slang and taboo words being used, as well as empty nonsense words (such as *thingummajig* and *whatchamacallit*), which would never be found in writing. Conversely, writing tends to make greater use of vocabulary whose meaning is precise. Writers can ponder a while, and look a word up before they write it. This option isn't usually available to speakers.

Punctuating speech with. Pauses.

The pauses, rhythms, and melodies of speech provide the basis of our punctuation system. There is usually a broad correspondence between the way we punctuate our sentences and the way we speak them. Each of the sentences in this paragraph, for example, would be spoken aloud with the punctuation marks expressed by different amounts of pause, or by variations in the rate of utterance. When speakers fail to preserve this correspondence, it tends to be noticed, and the speech style may be criticized, especially if it is used in public. The most noticeable instance of such a style is the 'on-the-spot' report given by radio and television reporters, which was amusingly satirized in this 1963 *Guardian* editorial. (It should be added that the style is by no means restricted to the BBC.)

The BBC has introduced a. New method of disseminating the spoken word at any rate we think it is new because we don't. Remember hearing it until a week or two ago it consists of. Putting the fullstops in the middle of sentences instead of at the end as we were. Taught at school as a corollary to this new sentences are run on without a break readers will say we are in. No position to talk but this appears to be a deliberate policy on the part of the BBC whereas our. Misprints are accidental.
 The practice seems to have started as a. Means of enlivening the reports of otherwise tedious football matches on a. Saturday afternoon now it has spread to the. News columns as it were and the effect is to make the subject matter. Confusing the interest of the listener is directed to the. Manner of delivery rather than the. Events recounted we tried to discover whether the ellipses or hiatuses followed a. Definite pattern or whether the breaks were made. Arbitrarily a pattern did emerge it seems that most of the breaks come after the. Definite or indefinite article or after a. Preposition sometimes they follow. Verbs but they always come when you. Least expect them and they constitute an outrage on what. We in the trade call the. Genius of the language.

● The interactive nature of conversation requires a great deal of 'manœuvring' which would not usually be found in writing (unless an author were trying to portray speech). There are special ways of opening a conversation (*Excuse me . . . , Guess what . . . , I say . . .*), of checking that the listener is following (*Are you with me? Let me put it another way . . .*); of changing a topic (*That reminds me . . . , By the way . . . , Where was I?*); and ending (*Nice talking to you; Gosh, is that the time?*). Such strategies are unnecessary in writing, which has its own ways of organizing the exposition of a text (e.g. prefaces, summaries, indexes, sub-headings, and cross-reference conventions like *see p. 33*).

● Conversation can use a wide range of tones of voice which are difficult to convey in writing (apart from through the use of a few typographical effects and punctuation marks). On the other hand, writing has a wide range of graphic features that do not exist in speech (such as colour, layout, capitalization). There are many vocal sound effects which cannot be satisfactorily written down, though novelists try. Equally, there are many written effects which cannot easily be spoken (such as train timetables, graphs, and formulae).

Written language is usually much more permanent and formal than speech. Because of its permanence, it also has a special status, being used where it is necessary to make something legally binding (as in

---

An unspeakable piece of writing

'We might go in your umbrella,' said Pooh.
'?'
'We might go in your umbrella,' said Pooh.
'??'
'We might go in your umbrella,' said Pooh.
'!!!!!!'
For suddenly Christopher Robin saw that they might.

A. A. Milne, *Winnie the Pooh*

And an unwritable piece of speech

Anthony Trollope describes a character in *Ralph the Heir* as having 'a soft, greasy voice, made up of pretence, politeness and saliva'. It is a splendid verbal picture, but it is not easy to decide exactly what type of voice is being described. Voice types defy precise verbal description.

contracts) or to provide a means of identity or authority (as in the sacred literature of a religious tradition). Because of its formality, it is more likely to be used to provide the standard which society values. Our speech is frequently judged by the standards of the written language – and found wanting.

GROUP IDENTITIES

The 'variety' of the English language encompasses all social situations. As soon as people come into regular contact with each other, the language they use is likely to develop features which reflect the bonds that exist between them, and which distinguish them from other social groups. When they need to write to each other or to outsiders, they may make use of special notepaper (if they can afford it), or a distinctive typography. When speaking, they may develop their own style of pronunciation. In both spoken and written language, there will emerge special vocabulary and grammatical constructions. In particular, they will develop their own slang. 'The chief use of slang', it has been said, 'is to show that you're one of the gang.' The point applies with equal force to families, schools, local clubs and societies, sports and games, jobs and professions, religious bodies, or any other context in which people come together. 'Gang' applies not only to youths on street corners, but to teachers, footballers, doctors, lawyers, the clergy – everyone. We all belong to a number of different 'gangs', and have learned the distinctive language of each of them.

The more a group of people are given the status of a social institution within a community, the more distinctive their language is likely to be. The most idiosyncratic varieties of English are those associated with the church and the law. In their traditional uses, both religious and legal English rely on archaic vocabulary and grammar, a wide range of special locutions, special tones of voice (in church services and courtrooms), and a distinctive written style (as in religious orders of service, or legal documents). Other well-recognized varieties of English include the language of government (Acts of Parliament, Civil Service prose), science, medicine, advertising, broadcasting and journalism. 'Domestic' varieties are also readily distinguishable, as seen in the language of recipes, instruction leaflets, and knitting patterns.

The best adjectives

In a study of the vocabulary used in television advertising, Geoffrey Leech found that the twenty most common adjectives, in order of frequency, were the following.

1. new	6. full	11. crisp	16. easy
2. good/better/best	7. sure	12. fine	17. bright
3. free	8. clean	13. big	18. extra
4. fresh	9. wonderful	14. great	19. safe
5. delicious	10. special	15. real	20. rich

No other language variety gives such prominence to 'positive' adjectives of this kind, to the exclusion of their 'negative' or 'neutral' counterparts (*old, bad, ordinary*, etc.).

Within each category, there may be many 'sub-varieties'. For instance, there are several styles of advertising, such as the difference between the 'hard sell' and the 'soft sell' approaches to marketing a product. The different domains of science and technology have their own vocabulary and conventions of presentation, and often display interesting grammatical differences. Journalism provides us with the distinction between the 'quality' press and the 'tabloids'. And within these sub-varieties there may be further distinctions – the style of individual newspapers or magazines, such as the *Daily Mail* or the *Sun*.

When writing a grammar or dictionary, it is easy to forget about the linguistic idiosyncrasies of the different varieties of English, and concentrate only on the 'common core' of words and structures which they contain. But this is to miss out a great deal of what makes the language real and dynamic. The abbreviated syntax of knitting patterns or cookery recipes is just as much a part of English as is the complex prose of a monograph or a formal speech. The news reporter who leaves out verbs (*Now over to John Brown in Birmingham*) is a long way from the legal draftsman who uses two or three verbs for the same meaning (*have and hold, made and signed*), but for both their language is shaped by their circumstances – the need for economical expression in the first case; the need to include different nuances of meaning in the second. There are vast differences in the range and organization of the many varieties of English. A small selection is illustrated in the remaining pages of this chapter.

The variety of English

A common exercise in stylistic analysis is to look at a sample of language, note its main linguistic features, and work out from these the kind of situation in which it would have been used. The answer is usually clear, even if the subject-matter clues are removed. For example, *O — the — of —, who hast — thine — ...* could only be traditional religious English.

O God the King of Glory, who hast exalted thine only Son Jesus Christ with great triumph unto thy kingdom in heaven, we beseech thee leave us not comfortless, but send to us thine Holy Ghost to comfort us, and exalt us into the same place, whither our Saviour Christ is gone before, who liveth and reigneth with thee and the Holy Ghost, one God, world without end, Amen. (*Prayer*)

Using No. 7 needles, cast on 45 sts. Work 6 rows in moss stitch (every row *K.1, P.1, rep. from * to last st., K.1). Proceed in lace and moss stitch patt. with moss stitch border as follows: **1st row** (K.1, P.1) twice, *K.1, w.f., K.3, w.f., sl.1, K.1, p.s.s.o., K.1 ... (*Knitting pattern*)

Whereas a proposal to effect with the Society an assurance on the Life Insured named in the Schedule hereto has been duly made and signed as a basis of such assurance and a declaration has been made agreeing that this policy shall be subject to the Society's Registered Rules (which shall be deemed to form part of this policy) to the Table of Insurance printed hereon and to the terms and conditions of the said Table ... (*Life insurance proposal*)

The photolytic decomposition of phenylazotriphenylmethane in benzene apparently follows a similar course to the pyrolytic decomposition discussed above. It has been investigated by Horner and Naumann (1954) and Huisgen and Nakaten (1954), and was found to involve a primary dissociation into phenyl and triphenylmethyl radicals and nitrogen, in the manner indicated in equation (8). (*Chemistry textbook*)

ANGLESEY S/C cottage slps 6, col. TV, tel., no dogs. Avail. Mar., Apr., Jun. Write Box 342 for brochure. (*Newspaper small ad*)

The judge in the mail train robbery trial at Aylesbury has ordered round-the-clock police protection for the families of the jury, all men, when they retire to consider their verdict. When Mr Justice Edmund Davis said this in court this morning, he referred to the fact that earlier this week one of the jurors had reported an attempt at bribery. The clerk of the court had told him, he said, that the jury were now asking for assurances that there would be no kind of interference with their families while they were in retirement . . . (*B B C radio news*)

Cream together butter, sugar and beaten yolks until smooth. Heat the chocolate and water in a bowl over boiling water, stirring to a creamy consistency. Add slowly to the first mixture, then fold in stiffly-beaten egg whites . . . (*Cookery book*)

And the score goes up to 34 for 2. Edrich 22. And Cowdrey out this morning, caught Burge, bowled Hawke, 10. And England now, of course, metaphorically speaking, on the back foot. The batsmen still to come, which many of you no doubt will be counting up – and some Englishmen may be glad that Jack Flavell was left out in favour of a batsman – Parfitt next, then Sharpe, then Parkes, then Titmus, Trueman, Gifford, Coldwell. Now a little fussing about someone behind the sight-screen before McKenzie bowls . . . (*Radio sports commentary*)

Ordinary dusting doesn't remove sticky marks. Now Pledge turns your duster into a magnet for dust and marks. With Pledge just a wipe picks up dust and sticky marks. Leaves a real wax shine instantly. So when you dust, turn your duster into a magnet for dust and marks, with Pledge. Worth every penny, because it cleans and shines as you dust. Pledge, from Johnsons. (*TV advertisement*)

My government reaffirm their support for the defence of the free world, the basic concept of the Atlantic alliance, and they will continue to play their full part in the North Atlantic Treaty Organization, and in other organizations for collective defence. They will review defence policy to ensure, by relating our commitments and our resources, that my armed forces are able to discharge their many tasks overseas with the greatest effectiveness and economy . . . (*Formal speech, opening of Parliament*)

A more detailed look at legal language

● Formal and ceremonial words and constructions are found both in written documents and in the spoken language of the courtroom:

Signed, sealed and delivered   *You may approach the bench*
Your Honour   *May it please the court*
. . . the truth, the whole truth, and nothing but the truth

● Frequent use is made of common words with uncommon meanings:

    action = law suit   *presents* = this legal document
    hand = signature   *said* = mentioned before

● Old and Middle English words are retained, though no longer in general usage:

    aforesaid   *heretofore*   *thereby*
    forthwith   *thenceforth*   *witnesseth*

● There are many Latin words and phrases, only a few of which have become part of the language as a whole (e.g. *alias*, *alibi*):

    corpus delicti   *nolle prosequi*   *sui juris*
    ejusdem generis   *res gestae*   *vis major*

● French is the source of much legal language, though many words are now in general use (e.g. *appeal*, *counsel*, *crime*, *plaintiff*):

    demurrer   *estoppel*   *lien*
    easement   *fee simple*   *tort*

● There are several technical terms with precise and well understood meanings ('terms of art'):

    appeal   *contributory*   *felony*   *injunction*
    bail   *defendant*   *negligence*

● Less precise terms and idioms, in standard use in daily legal discussion, are sometimes referred to as legal 'argot';

    alleged   *objection*   *superior court*
    issue of law   *order to show cause*   *without prejudice*

● Relatively vague words and phrases are often used deliberately, to permit a degree of flexibility in interpretation:

    adequate cause   *improper*   *nominal sum*
    as soon as possible   *malice*   *reasonable care*

Effective courtroom strategies

Television courtroom dramas have brought spoken legal language to the attention of millions who have never attended court themselves. William O'Barr has analysed some of the main linguistic strategies used in court by lawyers and witnesses.

Lawyers

1. Vary the way in which you ask questions.
2. Give your own witnesses a chance to speak at length; restrict the witnesses under cross-examination to short, direct answers to specific questions.
3. Convey a sense of organization in your interviews of witnesses and your remarks to the jury.
4. Adopt different styles of questioning with different kinds of witnesses (e.g. women, the elderly, children, experts).
5. Remain poker-faced throughout; do not reveal surprise even when an answer is totally unexpected; save dramatic reactions for special occasions.
6. Rhythm and pace are important; do not bore the jury with slowness; use silence strategically.
7. Repetition can be useful for emphasis but it should be used with care so as not to bore the jury.
8. Avoid interrupting a witness, especially a responsive answer; it gives the impression you want to hide some of the facts.
9. Use objections sparingly; they not only call attention to the material being objected to, but also convey an impression of attempting to conceal information.

Witnesses

1. Vary the way in which you give answers.
2. Give long answers wherever possible; make the opposition lawyer stop you frequently during cross-examination, to give the impression of reluctance to have your full story heard.
3. Try to confuse the organization which the opposition lawyer has planned for the cross-examination.
4. Adopt different styles of answering questions asked by different

questioners (e.g. deference to the judge, no hostile answers to the opposition lawyer).

5. Do not show surprise even when questions are unexpected; save dramatic reactions for special moments.

6. Use rhythm and pace to advantage. Upset the opposition lawyer's pace with variations in response timing (e.g. asking *Please repeat the question* after an especially long or complex question).

7. React to a cross-examiner's repetition of material, e. g. by saying *Why do you keep asking me the same question?*

8. Interrupt the opposition lawyer by volunteering answers, as soon as you can see the drift. This gives the impression that you are co-operative, and serves to confuse the lawyer's style.

9. Blurt out relevant facts and opinions on cross-examination, even though the opposition lawyer may attempt to limit your answer. These attempts will give the impression that the lawyer is trying to conceal some of your evidence.

Trucker Talk

One of the most distinctive varieties of contemporary English is the jargon of American truck drivers using citizen band radio. The language has been widely publicized since the medium became available in 1958, especially after the success of such films as *Convoy*. It contains a large number of stereotyped phrases for communicating routine messages, using a special numerical code (the CB–10 system).

Some trucker jargon			
affirmative	yes	*jockey*	driver
anklebiters	children	*lettuce*	paper money
barn	garage	*lollipop*	signpost
bear den	police station	*mobile*	car and caravan
bears	police	*mattress*	
big mama	a long aerial	*motion lotion*	fuel
boot rest	accelerator	*organ grinding*	making love
copy?	understand?	*pitstop*	lay-by
doughnuts	tyres	*rubber duck*	first convoy truck
drain the	stop for the	*slappers*	wipers
radiator	lavatory	*smokey on*	police on patrol
dusting	driving on hard	*rubber*	
	shoulder	*smokey's*	breath test
ears	CB set	*balloon*	
Evel Knievel	motorcyclist	*smokey with*	police car with CB
eyeballs	headlights	*ears*	
five-finger	stolen goods	*stack*	exhaust
discount		*super cola*	beer
grandma lane	slow lane	*tags*	plates
highballing	moving fast	*wrapper*	car

Some of the CB-10 codes

10–1	Poor reception	10–34	Trouble, need help
10–2	Good reception	10–35	Confidential
10–3	End transmission	10–36	Time is now
10–4	Message understood	10–37	Breakdown lorry needed
10–5	Relay message	10–38	Ambulance needed
10–6	Stand by	10–39	Message delivered
10–7	Leaving air	10–41	Tune to
10–8	In service	10–42	Traffic accident
10–9	Repeat	10–43	Traffic jam
10–10	Monitoring without transmitting	10–44	I have message for you
10–11	Transmitting too fast	10–45	Units within range help
10–12	Visitors present	10–46	Help motorist
10–13	Request for weather/ road conditions	10–50	Break channel
		10–60	Number of next message
10–16	Make collection at	10–62	Not understood, use telephone
10–17	Urgent		
10–18	Anything for me?	10–65	Waiting for next message
10–19	Nothing for you, return home	10–67	All units comply
		10–69	Message received
10–20	My position is	10–70	Fire
10–21	Call by telephone	10–73	Speed trap
10–22	Report in person	10–74	Negative
10–23	Stand by	10–77	Negative contact
10–24	Task completed	10–81	Reserve hotel room
10–25	Can you contact?	10–82	Reserve room
10–26	Disregard last message	10–84	My telephone number
10–27	Changing channel	10–85	My address
10–28	Identify your station	10–89	Radio mechanic required
10–29	Contact time up	10–91	Talk closer to microphone
10–30	Against regulations	10–92	Adjust transmitter
10–32	I will give you a radio check	10–93	Check my frequency
		10–99	Mission completed
10–33	Emergency traffic at this station	10–100	Stop at lavatory
		10–200	Police needed
		10–2000	Drug trafficker

More complex messages use everyday English, peppered with its own slang, which make it attractive to initiates and largely unintelligible to outsiders. There are now dialects of this variety: the UK system is not identical to the one used in the USA, because of differences in the two cultures.

7

೮ ೮ ೮ ೮ ೮ ೮ ೮ ೮ ೮ ೮

English at Play

Much of Chapter 6 dealt with the subject of English at work. The most distinctive and predictable varieties of the language are to be found in the vast range of jobs and professional activities which characterize modern society. The last part of the chapter began with the clergy and ended with truckers. But there are linguistic conventions to be followed for our leisure activities too – and especially whenever we 'play' with language, to convey effects which are intriguing, entertaining, endearing, or just plain funny.

The main characteristic of English at play is its readiness to depart from the norms of usage found elsewhere in the language. We break the rules to create a special effect – a strategy also found in literary writing (see Chapter 8). Jokes, riddles, graffiti, verbal contests, repartee, puns, and other forms of wit all rely on the speaker (or writer) doing something unexpected with language. The effect may be located at a single point, as in a pun or a 'punch line', or it may be a continuous, cumulative effect, as in the verbal repartee exchanged by rival street gangs, where each tries to out-swear the other.

In many cases there is a linguistic structure to the genre. Jokes often have stereotyped openings which make it possible to predict the sequence of events in the narrative. 'There was an Englishman, an Irishman, and a Scotsman . . .' means a three-part joke is to follow. Children's jokes rely greatly on a predictable internal structure:

> *A*: Knock knock.
> *B*: Who's there?
> *A*: Arthur.

From: *Cartoons from* Punch (Robson Books, 1979)

> *B*: Arthur who?
> *A*: Arthur ['alf a] minute and I'll find out.

Once the structure is well-established, it can accept deviations which break the expected sequence:

> *A*: Knock knock.
> *B*: Who's there?
> *A*: Doctor.
> *B*: Doctor who?
> *A*: That's right.

Graffiti rules OK

The '— rules OK' motif provides one of the best examples of a successful humour framework – used mainly as a source of graffiti. Here are a few examples, taken from walls in recent years. They clearly show the ingenious ways in which linguistic departures can be introduced from a simple norm.

Town criers rule, okez, okez, okez!
Sycophancy rules – if it's OK by you.
Scots rule, och aye!
Anarchy, no rules, OK?
Procrastination will rule one day, OK?
Apathy ru
Mañuel rules, Oh-Qué?
Synonyms govern, all right?
Roget's Thesaurus dominates, regulates, rules, all right, agreed.

Other well-known stereotyped structures include such openings as 'Waiter, there's a fly in my soup', 'What do you get if you cross an [ANIMAL] with an [ANIMAL]?', and 'What did the [NOUN] say to the [NOUN]?' In each case, a standard stimulus permits an almost infinite number of possible responses.

Riddles are more complex, from the point of view of meaning, but their structure often resembles that of a joke. Riddling is an intellectual verbal game: an utterance is made which is intended to mystify or mislead. Events, people, animals, or objects are described in such a way that the description suggests something different. The recipient of the riddle has to resolve the ambiguity. In English, riddles are usually quite short, and are found largely in children's games and conversation.

> What has two legs and flies? A pair of trousers.

But longer riddles can be found. 'Why are fire engines red?', in one version, has a twelve-line response:

> One and one are two.
> Two and two are four.
> Three times four is twelve.
> There are twelve inches in a ruler.
> Queen Mary was a ruler.
> Queen Mary ruled the sea.
> There are fish in the sea.
> The fish have fins.
> The Finns fought the Russians.
> The Russians are red.
> Fire engines are always rushin'.
> That's why fire engines are red.

Occasionally, riddles will express a more serious purpose, such as in narratives where they are a test of a hero's wisdom or worthiness. In one famous case, Oedipus was required to solve the riddle of the sphinx: 'What has one voice, and walks on four legs in the morning, on two at noon, and on three in the evening?' (The answer was a man, seen as a baby, an adult, and an old man with a stick.) Riddles of this kind are not restricted to single cultures, but turn up in riddle collections all over the world – including English.

The competitive element in riddling relates it to verbal duels and speech events where linguistic skill confers social status. In the USA, breakdancing has its correlate in fast-talking, or 'rapping', in which long sequences of rhyming lines are produced at speed to a fixed rhythm:

> . . . Always have fun
> Always on the run
> Can't rap now
> Till I see the sun
> You see twenty dollars
> Laying on the ground

The oldest English riddles

The Exeter Book, the oldest collection of English poetry, contains ninety-five riddles, probably dating from the eighth century. The riddles are generally written in the first person. Here is R. K. Gordon's translation of the 'Anchor' riddle:

Often I must war against the wave and fight against the wind; I contend against them combined, when, buried by the billows, I go to seek the earth; my native land is strange to me. If I grow motionless I am mighty in the conflict; if I succeed not in that they are stronger than I, and straightway with rending they put me to rout; they wish to carry off what I must keep safe. I foil them in that if my tail endures and if the stones are able to hold fast against me in my strength. Ask what is my name.

> Try to pick it up
> But it moved across town . . .

In more aggressive displays, taunts, boasts, name-calling, and various kinds of insult may be traded in lengthy exchanges. Among black American youths in ghetto areas, these exchanges are variously known as 'sounding', 'signifying', 'woofing' or 'playing the dozens'. A sequence of ritual insults ('raps') is followed by a series of replies ('caps'). Such duels seem to act as a way of finding out the social structure of the peer group. Members can discover and test the dominance of others, without recourse to fighting or bloodshed. Words not war.

Insult duels, politeness contests and boasting rituals have a long history in English. One of the earliest exchanges is recorded in the Old English poem the *Battle of Maldon* (AD 991) between the English and Danish leaders. In more recent times, the West Indian calypso was originally a type of verbal insult, directed at political figures. In the Middle Ages, these verbal attacks, known as 'flyting', were sometimes developed at length. Some of the best invective is found in William Dunbar's poem 'The Flyting of Dunbar and Kennedie' (early sixteenth century). The exact meaning of some of the words is uncertain, but there is no doubt about their purpose:

> Mauch muttoun, byt buttoun, peilit gluttoun, air to Hilhous;
> Rank beggar, ostir dregar, foule fleggar in the flet;

Chittirlilling, ruch lilling, lik schilling in the milhous;
Baird rehator, theif of natur, fals tratour, feyindis gett;
Filling of tauch, rak sauch, cry crauch, thow art oursett;
Muttoun dryver, girnall ryver, yadswyvar, fowll fell the;
Herretyk, lunatyk, puspyk, carlingis pet,
Rottin crok, dirtin drok, cry cok, or I sall quell the.

It is of course possible to insult people in more indirect and subtle ways, using sarcasm, loaded language, metaphor, puns, and other such devices. It is all word-play, whether the intent is jocular or serious. And word-play has an enormous range, being found in every conceivable linguistic context and used to express most emotions and subject-matters. Puns, for example, show this range very clearly. They are common enough in everyday contexts, where they are frequently heard (and enjoyed or condemned, according to taste) in conversation. They are the stock-in-trade of comedians ('What did the circus manager say to the human cannonball who wanted to leave? Where shall I find another man of your calibre!'). They are a fruitful source of effects in advertising ('Stick with us', advertising glue). And newspaper editors – in certain papers, at least – use them in headlines and sub-headings ('Check, mate', introducing an article about a chess-enthusiast not being allowed to leave the Soviet Union).

Too many of these examples would make us ill. For some people, puns are, as John Dryden claimed, 'the lowest and most grovelling form of wit'. They are not found with equal frequency in all parts of the English-speaking world: they are much less popular in the USA than in Britain, for example. On the other hand, word-play graces the most revered literature. Without puns, much of the pungency and humour of Shakespeare's writing would be lost. 'Ask for me tomorrow,' says the dying Mercutio in *Romeo and Juliet*, 'and you shall find me a grave man.' And possibly the most famous pun of all time is in the New Testament: 'Thou art *Peter*, and upon this *rock* I will build my church' – a pun which works better in French where, as in Latin, the same word is used for both *Peter* and *rock* (*pierre*).

ENGLISH LAUGHS AT ITSELF

The subject-matter of the jokes, puns, and riddles illustrated so far has been, in effect, life, the universe, and everything. But there is another level of linguistic play where the English language itself is the subject-matter. Under this heading come the many dialect joke-books, in which people laugh at the accents and vocal mannerisms of English users from different parts of the country or from different countries. Perhaps the most famous of these books was *Let Stalk Strine* (Australian), published in 1965, by Afferbeck Lauder, said to be Professor of Strine Studies at the University of Sinny. He uses standard spellings to represent the popular impression of a broad Australian accent (see p. 240), with bizarre results:

Jezz: Articles of furniture. As in: 'Set the tible, love, and get a coupler jezz'.
Scona: A meteorological term. As in: 'Scona rine'.
X: The twenty-fourth letter of the strine alphabet; also plural of egg; also a tool for chopping wood.

The same kind of satire has been levelled at Liverpool speech in *Lern Yerself Scouse* (1966), by Frank Shaw, Fritz Spiegl and Stan Kelly:

Ullo dur! Greetings; I am pleased to make your acquaintance.
Gisalite. Could you oblige me with a match, please.
Ere, tatty-head! I say, young woman.

And at Texas speech by Jim Everhart in *The Illustrated Texas Dictionary of the English Language* (1968):

all: petroleum, as in 'They found all on mah land!'
slave: the part of the garment covering an arm only.
stars: a flight of steps.

And at most British dialects by Sam Llewellyn, in *Yacky dar moy bewty!* (1985). East Anglian English, for instance:

Hilloo, bor!   Excuse me!
Oi oont noo where I em.   I am lost.
Blass that int noo bledda good.   Oh dear.

Or Hampshire English:

This be a jarming caddage.   What a charming cottage!
Thankee, muss.   Thank you, madam.
Un's got meece, vurlikely.   It has probably got mice.

Comic alphabets

The English alphabet has often been the butt of humour. There are hundreds of poems and puns based on reciting the letters in order. Widely known in the nineteenth century, they seem to have originated as an adult reflex of the rhyming alphabets which came to be used in schools ('A for an Apple, an Archer, and Arrow; B for a Bull, a Bear, and a Barrow', etc.). A selection of entries from Eric Partridge's *Comic Alphabets* (1961) runs as follows:

A for 'orses	N for mation
B for mutton	O for the rainbow
C for yourself	P for soup
D for dumb	Q for the bus
(deaf or dumb)	R for 'mo
E for brick	(half a moment)
(heave a brick)	S for you
F for vescence	(as for you)
G for police	T for two
(chief of police)	U for me
H for beauty	V for la compagnie
(age before beauty)	(Vive la compagnie)
I for Novello	W for a quid
J for oranges	(double you – betting)
(Jaffa oranges)	X for breakfast
K for teria	Y for mistress
(cafeteria)	(wife or mistress)
L for leather	Z for the doctor
M for sis	(send for the doctor)
(emphasis)	

But these are only some of the possibilities. Under A, for example, we find *A for ism*, *A for gardener* (Ava Gardner) and *A for mentioned*. Under N, *N for a dig* (infra dig), *N for a penny* (in for a penny), *N for lope* (envelope) and *N for laying*. Under Q, we also find *Q for billiards* and *Q gardens* (Kew). And under Y, several variants on 'wife' – *Y for lover*, *Y for husband*, *Y for secretary*, *Y for nagging* – as well as *Y for fishing* (Wye) and *Y for crying out loud*!

Few distinctive accents and dialects have escaped this kind of treatment. Nor are upper class accents exempt. If you want to learn to talk like the Queen, or like the Sloane Square set, there is no shortage of facetious manuals to help you on your way.

WORD GAMES

Another way in which we play with the English language is through the phenomenon of word games. People seem to delight in pulling words apart and reconstituting them in a novel guise, arranging them into clever patterns, finding hidden meanings in them, and trying to use them according to specially invented rules. Word puzzles and competitions are to be found in newspapers, at house parties, in schools, on radio and television, and in all kinds of individual contexts – as when an adult completes a crossword, or a child plays a game of Hangman. One of the most successful games on British television is 'Blankety Blank', in which people have to guess which word fills a blank in a familiar phrase. Another is 'Call my Bluff', where the participants have to decide which of three possible meanings belongs to an unfamiliar word. The majority of TV games, in fact, seem to contain some kind of language element.

The crossword is undoubtedly the most popular of all word games. It was devised in the USA in 1913 by a journalist, Arthur Wynne, as a newspaper puzzle called a 'word cross', and it quickly became a craze. But for anyone who has tried it, writing a good puzzle turns out to be far more difficult than solving it. The construction of the interlocking words within the puzzle is not the issue: the main problem is devising clues which are ingeniously ambiguous, but do not un-intentionally mislead. The more difficult puzzles make use of cryptic clues, which require the solver to understand several special conventions. An anagram might be signalled by a figure of speech expressing disorder, such as 'A youth is all mixed up . . .' If the clue contains a parenthetic phrase such as 'we hear', similar-sounding words are involved. Punning clues often end with an exclamation or question mark. And a large number of conventional expressions are used to symbolize certain letters, such as *left* (= L), *north* (= N), *a sailor* (= AB), or *a thousand* (= M). In the specialized world of the 'serious' crossword compilers, the rules governing the construction of clues are strictly adhered to, and much pleasure is obtained by making them really difficult and ingenious. In Britain, the symbol of this state of mind has been the choice of pseudonyms of some of the great compilers: Torquemada, Ximenes, and Azed (Deza in reverse) – all names of leaders of the Spanish Inquisition!

The boundary between word games and the world of secret messages and codes is a difficult one to draw. So is the boundary between a game, a hobby, and an obsession. Some of the examples below move in the direction of these other headings. And the last example in the chapter is very definitely not a game to those who practise it.

● *Acrostics* are compositions, usually in verse, which arrange certain letters within a text to form a word, phrase, or special pattern. Some are written as puzzles; in others, there is no attempt to conceal the 'answer'. Generally, the initial letter of each line provides the clue, but sometimes the pattern is based on the last letter of the line (a *telestich*), combinations of first and last letters (a *double acrostic*), or even more complex sequences. Acrostics are commonly used in mnemonics; for example, 'Every Good Boy Deserves Favour' is one way of remembering the names of the notes on the lines in the treble clef.

● *Word squares* are sequences of letters using words of equal length which read in horizontal, vertical, and occasionally diagonal directions. Usually the words are the same in each direction, but in *double word squares*, they read differently:

> O R A L
> M A R E
> E V E N
> N E A T

Some nine-word squares have been constructed in English, containing place names and several rare words, but so far no ten-word squares using ten different words have been completed, even with the help of a computer.

```
Q U A R E L E S T
U P P E R E S T E
A P P O I N T E R
R E O M E T E R S
E R I E V I L L E
L E N T I L L I N
E S T E L L I N E
S T E R L I N G S
T E R S E N E S S
```

● *Anagrams* rearrange the letters of a word or phrase to make new words – a procedure which at one time was thought to disclose significant information about a person's character or future, and even to carry mystical meaning or magical power. Jonathan Swift was one of many who ridiculed the pomposity and superstition of those who dealt in anagrams. In *Gulliver's Travels*, natives of Tribnia (Britain) discover plots using the 'anagrammatic method':

by transposing the letters of the alphabet in any suspected paper, they can lay open the deepest designs of a discontented party. So, for example, if I should say, in a letter to a friend, 'Our brother Tom has just got the piles', a skilful decipherer would discover that the same letters which compose that sentence, may be analysed into the following words, 'Resist – a plot is brought home – the tour'.

As a game, however, anagrams can provide a great deal of fun, especially by finding an anagram which relates to the original in some way:

astronomers – moon-starers
conversation – voices rant on
Margaret Thatcher – Meg, the arch-tartar
mother-in-law – woman Hitler
total abstainers – sit not at ale bars

● A *rebus* mixes letters, pictures, and graphic symbols to make words and sentences. Often, the sentences make sense only when read aloud in a certain way, as in this famous rebus:

YY U R	Too wise you are
YY U B	Too wise you be
I C U R	I see you are
YY 4 me	Too wise for me

Other ingenious constructions are shown below:

H&	hand
XQQ	excuse
reactions reac tions	split second reactions
stalH Pments	HP instalments

• *Tongue twisters* are one of the few word games which relate purely to the spoken medium. Words are juxtaposed which contain the same or similar sounds, and the exercise is to say them as rapidly as possible. Famous English examples include:

> The Leith police dismisseth us
> The sixth sheikh's sixth sheep's sick
> She sells sea-shells on the sea-shore

• *Palindromes* are words or phrases – and sometimes much larger units of language – which read the same in both directions. Simple examples are found in such everyday examples as *madam* and *Eve*, but the real challenge is to construct long sequences which make sense, such as *Draw, o coward!* and *Sex at noon taxes*. Longer sequences tend to deteriorate into nonsense, though there are exceptions: *Doc, note, I dissent. A fast never prevents a fatness. I diet on cod.* The longest palindrome is reputedly over 65,000 words.

• *Pangrams* are sentences which contain every letter of the alphabet – ideally, a single instance of each. The typist's sentence *The quick brown fox jumps over the lazy dog* satisfies the first criterion, but has several duplications. A 26-letter pangram devised in 1984 reads *Veldt jynx grimps waqf zho buck*, where there is undoubtedly a syntax, but a good dictionary is needed to establish the meaning.

• *Lipograms* are compositions which omit a letter of the alphabet. One of the most famous lipograms in English is *Gadsby* (1939), a 50,000-word novel by Ernest Wright, which makes no use of the most frequent letter of the English alphabet, *e*. A tiny extract from this remarkable work illustrates how it can be done:

> Upon this basis I am going to show you how a bunch of bright young folks did find a champion; a man with boys and girls of his own; a man of so dominating and happy individuality that Youth is drawn to him as is a fly to a sugar bowl. It is a story about a small town. It is not a gossipy yarn; nor is it a dry, monotonous account, full of such customary 'fill-ins' as 'romantic moonlight casting murky shadows down a long, winding country

road'. Nor will it say anything about twinklings lulling distant folds; robins carolling at twilight, nor any 'warm glow of lamplight' from a cabin window. No. It is an account of up-and-doing activity; a vivid portrayal of Youth as it is today . . .

● *Univocalics* are compositions which use only one vowel. The possibilities for expression are very limited, but several clever poems have been constructed in this way, as is illustrated by this sixteen-line work by C. C. Bombaugh called 'Incontrovertible Facts' (1890):

> No monk too good to rob, or cog, or plot.
> No fool so gross to bolt Scotch collops hot.
> From Donjon tops no Oronoko rolls.
> Logwood, not Lotos, floods Oporto's bowls.
> Troops of old tosspots, oft, to sot, consort.
> Box tops, not bottoms, school-boys flog for sport.
> No cool monsoons blow soft on Oxford dons,
> Orthodox, jog-trot, book-worm Solomons!
> Bold Ostrogoths, of ghosts no horror show.
> On London shop-fronts no hop-blossoms grow.
> To crocks of gold no dodo looks for food.
> On soft cloth footstools no old fox doth brood.
> Long storm-tost sloops forlorn, work on to no port.
> Rooks do not roost on spoons, nor woodcocks snort,
> Nor dog on snowdrop or on coltsfoot rolls,
> Nor common frogs concoct long protocols.

● *Doublets* is a game where one word is changed into another in a series of steps, each intervening word differing from its neighbours by only one letter. The challenge is both to form the chain of linked words, and to do so in as few steps as possible. The game was invented by Lewis Carroll, who gave as one of his first examples, 'Drive PIG into STY'. His answer involved five steps: PIG–WIG–WAG–WAY–SAY–STY.

● *Syzygies* is another Lewis Carroll game where one word is changed into another in a series of steps, with each intervening word having several letters in common with the preceding word. For example, MAN can be linked to ICE through the steps PERMANENT and ENTICE. Many other kinds of 'word-chains' have been invented, such as the construction of a chain of overlapping two-part words: FIREMAN–MANKIND–KINDNESS, etc.

● *Words within words* is a popular game, often chosen for competitions, whose aim is simply to make as many words as possible from the letters of a single word. To win is far more difficult than one might think – a comment which is true of many of the games in this chapter – and there are impressive scores to beat. One player, for example, has claimed there are 273 words in PSALTER – *rat, peat, repast* . . .

● *Grid games* all operate on the principle of building up words on a predetermined grid. Some are intended for individual use, such as Word Search (a large letter grid in which words have to be found by moving from one square to the next, in any direction). Others are for several players, such as Lexicon, Kan-U-Go, and Boggle. In Scrabble – the most famous game of this type – points are assigned based upon how many letters are used; the rarer letters score higher points, and certain squares in the grid are more valuable than others. This game now has its own national and international championships, in which expert players display rare feats of lexical awareness to achieve high scores.

● *Gematria* is a technique which substitutes numbers for letters, and compares the 'values' of words in order to provide insights into the meaning of life. The idea is very old. In the Middle Ages, there arose a Jewish (later a Christian) system of mystical practices based on an esoteric interpretation of Old Testament texts, known as the *Kabbala* (from Hebrew *qabbalah* 'something received'). It was thought that language in general, and biblical language in particular, contained coded secrets about God and the world, based on the way the letters of the text were arranged, and the numerical values which could be assigned to them.

In English, the twenty-six letters are valued 1 to 26, in order. On this basis, all kinds of curious and (some believe) significant correlations can be obtained. For example, it emerges that MAN and EDEN both score twenty-eight, BIBLE and HOLY WRIT are separated by 100, MOUNT SINAI and THE LAWS OF GOD both score 135, and JESUS, MESSIAH, SON GOD, CROSS and GOSPEL all score seventy-four. And in the secular domain, several mystical totals can be obtained, which adherents claim demonstrate the truth of the approach:

Clement Wood's 'Death of a Scrabble Master' cleverly portrays some of the special knowledge required to keep on winning:

This was the greatest of the game's great players:
If you played BRAS, he'd make it HUDIBRASTIC.
He ruled a world 15 by 15 squares,
Peopled by 100 letters, wood or plastic.

He unearthed XEBEC, HAJI, useful QAID,
Found QUOS (see pl. of QUID PRO QUO) and QUOTHA,
Discovered AU, DE, DA all unitalicized
(AU JUS, DA CAPO, ALMANACH DE GOTHA).

Two-letter words went marching through his brain,
Spondaic-footed, singing their slow litany:
AL (Indian Mulberry), AI (a sloth), EM, EN,
BY, MY, AX, EX, OX, LO, IT, AN, HE...

PE (Hebrew letter), LI (a Chinese mile), KA, RE,
SH (like NTH, spectacularly vowelless),
AY, OY (a cry of grief, pain or dismay);
HAI, HI, HO – leaving opponents powerless.

He, if the tiles before him said DOC TIME,
Would promptly play the elegant DEMOTIC,
And none but he fulfilled the scrabbler's dream,
When through two triple words, he hung QUIXOTIC.

The day his adversary put down GNASHED,
He laid – a virtuoso feat – beneath it GOUTIER,
So placed, that six more tiny words were hatched:
GO, NU, AT, SI, then (as you've seen, no doubt) HE, ER.

NOT + SAME	BOOK + LOAN	KEEP + OFF	KING + CHAIR	GOOD + DEEDS	ALL + VOTE
DIFFERENT	LIBRARY	GRASS	THRONE	SCOUT	DEMOCRACY

As is evident from the examples, a certain amount of linguistic manipulating sometimes has to take place for the numbers to come out right. SON OF GOD would not work; nor would BOOKS + LOAN. There has to be some numerical manipulating too – totals are allowed

Code games

Children often spontaneously play with spoken English by turning ordinary words back-to-front or inside-out. Most of these games are based on the word spelling. Even in the more complex cases, practitioners can teach themselves to talk at great speed. Records of some of the languages go back over 100 years. Some of the games are also heard in use among adults, especially in contexts where secrecy is required, such as in front of customers, or small children.

- In **back slang**, words are spelled backwards, and then the new arrangement of letters is given a plausible pronunciation. It has been observed among soldiers, barrow-boys, shopkeepers, thieves, and public-school pupils. First World War examples include *kew* (week), *neetrith* (thirteen), *tekram* (market) and *tenip* (pint).
- In what is sometimes called **centre slang**, the central vowel of a word, along with its following consonant, is placed at the beginning, and a nonsense syllable added, e.g. *eekcher* (cheek), *hoolerfer* (fool), *ightri* (right).
- In **eggy-peggy** or **aygo-paygo** speech, an extra syllable is added, e.g. *Pugut thagat begook dowgun* (Put that book down). Similar games insert an extra vowel or consonant between each syllable: using *f*, for example, 'Where are you going' becomes *Wheref aref youf gofing*.
- In **pig Latin**, the first consonants are put at the end of the word, and *ay* or *e* added, e.g. *Utpay atthay ookbay ownday*. In a variant of this, last consonants are put at the beginning of the word, with extra sounds to aid the pronunciation, e.g. *Teput tatha keboo nadaw*.
- In **t-ing in i** (talking in initials), certain words are replaced by their first letters. A case from a school in Texas showed examples such as *Some p l-ed the m* (Some people liked the movie), *She's a v p g* (She's a very pretty girl). Parents also sometimes use this form of abbreviation in front of their young children, along with other spelling conventions, such as *It's time for b,e,d*. This genre of secret language is perhaps not too far away from the widespread use of initials in technical slang, e.g. the medical *Very SOB* (short of breath).

to differ by certain amounts (for instance, if two words added up to fifty-three and fifty-four respectively, they would still be considered significant). And the cases where numbers coincide are far outnumbered by the cases where they don't. None the less, such calculations can persuade people to allow their lives to be influenced by the hidden numbers. For example, in deciding whether to carry out a certain activity at a certain time, believers may look to see whether the numerical value of their name and that of the day or date correspond in any way. In such cases, the English word game is no longer being played for fun.

Sound Symbolism

It is a basic principle of language study that sounds don't have a meaning. It doesn't make sense to ask 'What does *p* mean?' or 'What does *e* mean?'. On the other hand, we often encounter words where there *does* seem to be some kind of relationship between the sounds and what is going on in the real world. We link a particular kind of sound with a particular kind of meaning. When this happens, we talk about 'sound symbolism'. When it happens in poetry, it goes under the heading of 'onomatopoeia'.

Words with sound symbolism are very common in children's literature – the names of story-book characters (*Mr Pip*, *Mrs Snoozle*), or the sound effects in comic strips (*Pow! Zap! Screeeech!*). A number of everyday words also use sounds that seem to have a common meaning. Single-syllable words ending in a short vowel + *ck* often convey a sense of 'sudden movement or sound': *crack*, *click*, *cluck*, *flick*, *whack*, *prick*, *hack*, *peck*, *kick*, *nick*, *tick*. Words ending in *–le* often imply smallness or slightness: *bubble*, *trickle*, *rustle*, *needle*, *pebble*, *nibble*, *feeble*, *nimble*, *icicle*, *wiggle*, *tingle*, *pimple*, *little*, *beetle*. Words with *ee* are also sometimes associated with smallness: *wee*, *teeny*, *twee*, *peep*, *seed*, *peek*. On the other hand, there are many exceptions to each of these categories (*book*, *sock*; *castle*, *bustle*; *tree*, *beef*).

The *sl* consonant cluster is perhaps the best-known candidate for sound symbolism in English. Words beginning with *sl* are said to convey unpleasant or negative associations: *slimy*, *slob*, *slug*, etc. How far is this true? A list of the main *sl–* words given in one dictionary is printed opposite (ignoring compounds and derived words, e.g. *slow-coach*, *slowish*). There are forty-one words which have at least one sense with 'negative' associations, and twenty-seven which have none ('neutral'). There are even some with strongly positive associations (*sleek*). The situation, then, isn't totally straightforward. However, it does seem that *sl–* words are twice as likely to have a negative rather than a positive 'feel' to them. And if the word appears towards the end of the list (*slo–* or later), the correlation is very strong indeed.

Sl– *words in English*

	neg.	neut.		neg.	neut.		neg.	neut.
slab		+	sleeve		+	slop	+	
slack	+		sleigh		+	slope		+
slag	+		slender		+	slosh	+	
slake		+	sleuth		+	slot		+
slalom		+	slice		+	sloth	+	
slam		+	slick	+		slouch	+	
slander	+		slide		+	slough	+	
slang	+		slight	+		slovenly	+	
slant		+	slim		+	slow	+	
slap	+		slime	+		sludge	+	
slash	+		sling	+		slug	+	
slat		+	slink	+		sluggish	+	
slate (v.)	+		slip	+		sluice		+
slate (n.)		+	slipper		+	slum	+	
slattern	+		slit		+	slumber		+
slaughter	+		slither	+		slump	+	
slave	+		sliver		+	slur	+	
slay	+		slob	+		slurp	+	
sleazy	+		slobber	+		slurry	+	
sledge		+	sloe		+	slush	+	
sleek		+	slog	+		slut	+	
sleep		+	slogan		+	sly	+	
sleet	+		sloop		+			

However, when all the clear cases of symbolic words are gathered together – *teeny*, *crack*, *mumble*, *splash*, *cuckoo*, and the rest – the total is still very small. The vast majority of words in English are made up of sounds that bear no obvious relationship to the objects, events, sensations and ideas which give content to our physical and mental worlds.

Sound symbolism in practice

The symbolic value of sounds is nowhere better illustrated than in successful nonsense verse, the most famous example of which is Lewis Carroll's 'Jabberwocky'.

> 'Twas brillig, and the slithy toves
> Did gyre and gimble in the wabe:
> All mimsy were the borogoves,
> And the mome raths outgrabe.
>
> 'Beware the Jabberwock, my son!
> The jaws that bite, the claws that catch!
> Beware that Jubjub bird, and shun
> The frumious Bandersnatch!'
>
> He took his vorpal sword in hand:
> Long time the manxome foe he sought –
> So rested he by the Tumtum tree,
> And stood awhile in thought.
>
> And, as in uffish thought he stood,
> The Jabberwock, with eyes of flame,
> Came whiffling through the tulgey wood,
> And burbled as it came!
>
> One, two! One, two! And through and through
> The vorpal blade went snicker-snack!
> He left it dead, and with its head
> He went galumphing back.
>
> 'And hast thou slain the Jabberwock?
> Come to my arms, my beamish boy!
> O frabjous day! Callooh! Callay!'
> He chortled in his joy.
>
> 'Twas brillig, and the slithy toves
> Did gyre and gimble in the wabe:
> All mimsy were the borogoves,
> And the mome raths outgrabe.

Carroll (in the persona of Humpty Dumpty) also provided interpretations of some of the nonsense words, such as *slithy* = 'lithe and slimy', *mimsy* = 'flimsy and miserable', *mome* = 'from home', *outgrabe* = 'something between bellowing and whistling, with a kind of sneeze in the middle'.

8

ᘓ ᘓ ᘓ ᘓ ᘓ ᘓ ᘓ ᘓ ᘓ ᘓ

Personal English

English
British English
Twentieth-century British English
Twentieth-century British standard English
Twentieth-century British standard religious English
Twentieth-century British standard religious English as heard in sermons
Twentieth-century British standard religious English as heard in sermons
  given by the Reverend Fred Smith

'If you'll forgive the intervention, gentlemen, the mome raths did _not_ gyre and gimble. They outgrabe.'

Punch, 10 July 1985

In a sequence such as this, it is possible to see the way the study of English moves from the language as a whole to the language of an individual. Fred Smith's English has many features which will be shared by other language users in the categories named – other preachers, other clergy, other standard British speakers. There are certain features of the kind of language used for preaching – certain words, grammatical patterns and (especially) tones of voice – which will be found regardless of who is actually giving the sermon. These more-or-less predictable linguistic traits have been discussed in Chapter 6.

But Fred Smith is Fred Smith, linguistically as well as visually. His physique, personality, and background make him different from all other users of English. We can recognize him, in particular, from the quality of his voice or his handwriting. He may have a distinctive blend of regional accents (see p. 86), or a special way of pronouncing certain sounds. He will have his favourite words or turns of phrase, or a preference for certain kinds of grammatical construction. And, much less noticeable, he will have a predictable tendency to develop his points in a certain way – a penchant for analogies, perhaps, or certain kinds of metaphor. His congregation will undoubtedly be aware of some of these traits, especially if he has a vivid and memorable style – or, of course, if he hasn't.

These individualistic features of English deserve study too. For the most part, they are relatively unimportant. When we listen to people, we do not spend much time paying attention to what it is about their language that makes them different. Indeed, it is not at all easy to listen to or read anyone with frequent and prominent linguistic idiosyncrasies. An unusual voice quality is a distraction, as is eccentric handwriting, or a persistent use of a particular idiom. But there are several cases where the individuality of someone's use of English – their personal *style* – is considered to be a matter of importance.

AUTHORSHIP RESEARCH

Consider what would happen if you found an old manuscript in your attic which purported to be a previously unknown Shakespeare play. How would you decide whether the language was genuinely

Shakespeare's? The main way would be to select a number of stylistic features from the works definitely known to be Shakespeare's and compare their use with the same features in the new text. Are they used with the same frequency, and in the same way? Depending on the degree of similarity, a plausible case for Shakespearean authorship could be established.

Such techniques never make a cast-iron case. If the style of the new text were identical, it wouldn't rule out the possibility that someone had made a forgery – a successful copy of Shakespeare's style. And if it were very different, it wouldn't rule out completely the possibility that Shakespeare had written it – it might have been a product of an 'early', immature period, for example, or perhaps he was experimenting with a new style (something authors often do). None the less, if the stylistic features have been carefully chosen, and if the texts are long enough for some serious counting to be done, a close stylistic correspondence would make a very strong case for identical authorship.

An investigation of this kind was carried out by the Swedish linguist Alvar Ellegård in 1962, in an attempt to discover the authorship of a series of political letters which appeared in the London daily paper the *Public Advertiser* between 1769 and 1772. The letters were signed 'Junius'. Their criticisms of the government made them very popular, and they were often reprinted in pamphlet form. But it was never discovered who Junius was. Ellegård counted the words in the letters (over 80,000), and compared them with a million-word norm of political literature from the same period. Some words were found to be more common in the letters than in the norm, and some were found to be less common. Altogether, 458 lexical features were used, along with fifty-one synonym choices (such as whether Junius used *on* or *upon*, *commonly* or *usually*, *till* or *until*, *know not how* or *do not know how*. For example, Junius preferred *until* to *till* in 78 per cent of possible instances – a feature shared by only one in seven contemporary writers in Ellegård's sample. These features were then compared with a sample of over 230,000 words taken from the known works of the most likely contender for authorship, Sir Philip Francis. The similarities were so significant that Ellegård was able to conclude with confidence, 'We have identified Junius with Francis'.

An extract from the 'Junius' letters

If we see them [the people] obedient to the laws, prosperous in their
industry, united at home, and respected abroad, we may reasonably pre-
sume that their affairs are conducted by men of experience, abilities and
virtue. If, on the contrary, we see an universal spirit of distrust and dis-
satisfaction, a rapid decay of trade, dissensions in all parts of the empire,
and a total loss of respect in the eyes of foreign powers, we may pronounce, without hesitation, that the government of that country is weak,
distracted and corrupt.

Another case of this sort of reasoning – much more famous in
its day – was the controversy over whether Shakespeare's plays
could have been written by his contemporary Francis Bacon. An
American geophysicist, T. C. Mendenhall, investigated the question
by using 'word spectra' – profiles of the way in which authors used
words of different lengths, which he thought could be as uniquely
identifying as metallurgic spectrograms. He counted the length of
about 400,000 words from Shakespeare's plays and an unspecified
but very large sample from the writings of Bacon (see p. 129). He
broke the sample down into smaller counts, based on single works,
and found that in each single count from Shakespeare there were
significantly more four-letter words than three-letter words.
Bacon, however, used more three-letter words than four-letter
words, and also had a higher proportion of longer words. However,
statistical evidence does not convince everyone. As one sceptic
remarked when Mendenhall's findings were published in 1901: if
Bacon could not have written the plays, 'the question still remains,
who did?'!

An interesting application of authorship research in recent years
has been in connection with court cases – an application that sometimes goes under the name of 'forensic linguistics'. In a typical situation, the prosecution argues that incriminating utterances heard on a
tape-recording have the same stylistic features as those used by the
defendant, or, conversely, the defence argues that the differences are
too great to support this contention. A common defence strategy is to
maintain that the official statement to the police, 'written down and

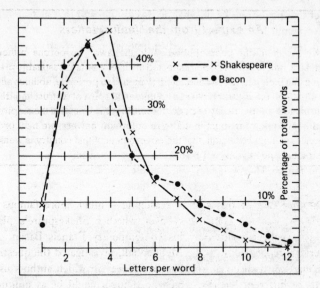

used in evidence', is a misrepresentation, containing language which would not be part of the defendant's normal usage.

Arguments based on stylistic evidence are usually very weak, because the sample size is small, and the linguistic features examined are often not very discriminating. But in several cases they have certainly influenced the verdict, and in one well-known case, subsequent analysis definitely supported the contention that there had been a miscarriage of justice. This was the Timothy Evans case. In 1950, Evans was hanged for the murder of his wife and child at 10 Rillington Place in London. Three years later, following the discovery of several bodies at the house, John Christie was also hanged. After considerable discussion of the case, a public inquiry was held, which led to Evans being granted a posthumous pardon in 1966.

A central piece of evidence against Evans was the statement he made to police in London on 2 December 1949, in which he confessed to the murders. Evans was largely illiterate, so the statement was made orally, and written down by the police. At the trial, he denied having anything to do with the murders, claiming that he was so upset that he did not know what he was saying, and that he feared the police would beat him up if he did not confess.

In 1968, Jan Svartvik, a Swedish linguist, made an analysis of the Evans statements, amounting to nearly 5,000 words. It proved possible to show that the language contained many conflicting stylistic features, such as those italicized below. Utterances 1–3 contain several examples of non-standard speech; utterances 4–6 contain items that would be somewhat unexpected from an illiterate person.

1. I *done* my day's work and then had an argument with the *Guvnor* then I left the job. He *give* me my wages before I went home . . .
2. I said, 'I thought you *was* going to Brighton' . . .
3. I did*n't* want *nothing* to do with it . . .
4. She was *incurring* one debt after another and I could not stand it any longer so I strangled her with a piece of rope and took her down to the flat below the same night *whilst* the old man was in hospital . . .
5. I *accused* her of *squandering* the money . . .
6. He handed me the money which I counted *in his presence* . . .

The incriminating statement was analysed into five sections, three of which contained background information (Type A), and two of which contained the details of the murders (Type B). Evans later denied that the latter paragraphs were his. Can this be shown from the style?

Svartvik examined just six grammatical features, all to do with the way Evans connected his clauses:

1. Clauses not linked to any other clauses, e.g. 'He paid me the money.'
2. Clauses linked by *and*, *or*, *but*, or *so*, e.g. 'My wife was always moaning about me working long hours *so* I left . . .'
3. Clauses linked by words like *then* or *also*, e.g. 'I *then* made my baby some food and fed it . . .'
4. Clauses linked by sharing the same subject, e.g. '*The van* come Monday afternoon and cleared the stuff out.'
5. Clauses linked by words like *if*, *when*, *before*, *that*, etc., e.g. 'He then asked me *if* it was paid for'.
6. Clauses linked by words like *who* or *which*, e.g. 'He handed me the money *which* I counted . . .'

The results were as follows:

Type A			Type B	
		(%)		(%)
1.	92	37.1	10	20.0
2.	17	6.9	15	30.0
3.	30	12.1	1	2.0
4.	50	20.2	17	34.0
5.	45	18.1	5	10.0
6.	14	5.6	2	4.0
Total	248		50	

The differences turn out to be highly significant. For example, note the way Type A paragraphs are linked by words like *then* (criterion 3); these are hardly ever used in Type B. And the proportion of the *and* type (criterion 2) is also very different.

The samples are very small, so the conclusions must be tentative. But the analysis undoubtedly corroborates Evans's denial: from a linguistic point of view, the paragraphs which he later claimed were untrue are very different indeed from the rest of his statement, which to the end he continued to assert was the truth.

DEVIANT ENGLISH

Stylistic analyses of the above kinds need large samples to work on, because the features of language they are looking for are part of the basic structure of English. Everyone uses such words as *and* or *then*, so any idiosyncratic use of these words is unlikely to show up until a great deal of usage has been processed. But there is another way in which personal linguistic identity can be established, and that is to find features which are unique – deviations from the normal structure of the language that are used by only one person (or, of course, by people imitating that person). This kind of evidence can be discovered from very small samples. Sometimes, just one sentence can be enough, as in this example:

> we)under)over,the thing of floating Of
> ;elate
> shyly a-live keen parallel specks float-ing create
> height,

No one but e. e. cummings has played with the typographic features of the language to such an extent. It is a distinctive feature of his poetry, and – whether we understand and like it, or not – it uniquely identifies his style.

Literature – and poetry in particular – is the domain where English deviates most markedly from the norms we are used to in everyday conversation. But it is not the only domain to break the normal rules of the language, of course. Humour regularly bends or breaks linguistic rules, as we have seen (p. 105), as does advertising. *Beanz meanz Heinz* breaks a spelling rule. *Drinka pinta milka day* breaks the word-spacing rule. *Why do you think we make Nuttall's Mintoes such a devilishly smooth cool creamy minty chewy round slow velvety fresh clean solid buttery taste?* doesn't actually break any rule, but it does stretch our ability to cope with a long sequence of adjectives almost to breaking-point.

Less noticeably, religious language deviates from normal usage: those who believe in God, it has been observed, are continually trying to say what cannot be said, and thus have to bend the language in order to express their sense of something that exists beyond language. Theologians are repeatedly having to walk along the 'edges' of language in an attempt to talk about spiritual realities; *The Edges of Language* is in fact the title of a book on the subject by the American theologian Paul van Buren (1972). And in everyday religious contexts, too, words which in other situations would seem meaningless, absurd, or self-contradictory are accepted as potentially meaningful. A sentence such as *I eat your body and drink your blood* would normally be expected only in the worst kind of horror movie; but in a Christian religious context, the words operate on a different level of meaning, conveying different associations. And John Donne concludes one of his 'Divine Meditations' (XIV) with a series of paradoxes:

> Take mee to you, imprison mee, for I,
> Except you' enthrall mee, never shall be free,
> Nor ever chast, except you ravish mee.

Deviant English can be found in yet other areas. In the clinical field of language disability, for example, a major preoccupation is to draw up profiles of people whose command of English is inadequate, in order to define precisely the symptoms of their condition. Adults who have suffered brain damage, such as a stroke, commonly come out with markedly deviant language. Children, too, can fail to learn English along normal lines, and produce language which is bizarre. Here is an example of the latter – from an essay written by a profoundly deaf sixteen-year-old on the film *Star Wars*:

The Star Wars was the two spaceship a fighting opened door was coming the Men and Storm trooper guns carry on to Artoo Detoo and threepio at go the space. The Earth was not grass and tree but to the sand, R2D2 and C3PO at going look for R2D2 walk the sand people carry away Artoo Detoo sleep.

The field of psychiatric disturbance also provides many examples of language which deviates – often in meaning rather than in structure – from the patterns we expect to find in normal conversation.

But it is in poetry where deviant uses of English really come into their own. Distinctiveness can be found at any of the levels of structure discussed in Part I, and often involves several levels at work together. An obvious way in which poetry deviates from other forms of writing is in its use of lines and (less predictably) verses. The line is the critical factor.

> Almost anything
> Can be made to look
> Poetic,
> As long as it is
> Written in lines.

Sometimes the line length itself becomes part of the poem – as in the visual effects of the school of concrete poetry. More usually, the lines have a rhythmical identity, and provide a means of distributing the meaning into units of different 'weights'. In its most straightforward form, the rhythm is predictable, line by line; each line coincides with a unit of meaning, and may be reinforced by a fixed rhyme scheme:

As for Venice and her people, merely born to bloom and drop,
Here on earth they bore their fruitage, mirth and folly were the crop:
What of soul was left, I wonder, when the kissing had to stop?
      Robert Browning, 'A Toccata of Gallupi's'

In less obvious cases, the rhythm varies from line to line, and there may be a carrying-over of meaning from one line to the next:

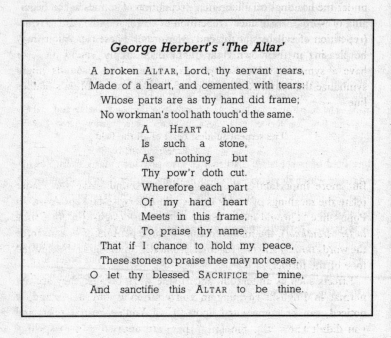

George Herbert's 'The Altar'

A broken ALTAR, Lord, thy servant rears,
Made of a heart, and cemented with tears:
  Whose parts are as thy hand did frame;
  No workman's tool hath touch'd the same.
            A   HEART   alone
            Is   such   a   stone,
            As   nothing   but
            Thy pow'r doth cut.
            Wherefore each part
            Of my hard heart
            Meets in this frame,
            To praise thy name.
  That if I chance to hold my peace,
  These stones to praise thee may not cease.
O let thy blessed SACRIFICE be mine,
And sanctifie this ALTAR to be thine.

> April is the cruellest month, breeding
> Lilacs out of the dead land, mixing
> Memory and desire, stirring
> Dull roots with spring rain.
>   T. S. Eliot, *The Waste Land*

A marked contrast in semantic (and rhythmical) weight can be seen in the final line of this extract:

> Interruption looms gigantified,
> Lurches against, treads thundering through,
> Blots the landscape, scatters all,
> Roars and rumbles like a dark tunnel,
> Is gone.
>   Robert Graves, 'Interruption'

The repetitive use of sounds within and between lines is a major characteristic of poetic language. The effects are usually referred to under the headings of 'alliteration' (repetition of sounds at the beginning of words), 'assonance' (repetition of vowel sounds), and 'rhyme' (repetition of syllables at the ends of words). These repetitions may be pleasing in their own right. They may simply 'sound nice', or have a symbolic value (see p. 122). A series of *s* sounds might symbolize the sound of the sea, or of a snake, as in Milton's famous line:

> The serpent subtlest beast of all the field
> *Paradise Lost*, ix, 86

But more importantly, the similarities of sound make the reader relate the meanings of words that would otherwise be kept apart. In Pope's line 'Thron'd in the centre of his thin designs' (in *An Epistle to Dr Arbuthnot*), the main function of the repetition of *th* is to force the words *thron'd* and *thin* together, ironically diminishing the elevated tone of the former.

Effects such as alliteration and rhyme work because they are not normal in English: rhyming in conversation is unusual – and, if noticed, can be commented upon ('Coo! You've been a poet, and you didn't know it!'). Similarly, there are unusual uses of spelling and typography, most of which would be impossible to 'translate' into spoken form. Look at the way in which the medieval associations are conveyed in this extract from T. S. Eliot's 'East Coker', for example:

> And see them dancing around the bonfire
> The association of man and woman
> In daunsinge, signifying matrimonie –
> A dignified and commodious sacrament.
> Two and two, necessarye coniunction,
> Holding eche other by the hand or the arm
> Whiche betokeneth concorde.

The e. e. cummings extract on p. 131 provides a further example of graphic deviance.

A deviant use of punctuation – in this case, not using any at all – is found in Molly Bloom's soliloquy in the final pages of James Joyce's *Ulysses*:

. . . of course shes right not to ruin her hands I noticed he was always talking to her lately at the table explaining things in the paper and she pretending to understand sly of course that comes from his side of the house and helping her into her coat but if there was anything wrong with her its me shed tell not him he cant say I pretend things can he Im too honest as a matter of fact I suppose he thinks Im finished out and laid on the shelf well Im not no not anything like it well see well see now shes well on for flirting too with Tom Devans two sons . . .

Deviant grammar and vocabulary (poetic 'diction') have long been recognized as other ways of identifying an author's style. The constraints of working within a fixed rhythm or rhyme scheme can force the grammar in all kinds of unexpected directions:

> How like a winter hath my absence been
> From thee, the pleasure of the fleeting year!
> What freezings have I felt, what dark days seen!
> What old December's bareness everywhere!
>   William Shakespeare, *Sonnets*

Often an abnormal use is made of a specific construction. In 'Fern Hill', Dylan Thomas takes the phrase 'all the [NOUN] long', and replaces the expected nouns of time:

> All the sun long it was running, it was lovely, the hay
> Fields high as the house, the tunes from the chimneys, it was air
>   And playing, lovely and watery
>   And fire, green as grass.
>   And nightly under the simple stars
> As I rode to sleep the owls were bearing the farm away,
> All the moon long I heard, blessed among stables, the nightjars
>   Flying with the ricks, and the horses
>   Flashing into the dark.

For abnormally constructed vocabulary, there are such extremely deviant cases as the wild words of Joyce's *Finnegans Wake*:

Oftwhile balbulous, mithre ahead, with goodly trowel in grasp and ivoroiled overalls which he habitually fondseed, like Haroun Childeric Eggeberth he would caligulate by multiplicables the alltitude and malltitude until he seesaw by neatlight of the liquor wheretwin 'twas born . . .

Or the powerful compounds of Gerald Manley Hopkins:

> Now burn, new born to the world,
> Double-naturéd name,
> The heaven-flung, heart-fleshed, maiden-furled
> Miracle-in-Mary-of-flame,
> Mid-numbered He in three of the thunder-throne!
> Not a dooms-day dazzle in his coming nor dark as he came;
> Kind, but royally reclaiming his own;
> A released shower, let flash to the shire, not a lightning
> of fire hard-hurled.
> 'The Wreck of the Deutschland'

Literary linguistic ingenuity, and thus identity, knows no bounds. Rules are there to be broken in the interests of insight. But the process is not random, nor arbitrary. At every point, with every example, there is a unifying theme. It has been neatly summarized by Robert Graves: a poet needs to 'master the rules of grammar before he attempts to bend or break them'. So too it is, or should be, for anyone who evaluates, or simply reads, English literature.

Statistical Laws?

There is another side to statistical work with English, apart from the study of individual differences. This is the investigation of whether there are properties of the language which do not vary *at all* – whatever the time or place, whoever the person. Several researchers have tried to find 'laws' governing the way people use sounds, letters and words – laws, moreover, which will hold not only for English, but for all languages.

A good example of a strong statistical tendency in language is the relationship between how long a word is and how often it occurs. According to the American philologist George Zipf, there is an inverse relationship between these two factors – that is, the more frequently a word is used in a language, the shorter it will be. The theory can be tested on any sample of English vocabulary, though it needs to be quite a large sample before the results begin to show up clearly.

Opposite is a small selection of words taken from the beginning of letter C in E. L. Thorndike's and I. Lorge's *The Teacher's Word Book of 30,000 Words* (New York, 1944). The first column gives words which occurred among the top 500 words of their sample; the second, words which occurred in the next 500; the third shows words that occur on average once in 4 million running words; and the fourth shows words that occur slightly less frequently than this. The average word length, in letters, is given beneath each column. Zipf seems to be right.

There are other interesting statistical correlations. For instance, if you count the words in a text and list them in order of decreasing frequency (as on p. 141), the same pattern keeps turning up. The first fifteen words will account for 25 per cent of all the words in the text. The first 100 words will account for 60 per cent. And the first

1–500	501–1,000	1 in 4 million	4 in 18 million
call	cannot	Ca	calash
came	can't	cabalistic	calibrate
can	captain	caballero	calif
car	catch	cabby	calliopsis
care	caught	cabin-boy	callisthenic
carry	cent	cabinetmaker	calumniator
case	center	caboose	calx
cause	century	cacao	camelopard
chance	certain	cachet	canalize
change	certainly	cadaverous	canard
4.4	6.1	7.4	8.1

1,000 words for 85 per cent. These proportions can be found in any text (as long as it is not too short), in any language.

Or take this kind of relationship, also observed by Zipf. Here are five words taken from a very large sample of English conversation. The words have been ordered in terms of their frequency ('rank order'). *Very* was the thirty-fifth most frequent word in the sample, turning up 836 times in all. *See* was the forty-fifth most frequent word, turning up 674 times. And so on.

	Rank order [r]	Total frequency [f]
very	35	836
see	45	674
which	55	563
get	65	469
out	75	422

If you now multiply the rank order by the frequency ($r \times f$) the total in each case is very similar, around 30,000:

	$r \times f$
very	29,260
see	30,330
which	30,965
get	30,485
out	31,650

As statisticians would say, the relationship between rank order and frequency is inversely proportional.

However, when this kind of relationship is investigated thoroughly, it turns out to be less simple. The figures don't always come out to 30,000. Words of very high frequency or very low frequency produce some different results. For instance, the r × f figure for the most frequent word in the sample, *I*, is 5,920. And generally speaking, it is very difficult to discover simple statistical regularities that work for all kinds of text. It is even a problem making a basic statement of frequency. What are the most frequent letters in English? What are the most frequent words? It depends, as the following tables show.

Arne Zettersten compared the frequency orders of the letters in the English alphabet in several styles of American English (totalling over a million words of text). The average order is given first, followed by the order found in press reporting, religious writing, scientific writing, and general fiction. The last line gives the order used by Samuel Morse in compiling the Morse Code, which was based on the quantities of type found in a printer's office. Apart from E and T (partly accounted for by the frequency of *the*), no two lines are the same.

Average	E T A O I N S R H L D C U M F P G W Y B V K X J Q Z
Press reporting	E T A O N I S R H L D C M U F P G W Y B V K J X Q Z
Religious writing	E T I A O N S R H L D C U M F P Y W G B V K X J Q Z
Scientific writing	E T A I O N S R H L C D U M F P G Y B W V K X Q J Z
General fiction	E T A O H N I S R D L U W M C G F Y P B K V J X Z Q
Morse Code	E T A I N O S H R D L U C M F W Y G P B V K Q J X Z

Similar differences emerge when we try to find out the frequency of English words. A great deal depends on the kind of material used. The following counts, based on British English sources, show the twenty most frequently occurring words. There are some important differences between the spoken and the written samples – note especially the frequency of *I*, *yes*, and *well* in adult speech, and the much more specific vocabulary in the child writing. Also note the way *he* and *his* appear, whereas *she* and *her* do not – a point reflecting the male bias found in the language (see p. 256). The greater frequency of *no* as opposed to *yes* in the child speech sample may or may not be significant!

Written English (newspapers)	Spoken English (conversation)	Spoken English (5-year-olds)	Written English (5-year-olds)
1. the	the	I	a
2. of	and	you	the
3. to	I	it	I
4. in	to	the	play
5. and	of	to	is
6. a	a	a	and
7. for	you	that	to
8. was	that	and	my
9. is	in	one	house
10. that	it	no	in
11. on	is	on	go
12. at	yes	got	on
13. he	was	in	this
14. with	this	what	with
15. by	but	do	went
16. be	on	this	are
17. it	well	my	am
18. an	he	yes	it
19. as	have	oh	at
20. his	for	there	some

PART III

໕ ໕ ໕ ໕ ໕ ໕ ໕ ໕ ໕

The History of English

We now look at the way the English language has changed over the centuries, from the days when it first arrived in Britain to its current status as a world language. Chapter 9 investigates the state of the language in Anglo–Saxon times: it examines the structure of Old English, its various dialects, and the social and historical pressures which affected the language between the fifth and the eleventh centuries. The final section introduces the runic alphabet, to permit access to the earliest inscriptions.

Chapter 10 continues the account into the Middle English period, from the eleventh to the fifteenth centuries. It deals with the main linguistic consequences of the Norman invasion, looking at the great changes in vocabulary which took place during this period, and also at aspects of the grammar, pronunciation, and spelling. We look at the origins of the modern standard language.

In Chapter 11, we follow English from Caxton and the Renaissance through Shakespeare and the Authorized Version of the Bible to the age of Johnson and the first major dictionaries and grammars. The way vocabulary changes is a special theme, and this is shown continuing right through the nineteenth century.

In the next chapter, we retrace our steps, and examine the way in which other varieties of English developed in parallel with that found in England. We look in turn at Scotland, Ireland, America, Canada, the Caribbean, Australia, New Zealand and South Africa. There is a special feature on British v. American dialect differences today.

With Chapter 13, we have reached the present day. We look at some of the factors which are affecting the way in which English is viewed in the world – the impact it is having on other languages (Franglais, Spanglish, etc.), the new social pressures which are causing it to change (feminism, the plain English campaigns), new regional Englishes (in India and elsewhere), and the development of a world standard. Then, in a last, short chapter, I raise the question of the future of the language in the twenty-first century and beyond.

9

ᛒ ᛒ ᛒ ᛒ ᛒ ᛒ ᛒ ᛒ ᛒ ᛒ

Old English

> What's in a name? That which we call a rose
> By any other name would smell as sweet.
>
> *Romeo and Juliet, II, ii*

When we look at the first years of the English language, the most immediate question is what to call it. Should we talk about 'Anglo-Saxon' or 'Old English'? Both labels are widely used.

The historical events are clear. There is an account in Bede's

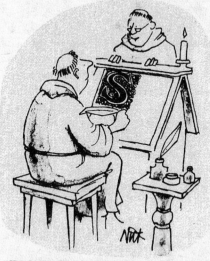

'How's the Psalms' title-page coming along?'

Punch, 12 November 1986

In the year of our Lord 449 . . . the nation of the Angles, or Saxons, being invited by the aforesaid king [Vortigern], arrived in Britain with three long ships . . . they engaged with the enemy, who were come from the north to give battle, and obtained the victory; which, being known at home in their own country, as also the fertility of the country, and the cowardice of the Britons, a more considerable fleet was quickly sent over, bringing a still greater number of men, which, being added to the former, made up an invincible army . . . Those who came over were of the three most powerful nations of Germany – Saxons, Angles, and Jutes. From the Jutes are descended the people of Kent, and of the Isle of Wight, and those also in the province of the West-Saxons who are to this day called Jutes, seated opposite to the Isle of Wight. From the Saxons . . . came the East-Saxons, the South-Saxons, and the West Saxons. From the Angles . . . are descended the East-Angles, the Midland-Angles, Mercians, all the race of the Northumbrians, that is, of those nations that dwell on the north side of the river Humber, and the other nations of the English.

Ecclesiastical History of the English Nation reporting the invasion of Britain in AD 449 by warlike tribes from north-west Europe – the Saxons, Angles, and Jutes, who lived in the regions now known as the Netherlands, Germany, and Denmark. Bede's account was written in Latin in about AD 731.

The invaders were first called 'Saxons', but Latin writers later began to refer to them as 'Angles' (*Angli*), regardless of which tribe they belonged to. Until around AD 1000, the nation was called *Angelcynn* (nation of the Angles), and then *Englalond* (land of the Angles). The language was always referred to as *Englisc* (the *sc* spelling was used for the sound *sh*), and this has led to the modern name.

During those early centuries, the name 'Anglo-Saxon' did not exist. This label began to be used after the Renaissance, when it referred to all aspects of the period – people, culture, and language. It is still the usual way of talking about the cultural history, but since the nineteenth century, when the history of languages came to be studied in detail, 'Old English' has been preferred for the name of the language. This name emphasizes the continuing development of the language from Anglo-Saxon times through 'Middle English' (see Chapter 10) to the present day.

So do we call the language 'Old English' or 'Anglo-Saxon'? If we want to stress the *continuity*, the points of similarity between the modern and older periods of the language, we will use the first term. If we want to stress the *contrast* between Anglo-Saxon and present-day culture, and the linguistic differences, we will use the second. This book is emphasizing the theme of continuity, so the chapter is headed 'Old English'. But this mustn't tempt us to play down the differences.

SOME FEATURES OF OLD ENGLISH

In fact, it is the differences which strike us most forcibly when we first encounter Old English. The language looks alien because of its distinctive spelling, there is a great deal of unfamiliar vocabulary, and there are many points of grammatical difference. On the other hand, with a relatively small amount of training, it proves possible for English-speakers to 'translate' Old English quite well. As we become used to the appearance of the texts, we begin to note a very large number of points of similarity. And even a word-for-word gloss of an extract (below) quickly develops in an English reader an immediate 'feel' for the language.

The extract is taken from the Venerable Bede's *Ecclesiastical History* (Book IV, Chapter 24). It tells the story of Caedmon, the

---

wæs he se mon in weoruldhade geseted oð þa tide þe he
Was he the man in secular life   settled until the time that he

wæs gelyfdre ylde; ond næfre nænig leoð geleornode, ond he
was of-infirm age; and never any   poem learned,   and he

for þon oft in gebeorscipe, þonne þær wæs blisse intinga
therefore often at banquet,   when there was of-joy occasion

gedemed, þæt heo ealle sceolden þurh endebyrdnesse be hearpan
decided, that they all   should   by   arrangement with harp

singan, þonne he geseah þa hearpan him nealecan, þonne aras he
to sing, when he saw   the harp   him approach, then   arose he

for scome from þæm symble, ond ham eode to his huse. þa   he
for shame from the feast,   and home went to his house. When he

þæt þa sumre tide dyde, þæt he forlet þæt hus   þæs
that a certain time did, that he left   the house of the

gebeorscipes, ond ut wæs gongende to neata   scipene,
banquet,   and out was going   to of-cattle stall

þara   heord . him wæs þære neahte beboden; þa   he ða þær
of which keeping him was that night   entrusted; when he   there

in gelimplice tide his leomu on ræste gesette ond onslepte,
at suitable   time his limbs   at rest   set   and fell asleep,

þa stod him sum   mon æt   þurh swefn, ond hine halette
then stood him a certain man beside in   dream, and him hailed

ond grette, ond hine be his noman nemnde, 'Cædmon, sing me
and greeted, and him by his name   called.   'Cædmon, sing me

hwæthwugu.' þa   ondswarede he, ond cwæð, 'Ne con ic noht
something.'   Then answered   he, and said,   'Nor can I nothing

singan; ond ic for þon of   þeossum gebeorscipe ut eode ond hider
sing;   and I for that from this   banquet   out went and hither

gewat, for þon ic naht   singan ne cuðe.'   Eft   he cwæð,
came, because I nothing to sing not knew how.' Again he spoke,

se ðe   wið hine sprecende wæs, 'Hwæðre þu me   meaht
he that with him speaking   was, 'However you for-me can

singan.' þa   cwæð he, 'Hwæt sceal ic singan?' Cwæð he, 'Sing
sing.'   Then said   he, 'What shall I sing?'   Said   he, 'Sing

me frumsceaft.' þa   he ða þas andsware onfeng, þa   ongon he
me creation.' When he   this answer   received, then began he

sona   singan in herenesse Godes Scyppendes, þa   fers
immediately to sing   in praise   of God Creator,   these verses

ond þa   word þe he næfre gehyrde . . .
and these words that he never had heard . . .

unlettered cowherd who became England's first Christian poet,
sometime in the seventh century. The translation into Old English
may have been made by King Alfred, in the ninth century.

The extract is printed here in an edited form. In the original manuscript, which dates from around the end of the ninth century, there

are no punctuation marks or capital letters, and there were many variations in the spaces between words. Compound words are sometimes divided differently from the way they would be today. Also, the Anglo-Saxon scribes used a number of abbreviations, to speed up the copying of manuscripts, and these have here been replaced by the full words. For example, the word *ond* (and) was often written with a shorthand sign 7, much as we use '&' today, and this time-saver was carried through to other words – *andswarede*, for example, was often written 7*swarede*. Other graphic differences, such as the use of the runic symbol ρ (wyn) for *w*, and the use of 3 (yogh) for *g*, are also not shown in this extract, as is standard practice in editions of Old English texts.

The word-by-word translation needs to be polished up, of course, before it reads acceptably in modern English. One such version of the story goes like this:

He was a man settled in the secular life until he was of an advanced age; and he had never learned any poems. He therefore often found himself at a banquet, when there was to be a time of joyfulness, and they all had to take it in turns to sing with the harp. When he saw the harp approach him, then out of shame he arose from the feast, and went home to his house. On one occasion when he did this, he left the house of the banquet, and went out to the cattle stall, which had been entrusted to him to look after for the night. At a suitable time he settled down to rest and fell asleep. Then in a dream someone stood beside him, who hailed him and greeted him by his name, calling, 'Caedmon, sing me something.' Then he answered, and said, 'I cannot sing anything; and for that reason I left the banquet and came here, because I did not know how to sing.' The one who was speaking to him spoke again, 'However, you can sing for me.' Then he said, 'What shall I sing?' He said, 'Sing me the Creation.' When he received this answer, he immediately began to sing in praise of God the Creator these verses and words, which he had never before heard . . .

If we look at these three versions together – the Old English, the literal translation, and the free translation – it's possible to see some of the important similarities and differences between the language then and now.

● The spelling has an alien appearance, but this is a fairly superficial difference. Most of the strangeness is due to the use of the symbols representing sounds not present in the Latin alphabet (p. 74): þ (known as 'thorn'), ð (now known by its Scandinavian name, 'eth'), and æ ('ash'). The first two had the sounds of the *th* letters in *this* and *thin*, and have since been replaced by *th*. The sound æ was mid-way between *a* and *e* – to modern ears, more like the vowel of *set* than of *sat*. If we were to replace the Old English letters by modern ones, turning *ƿæs* into *was*, *þæt* into *that*, and so on, the spelling immediately becomes less fearsome.

• The vocabulary presents a mixed picture. The majority of the words in the extract are closer than we might think to present-day English. The similarity is sometimes obscured by the spelling, or by the use of a prefix or suffix that has since disappeared. There would be little difficulty over recognizing *singan* as *sing*, or *grette* as *greeted*, for instance. *Ondswarede* is very close to *answered*, *onslepte* to *asleep*, and *geleornode* (beginning with the prefix *ge-*, still used in modern German) to *learned*. If the *ge-* prefix is dropped from *geseted*, we are very close to *seated*; *geseah* is close to *saw*; and *gehyrde* to *heard*. Most of the prepositions and pronouns in the extract are identical in form (though not always in meaning): *for*, *from*, *in*, *æt* ('at'), *he*, *him*, *his*.

On the other hand, some of the words look very strange, because they later fell out of use. *Gelimplice*, which means 'fitting' or 'suitable', has disappeared from the language, as has *neata* 'cattle', *swefn* 'dream, sleep', *beboden* 'entrusted', and *frumsceaft* 'beginning, creation', as well as some of the 'small' words, like *þa* 'when' and *se* 'the'. Some words begin to make sense only when we take them apart: for example, *gebeorscipe* seems to have nothing to do with 'banquet', until we see that *beor* is the Old English word for 'beer'. Likewise, *endebyrdnesse* 'arrangement, order' is based on a combination of *ende* 'end', *byrd* 'birth' or 'rank', and the noun ending *-ness*. The language contains many long compound words, especially in its poetry, where the coining of vivid figurative phrases (or 'kennings') was a particular feature – the sea is described as a 'whale-road' (*hronrad*), a person's body as a 'bone-house' (*banhus*), and a sword as a 'battle light' (*beadoleoma*). Unless one becomes a specialist, it is always necessary to have an Old English dictionary to hand to cope with these coinages when reading the literature of the age.

• From the point of view of grammar, the extract shows a fascinating mixture of (to modern eyes and ears) the familiar and the unfamiliar. The word order is much more varied than it would be in present-day English, but there are several places where it is strikingly similar. Adjectives usually go before their nouns, as do prepositions, articles and similar words (*the*, *this*, etc.), just as they do today. Sometimes, whole sentences are identical in the order of words – or nearly so.

Hwæt sceal ic singan?
What shall I sing?

þonne aras he for scome from þæm symble
then arose he for shame from the feast

The main differences in word order affect the placing of the verb in the sentence. Quite often, the verb appears before the subject (especially when the sentence begins with such words as 'then' or 'when' (*þa*)):

wæs he   *was he* (= he was)
þa ongon he singan   *then began he to sing* (= he began)

And the verb is also often put at the end, with the object and other parts of the sentence coming before it. This is probably the most noticeable feature of the language of the Caedmon story.

þa he þæt þa sumre tide dyde
when he that a certain time did

ond hine be his noman nemnde
and him by his name called

In present-day English, word order is relatively fixed. The reason why the order in Old English could vary so much is that the relationships between the parts of the sentence were signalled by other means. Old English was an *inflected* language: the job a word did in the sentence was signalled by the kind of ending it had. Today, most of these inflections have died away. The difference between *the man saw the messenger* and *the messenger saw the man* is now signalled solely by the order of the words. The person doing the action (the 'subject' of the sentence) comes first; the person receiving the action (the 'object') comes last. In Old English, the endings would vary. The first sentence would be *se guma geseah þone bodan*; the second would be *se boda geseah þone guman*. There are two changes to note. The word for *the* changes from *se* to *þone*, and the nouns add an *-n* ending when they change from subject to object. As a result, it is always clear who is doing what to whom, regardless of the order in which the words appear: *se guma geseah þone bodan* would mean the same as *þone bodan geseah se guma*, or any other sequence. There would be some change of emphasis, but there would be no real ambiguity.

Getting used to the word endings is the main problem facing anyone wanting to learn Old English grammar. It is necessary to learn the different forms taken by the verbs, nouns, pronouns, adjectives, and the definite article. The irregular verbs, which change their form from present to past tense (e.g. *see – saw*), are a particular nuisance – as indeed they continue to be for foreign learners of modern English. There are far more irregular verbs in Old English than in the language today. But it should none the less be plain from reading the glosses to the Caedmon extract that present-day English speakers already have a general grasp of the 'feel' of Old English grammar. We know more of the ancestral language than we think.

THE STORY OF OLD ENGLISH

Before the Anglo-Saxon invasions, the languages of Britain were Celtic, spoken in many dialects by people who had themselves invaded the islands several centuries before. Many Celtic tribes had in turn been subjugated by the Romans, but it is not known just how much Latin – if any – was spoken in daily life in the province. When the Roman legions left, in the early fifth century (to help defend other parts of the Roman Empire), the only permanent linguistic sign of their presence proved to be the place names of some of their major settlements – such as the towns now ending in *-chester* (derived from the Latin word for 'camp', *castra*), and a small number of loan words, such as *stræt* (street, road).

The linguistic effects of the Anglo-Saxon wars were just as clear-cut. Many Celtic communities were destroyed, assimilated, or gradually pushed back westwards and northwards, into the areas we now know as Cornwall, Wales, Cumbria, and perhaps also Scotland. Here the Celtic dialects were to develop in separate ways, resulting in such modern languages as Welsh and Gaelic. We do not know if many

Celts stayed in the east and south, but if they did, they would soon have lost their identity within the dominant Anglo-Saxon society. One thing is clear: the Celtic language of Roman Britain had hardly any influence on the language spoken by the Anglo-Saxons. Only a handful of Celtic words came into English at the time – such as *crag*, *combe*, *bin*, *cross*, *brock* (badger), and *tor* (peak). And there are even very few Celtic place names in what is now southern and eastern England (though these are much more common in Cornwall and Devon, and of course in Wales and Scotland). They include such river names as *Thames*, *Avon* (from the word for 'river'), *Exe*, *Usk*, and *Wye*. Town names include *Dover* (water), *Pendle* (*pen* is 'top' in Welsh), and *Kent* (whose meaning is unknown).

There is a 'dark age' between the arrival of the Anglo-Saxons and the first Old English manuscripts. There are a few scattered inscriptions in the language, dating from the sixth century, and written in the runic alphabet which the invaders brought with them (p. 161), but these give very little information about what the language was like. The literary age began only after the arrival of the Roman missionaries, led by Augustine, who came to Kent in AD 597. Large numbers of Latin manuscripts were produced, especially of the Bible and other religious texts.

Old English manuscripts also began to be written. The earliest texts are glossaries of Latin words translated into Old English, and a few early inscriptions and poems, dating from around AD 700. But very little material remains from this early period. Doubtless many manuscripts were burned during the eighth-century Viking invasions. The main literary work of the period, the heroic poem *Beowulf*, survives in a single copy, made around AD 1000 – possibly some 250 years after it was first composed (see p. 154). Most extant Old English texts date from the period following the reign of King Alfred (849–899), who arranged for many Latin works to be translated – including the Bede *Ecclesiastical History*. But the total corpus is extremely small. The total number of words in the Toronto corpus of Old English texts, which contains all the texts (but not all the alternative manuscripts of a text) is only three and half million – the equivalent of about thirty medium-sized modern novels.

The texts which have survived come from all over the country, and from the way they are written they provide evidence that there were

... hrægl þe him . . . asetton ge[aron?]
denne heah ofer heafod leton holm ber[an]
geafon on garsecg him wæs geomor sefa
murnende mod men ne cunnon secgan
to soðe selerædenne hæleð under heofen[um]
hwa þæm hlæste onfeng

       .I.

Ða wæs on burgum beowulf scyldinga
leod cyning longe þrage folcum gefræ[ge]
fæder ellor hwearf aldor of earde
oþ þæt him eft onwoc heah healfdene heold
þenden lifde gamol ⁊ guðreouw glæde scyl
dingas ðæm feower bearn forð gerimed in
worold wocun weoroda ræswa heoroga[r] ⁊
hroð gar ⁊ halga til hyrde ic . . . wæs . . . elan cwen
heaðo scilfingas heals gebedda þa wæs hroð
gare here sped gyfen wiges weorð mynd þ[æt]
him his wine magas georne hyrdon oð þ[æt]
seo geogoð geweox mago dryht micel him
on mod bearn þ heal reced hatan wolde

several dialects of Old English. There was no single system of spelling at the time. Scribes would spell words as they sounded, and these spellings suggest different accents. Thus in the south-east of the country, the word for 'evil' was written *efel*, whereas in other places it was written *yfel*. Hundreds of such spelling differences exist.

The main dialect divisions (see map, p. 156) reflect the settlements of the invading tribes, with their different linguistic backgrounds, and these divisions are still apparent in the country today. The area occupied by the Angles produced two main dialects: *Mercian* was spoken in the Midlands, roughly between the River Thames and the River Humber, and as far west as the boundary with present-day Wales; *Northumbrian* was spoken to the north of Mercian, extending into the eastern lowlands of present-day Scotland, where it confronted the Celtic language of the Britons of Strathclyde. *Kentish*, spoken by the Jutes, was used mainly in the area of present-day Kent and the Isle of Wight. The rest of England, south of the Thames and west as far as Cornwall (where Celtic was also spoken), was settled by Saxons, the dialect being known as *West Saxon*. Most of the Old English manuscripts are written in West Saxon, because it was the kingdom of Wessex, under King Alfred, which became the leading political and cultural force at the end of the ninth century. However, modern standard English is descended not from West Saxon, but from Mercian, as this was the dialect spoken in the area around London, when that city became powerful in the Middle Ages (p. 185).

There is a clear line of descent from Old English to the English of the present day, in sounds, spelling, grammar, and vocabulary. About a third of the words we use on any page are of Old English origins. But what of the other two-thirds?

Left: A page from *Beowulf*, taken from the manuscript now lodged in the British Library. The manuscript was damaged by fire in 1731, hence the odd shape to the page. The story is about a Scandinavian hero, Beowulf, who fights and kills a monster, Grendel, in Denmark. He is later made king of the Geats, in southern Sweden. There, as an old man, he kills a dragon in a fight that leads to his own death. Poetry of this kind was recited from memory ('sung', as Caedmon puts it) to the accompaniment of the harp – no small achievement, given that the poem contains over 3,000 lines.

The origins and distribution of the main dialects of Old English

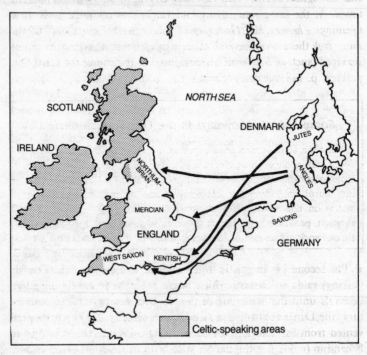

The history of English is one of repeated invasions, with new-comers to the islands bringing their own language with them, and leaving a fair amount of its vocabulary behind when they left or were assimilated. In the Anglo-Saxon period, there were two major influences of this kind.

• The Christian missionaries not only introduced literacy. They also brought a huge Latin vocabulary, some of which was taken over into Old English. The Anglo-Saxons had encountered Latin before, in Europe, when several Latin words entered their language – such as *weall* 'wall', *stræt* 'street', *ceap* ('bargain', 'cheap'), and *win* ('wine'), and they brought these words with them to Britain. But there were only a few dozen such words. By contrast, the missionary influence resulted in around 450 new words coming into the language, mainly to do with the church and its services, but including many domestic and biological words. The vast majority have survived in modern times. At the same time, many Old English words were given new meanings – *heaven*, *hell*, *God*, *gospel* ('good news'), *Easter*, *Holy Ghost*, *sin* – and there were several other usages, most of which have not survived (such as *Scyppend* 'shaper', used at the end of the Caedmon passage, p. 148, meaning 'Creator').

Some Latin borrowings in the Old English period

abbot, alms, altar, anchor, angel, apostle, ark, cancer, candle, canon, cap, cedar, cell, chalice, chest, cleric, creed, cucumber, deacon, demon, disciple, elephant, epistle, fever, font, giant, grammatical, history, hymn, idol, laurel, lentil, lily, litany, lobster, marshmallow, martyr, mass, master, mat, noon, nun, offer, organ, oyster, paper, place, plant, pope, priest, prophet, psalm, purple, radish, relic, rule, sabbath, school, scorpion, shrine, sock, temple, tiger, title, tunic, verse.

● The second big linguistic invasion came as a result of the Danish (Viking) raids on Britain, which began in AD 787 and continued at intervals until the beginning of the eleventh century. Within a century, the Danes controlled most of eastern England. They were prevented from further gains by their defeat by King Alfred in 878 at Ethandun (modern Edington, in Wiltshire). A treaty was then drawn up in which the Danes agreed to settle only in the north-east third of the country – east of a line running roughly from Chester to London – an area that was subject to Danish law, and which thus became known as the Danelaw. In 991 a further invasion brought a series of victories for the Danish army, and resulted in the English king, Æthelred, being forced into exile, and the Danes seizing the throne. England stayed under Danish rule for twenty-five years.

The result of this prolonged period of contact was a large number of Danish settlements with Scandinavian names. There are over 1,500 place-names of Scandinavian origin in England, especially in Yorkshire and Lincolnshire. Over 600 places end in *-by*, the Danish word for 'farm' or 'town' – *Derby*, *Grimsby*, *Rugby*, etc. Many of the remainder end in *-thorp* ('village'), as in *Althorp* and *Linthorpe*; *-thwaite* ('an isolated area'), as in *Braithwaite* and *Langthwaite*; or *-toft* ('a piece of ground'), as in *Lowestoft* and *Nortoft*. Many Scandinavian personal names (e.g. surnames ending in *-son*, such as *Davidson* and *Henderson*) are also found in these areas (see p. 159).

In the long term, over 1,800 words of definite or probable Scandinavian origin entered the language during this period, and are still to be found in present-day standard English. Several thousand more

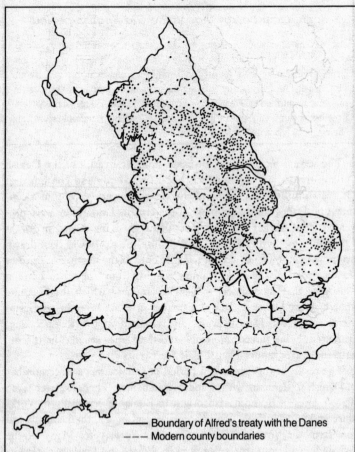

Scandinavian parish names in England, related to the boundary line of the Danelaw

——— Boundary of Alfred's treaty with the Danes
– – – Modern county boundaries

The distribution of English family names ending in -son.

The figures give the number of different surnames which are thought to have come from each county. The Scandinavian influence in the north and east is very clear.

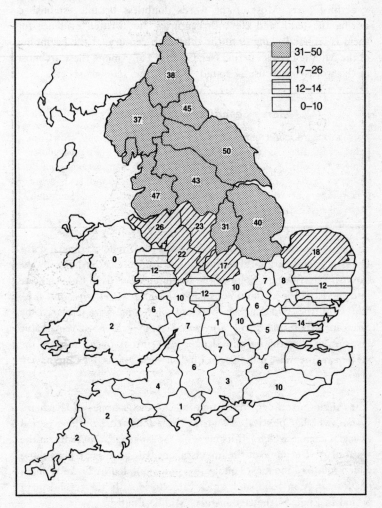

continued to be used in regional dialects, especially those of the north-east. In fact, hardly any of these words actually turn up in Old English manuscripts, which shows the time it takes for words to become established, and to be used in literature (among the exceptions are *law* and *riding*, as in the 'West Riding' of Yorkshire, from *þriding* – a third part). Most of the words doubtless became established during the tenth and eleventh centuries, but written evidence for them is largely lacking until the thirteenth century, at the beginning of the Middle English period (see Chapter 10). Among these are most of the words which use *sk* sounds – *skirt*, *sky*, *skin*, *whisk*, etc.

Some Scandinavian loan words

are, awkward, band, bank, birth, both, brink, bull, call, clip, crawl, die, dirt, drag, dregs, egg, fellow, flat, freckle, gap, gasp, get, give, glitter, guess, harbour, hit, ill, keel, keg, kid, knife, leg, lift, loan, low, meek, muck, odd, race, raise, ransack, reindeer, root, rotten, rugged, scab, scare, score, scowl, scrap, seat, sister, sky, slaughter, sly, stack, steak, take, their, they, thrust, tight, trust, want, weak, window

---

The closeness of the contact between the Anglo-Saxons and the Danish settlers during this period of 250 years is clearly shown by the extensive borrowings. Some of the commonest words in English came into the language at the time, such as *both*, *same*, *get*, *give*, and *take*. Three of the Old English personal pronouns were replaced by Scandinavian forms (*they*, *them*, *their*). And – the most remarkable invasion of all – the invading language even took over a form of the verb *to be*, the most widely used English verb. *Are* is of Scandinavian origin.

The Anglo-Saxon age was a time of enormous upheaval. Each invasion, whether physical or spiritual, was followed by a long period of social change which left its mark on the language, especially on the vocabulary. But none of the linguistic changes were as great as those which followed the most famous invasion of all, led by Duke William of Normandy in 1066, and which came to identify the second main period in English language history, Middle English.

Casting the Runes

Old English was first written using the runic alphabet. This alphabet was used in northern Europe, in Scandinavia, present-day Germany, and the British Isles, and it has been preserved in about 4,000 inscriptions and a few manuscripts. It dates from around the third century AD. No one knows exactly where the alphabet came from. It is a development of one of the alphabets of southern Europe, probably the Roman, which runes resemble closely. The runic script could well have been invented in the Rhine area; we know that there were lively trade contacts here between Germanic people and Romans in the first centuries of our era.

The common runic alphabet used throughout the area consisted of twenty-four letters. It is written both from left to right and from right to left. Each letter had a name, and the alphabet as a whole is called the 'futhorc' (in Britain), from the names of its first six letters (in a similar way to our name 'alphabet', derived from the first two letters of the Greek alphabet, alpha and beta). The version found in Britain used extra letters to cope with the range of sounds found in Old English, and at its most developed form, in ninth century Northumbria, consisted of thirty-one letters. This alphabet is illustrated on p. 162, along with the names of the symbols in Old English and their meanings (where these are known). However, this list does not give all the variant shapes which can be found in the different inscriptions.

The inscriptions in Anglo-Saxon date from the fifth or sixth centuries AD. They are found on weapons, jewellery, monuments, and other artefacts. Sometimes they simply tell who made or owned the object. Most of the Old English rune stones say little more than 'X raised this stone in memory of Y'. Often the message is unclear.

The Old English runic alphabet

Rune	Anglo-Saxon	Name	Meaning (where known)
ᚠ	f	feoh	cattle, wealth
ᚢ	u	ūr	bison (aurochs)
ᚦ	þ	þorn	thorn
ᚩ	o	ōs	god/mouth
ᚱ	r	rād	journey/riding
ᚳ	c	cen	torch
ᚷ	g [j]	giefu	gift
ᚹ	w	wyn	joy
ᚻ	h	hægl	hail
ᚾ	n	nied	necessity/trouble
ᛁ	i	is	ice
ᛡ	j	gear	year
ᛄ	3	ēoh	yew
ᛈ	p	peor	?
ᛇ	x	eolh	?sedge
ᛋ	s	sigel	sun
ᛏ	t	tiw/tir	Tiw (*a god*)
ᛒ	b	beorc	birch
ᛖ	e	eoh	horse
ᛗ	m	man	man
ᛚ	l	lagu	water/sea
ᚸ	ng	ing	Ing (*a hero*)
ᛟ	oe	eþel	land/estate
ᛞ	d	dæg	day
ᚪ	a	ac	oak
ᚫ	æ	æsc	ash
ᛣ	y	yr	bow
ᛠ	ea	ear	?earth
ᚷ	g [ɣ]	gar	spear
ᛢ	k	calc	?sandal/chalice/chalk
ᛤ	k̄	(*name unknown*)	

ᚢ ᛞ ᛖ ᛗᚱᛟᚷ ᚷ ᛗᚱᛟᚷ ᚷᚷ

14 13 12 11 10 9 8 7 6/5 4/3 2/1
u d e m ● æ g æ m ● æg og æ g

= gægogæ mægæ medu
= ?she-wolf reward to kinsman
= This she-wolf is a reward to my kinsman

The Undley bracteate (twice real size), and the runic transcription, transliterated into Old English. The image to the left of the helmeted head shows a she-wolf suckling two children – presumably a representation of the Romulus and Remus myth. The first six runes have been written as three groups of two – presumably because the rune-master wanted to be sure he had enough space for the whole inscription. The two small circles show the divisions between the words. With so little linguistic evidence to go on, the translation is uncertain – *gægogæ*, for example, may be a magical formula. The translation given here was made by Bengt Odenstedt.

They would be used in rituals by rune-masters, where the symbols would be given magical or mystical significance. The very name 'runes' means 'secret'.

When runes came to be used in manuscripts, they were commonly used to convey 'secret' information. In one manuscript, a collection of riddles contains items in which runes are used to provide clues to the solution. In another, an author's name is hidden – written in runic letters interspersed throughout a text. Over the centuries, the symbolic power of runes (perhaps arising from the way each symbol had a name, and represented a concept) has often been recognized. Runes continued to be used in Scandinavia until as late as the nineteenth century. Even in the twentieth century, they can be found in tales of mystery and imagination (such as the work of J. R. R. Tolkein).

The most famous runic inscriptions in Britain appear on the Ruthwell Cross, near Dumfries, a stone monument some 5 metres tall, and around the sides of a small bone box known as the Franks Casket. These both date from the early eighth century, and represent the Northumbrian dialect (p. 155). The earliest evidence of Old English is a runic inscription on a gold medallion (or bracteate) found at Undley in Suffolk in 1982, which has been dated AD 450–80.

Krist	wæs	on	rodi
Christ	*was*	*on*	*the cross*

ᚪᚱᛁᛋᛏ   ᚹᚫᛋ ᛗᛏ ᚱᛖᚻᛁ

ic	wæs	miþ	blodæ	bistemid
I	*was*	*with*	*blood*	*bedewed*

ᛁᚻ ᚹᚫᛋ ᛗᛁᚦ ᛒᛚᚫᚻᚪᚠ ᛒᛁᛋᛏᛗᛈᛁᚻ

Two sentences from the Ruthwell Cross, which has engraved upon it part of the Old English poem 'The Dream of the Rood'. There are no spaces between the words in the original inscription.

The Ruthwell Cross, Ruthwell Church, Dumfriesshire, Scotland

10

ᚷ ᚷ ᚷ ᚷ ᚷ ᚷ ᚷ ᚷ ᚷ ᚷ

Middle English

The year 1066 marks the beginning of a new social and linguistic era in Britain, but it does not actually identify the boundary between Old and Middle English. It was a long time before the effects of the invasion worked their way into the language, and in the meantime, Old English continued to be used. Well past 1100, texts were still being composed in the West Saxon variety that had developed in the years following the reign of King Alfred.

'Most of this is just a figure of speech now!'

Punch, 25 July 1984

An extract from the Peterborough Chronicle, for the year 1137

I ne can   ne I ne mai tellen alle þe wunder   ne alle þe
I not know nor I not can tell   all the atrocities ·nor all the

pines   ðat hi   diden wreccemen   on þis land, and ðat
cruelties that they did to wretched people in this land, and that

lastede þa xix intre   wile Stephne was king, and æure   it was
lasted   the 19 winters while Stephen was king, and always it was

uuerse and uuerse. Hi   læiden gæildes on the tunes
worse and worse. They imposed payments on the villages

æure   umwile, and clepeden it tenserie.   þa   þe
at regular intervals, and called   it protection money. When the

uureccemen   ne hadden nan more to gyuen, þa   ræueden hi
wretched people not had   no   more to give,   then robbed   they

and brendon alle the tunes,   ðat   wel þu myhtes faren
and burned   all the villages, so that well you might   go

al a dæis fare   sculdest thu neure finden man   in tune
all a day's journey should   you never find   anyone in village

sittende, ne land tiled.   þa   was corn dære and flesc and
dwelling, nor land cultivated. Then was corn dear and meat and

cæse and butere, for nan ne was o þe land. wreccemen
cheese and butter, for none not was in the land. Wretched people

sturuen of hungær; sume ieden on ælmes þe   waren sumwile
died   of hunger; some went on charity that were   formerly

ricemen, sume flugen ut of lande. wes næure gæt mare
great men, some fled   out of country. Was never yet more

wreccehed on land, ne næure hethen men werse ne diden þan
misery   in land, nor never heathen men worse not did   than

hi diden, for ouer   sithon ne forbaren hi   nouther
they did,   for contrary to custom not spared   they neither

circe ne cyrceiærd, oc namen al þe god   ðat þarinne
church nor churchyard, but seized all the property that therein

was, and brenden sythen   þe cyrce and altegædere. Ne
was, and burned   afterwards the church and everything. Neither

hi   me forbaren biscopes land ne abbotes ne preostes, ac
they not spared   bishop's land nor abbot's nor priest's, but

ræueden munekes and clerekes, and æuric man other   þe
robbed   monks   and clerics,   and every man another who

ouermyhte.
had the power.

The series of manuscripts which form the Anglo-Saxon Chronicle
clearly illustrate the period of change. This long work, which began
to be compiled in Alfred's time, recounts events in the history of
Britain from the time of the Anglo-Saxon invasions until the middle
of the twelfth century. In 1116, most of the monastery at Peterborough was destroyed by fire, along with many manuscripts. The
monks immediately began to replace the writings which had been
lost. They borrowed the text of the Chronicle from another monastery, copied it out, and then carried on writing the history themselves.
They continued until 1131, but then the writing stopped – doubtless
because of the chaotic conditions of civil war which existed in the
reign of King Stephen.

When the writing begins again, in 1154, after the death of Stephen,
the style is quite different. There are points of similarity with the
previous work, but the overall impression is that the writers were
starting again, using vocabulary and grammatical patterns which reflected the language of their time and locality, and inventing fresh
conventions of spelling to cope with new sounds. The above extract
has been set out in the same way as the Old English extract in the
last chapter, using a word-for-word translation, but it is no longer
necessary to add a free translation as well. Apart from a few phrases,
the language now seems much closer to modern English; indeed, the
Peterborough Chronicle is the earliest extensive text written in the
East Midland dialect, from which modern standard English
developed.

hæued. 7 uuryþen it ðat it gæde to þe hærnes. Hi diden heom in quar-
terne þar nadres 7 snakes 7 pades wæron inne. 7 drapen heom spa.
Sume hi diden in crucethus, ðis in an ceste þat was scort 7 nareu
7 un dep. 7 dide scærpe stanes þer inne. 7 þrengde þe man þær
inne. ð hi bræcon alle þe limes. In mani of þe castles wæron lof
7 gri. ð wæron rachenteges ð twa oþer thre men hadden onoh to
bæron onne. þar was sua maced ð is fæstned to an beom, 7 diden an
scærp iren abuton þa mannes throte 7 his hals. ð he myhte nowi-
der wardes. ne sitten ne lien ne slepen. oc bæron al ð iren. Mani
þusen hi drapen mid hunger. I ne can ne I ne mai tellen alle þe
wunder ne alle þe pines ð hi diden wrecce men on þis land. 7 ð lastede
þa xix wintre wile Stephne was king. 7 æure it was uuerse 7
uuerse. Hi læiden gæildes on the tunes æure umwile 7 clepeden it
tenserie. þa þe wrecce men ne hadden nammore to gyuen. þa ræueden hi 7 brendon alle the tunes. ð wel þu myhtes faren al a dæis
fare sculdest thu neure finden man in tune sittende. ne land tiled. þa was corn dære. 7 flec 7 cæse 7 butere. for nan ne wæs o þe land.
Wrecce men sturuen of hunger. sume ieden on ælmes þe waren sum
wile rice men. sume flugen ut of lande. Was neure gæt mare wreccehed on land. ne næure hethen men werse ne diden þan hi diden.
For ouer sithon ne forbaren nouther circe ne circeiærd. oc namen
al þe god ð þar inne was. 7 brenden sythen þe cyrce 7 alte gædere.
Ne hi ne forbaren b land ne abb ne preostes. ac ræueden munekes
7 clerekes. 7 æuric man other þe ouermyhte. Gif twa men oþer iii
coman ridend to an tun. al þe tunscipe flugæn for heom. wenden ð
hi wæron ræueres. þe biscopes 7 lered men heom cursede æure. oc was
heom naht þar of. for hi uueronal for cursæd 7 forsuoren 7 for lo-
ren. War sæ me tilede. þe erthe ne bar nan corn. for þe land was al
fordon mid suilce dædes. 7 hi sæden openlice ð crist slep 7 his ha-
lechen. Suilc 7 mare þanne we cunnen sæin. we þolenden xix wintre
for ure sinnes.

• There are several important grammatical developments shown in the extract. The system of Old English word endings is beginning to die away. Several of the old endings are still present, especially on verbs, but they are not used with as much consistency, and they no longer seem to play an important role in conveying meaning. The word order is now critical, and in most respects is very similar to that in use today. There is no sign in the extract of the Old English tendency to put the object before the verb, which was such an important feature of the Caedmon text. On the other hand, there are still several places where the grammar continues to show the older pattern, including a number of instances where the subject follows the verb:

> ræueden hi   *they robbed*
> forbaren hi   *they spared*
> man in tune sittende   *anyone sitting in* (i.e. 'inhabiting') *a village*
> was corn dære   *corn was dear*
> werse ne diden   *did not worse* (i.e. 'didn't do worse things')

There are also a number of phrases where the tight style of the writer makes the immediate sense unclear:

and æuric man other þe ouermyhte   *and every man who had the power* (literally, 'over-might') *robbed another*

And this particular extract makes a lot of use of 'double negatives' (and even triple negatives), another link with Old English. These need to be correctly interpreted, to follow the sense of the passage. There should be no temptation to 'cancel out' – using the mathematical rule that 'two negatives make a positive'. That is not how negative words worked in early English (nor, for that matter, in most of modern English). The principle is simple: the extra negative words increase the emphasis, making the negative meaning stronger. So, the multi-negative phrases should be interpreted as follows:

I ne can ne I ne mai tellen   *I don't know how to, nor am I able to tell of* . . .
þa þe uureccemen ne hadden nan more to gyuen   *when the wretched people
    had no more to give*
for nan ne wæs o þe land   *for there was none in the land*
ne næure hethen men werse ne diden   *nor did heathen men ever do worse*
ne hi ne forbaren   *neither did they spare*

• The spelling is a curious mixture. There are some special features, such as the use of *g* for a sound that most other texts of the time were spelling with the symbol ʒ ('yogh'). The old English runic symbols are still being used, but there is inconsistency. The *th* spelling is occasionally used (though this doesn't become widespread until the fourteenth century). The word for *was* is sometimes spelled with *a* and sometimes with *æ*. The runic symbol *ρ* is used in the manuscript, and is here shown as *w* (as is usual in modern editions of these texts), but *uu* is also a common spelling for this sound; the word for 'wretched people', for example, is spelled both ways in the extract. In addition, *u* is used where we would now find *v*, in such words as *æure* 'ever' and *gyuen* 'give'.

• There are still many words which need to be glossed for their meaning to be clear. Several words have since dropped from the language. We no longer use *pines* (cruelties), *gæildes* (forced payments), *tenserie* (protection money), *fare* (journey), *sturuen* (died), *ieden* (went), *sithon* (experience, custom), or *namen* (took, seized). And of the words which are still found today, several have altered meanings. The best examples in the extract are *wunder* (wonder), which could mean 'atrocities' as well as 'marvels', *flesc* (flesh) meaning 'meat', and *tunes* (villages), which developed into *towns*. Words like these are always a problem when reading a Middle English text. Because they look the same as the modern English equivalents, we can be fooled into thinking that they mean the same, whereas the meaning is in fact different. This problem of 'false friends' does not happen so often in reading Old English, where the vocabulary looks less familiar (see p. 150).

At the same time, because of the spelling, several words look stranger than they really are. The odd-looking word *wreccemen*, for instance, would have been pronounced very like *wretch-man* (but with the *w* sounded) and is thus very close to modern *wretched*. *Cyrceiærd* likewise would have been close to the modern pronunciation of *churchyard*, because the two *c* spellings represented the *ch* sound, and the *i* stood for the same sound as modern *y*. The same *ch* sound turns up in *cæse* (cheese). And *altegædere* is not far from *altogether*, nor *læiden* from *laid*.

Perhaps the most important point about the vocabulary of this text is the absence of French words. It is almost a century since the

French arrived, but you would never guess from the language of this Chronicle.

The Peterborough Chronicle looks back towards Old English and ahead towards Middle English. In fact, scholars have argued at length about whether it is best to call it 'late Old English' or 'early Middle English'. Some stress the archaic features of the text, pointing to similarities with Old English; others stress the differences. The text illustrates very clearly the difficulty of drawing a sharp boundary between different stages in the development of a language – which is why I have chosen it. But it does not take much longer before the ambiguity is resolved. Other texts from the twelfth century confirm the new direction in which the language was moving. When we look at manuscripts 100 years later, there is no doubt that a major change has taken place in the structure of English.

THE STORY OF MIDDLE ENGLISH

The period we call Middle English runs from the beginning of the twelfth century until the middle of the fifteenth, with the manuscripts at either end of this period showing the language in a state of change. The main influence on English was, of course, French – the language introduced to Britain by the Normans. Following the accession of William of Normandy, French was rapidly established in the corridors of power. William appointed French-speaking barons, and this was rapidly followed up by the appointment of French-speaking abbots and bishops. The links remained strong with Normandy, where the nobles retained their estates, and many of the kings spent long periods of time there. The written records show that there was very little use of English among the hierarchy. We are told that William himself tried to learn English at one point, but without success. Most of the Anglo-Norman kings were unable to communicate in the language – though it is said that some used it for swearing!

In 1204, the situation changed. King John of England came into conflict with King Philip of France, and was obliged to give up control of Normandy. The English nobility lost their estates in

France, and antagonism grew between the two countries (leading ultimately to the Hundred Years War, which began in 1337). The status of French diminished as a spirit of English nationalism grew. During the twelfth century, English became more widely used among the upper classes. There was an enormous amount of intermarriage with English people. Scaccario, a chronicler writing in 1177, has this to say:

Now that the English and Normans have been dwelling together, marrying and giving in marriage, the two nations have become so mixed that it is scarcely possible today, speaking of free men, to tell who is English, who of Norman race.

By the end of the twelfth century, contemporary accounts suggest that some children of the nobility spoke English as a mother tongue, and had to be taught French in school. French continued to be used in Parliament, the courts, and in public proceedings, but translations into English increased in frequency through the period, as did the number of handbooks written for the teaching of French. In 1362 English was used for the first time at the opening of Parliament. By the end of the century, when Richard II was deposed, Henry IV's speeches at the proceedings were made in English. By about 1425 it appears that English was universally used in England, in writing as well as in speech.

How had the language managed to survive the French invasion? After all, Celtic had not survived the Anglo-Saxon invasions 500 years before (see Chapter 9). Evidently the English language in the eleventh century was too well established for it to be supplanted by another language. Unlike Celtic, it had a considerable literature and a strong oral tradition. It would have taken several hundred years of French immigration to have changed things – but the good relations between England and France lasted for only 150 years.

This 150 years, none the less, is something of a 'dark age' in the history of the language. There is hardly any written evidence of English, and we can thus only speculate about what happened to the language during that period. Judging by the documents which have survived, it seems that French was the language of government, law, administration, and the church, with Latin also used as a medium of education and worship. The situation becomes clearer in the thirteenth century, when we find an increasing number of sermons, prayers, romances, songs, letters, wills, and other documents. And then in the fourteenth century, we have the main achievements of Middle English literature, culminating in the writing of Geoffrey Chaucer (?1340–1400).

VOCABULARY

The linguistic influence of this period of French rule took time to make itself felt, but it becomes increasingly evident in the English manuscripts of the thirteenth century. The main effect was the enormous number of French words which came into the language – around 10,000, according to one estimate. The words were largely to do with the mechanisms of law and administration, but they also included words from such fields as medicine, art, and fashion. Many of the new words are quite ordinary, everyday terms. Most have stood the test of time, about three-quarters of them still being in use today. A general impression of the great range covered by this new vocabulary can be obtained from the selection below (though this is only about a fiftieth of the French borrowings made during the Middle English period).

Some French loan words in Middle English

Administration
bailiff, baron, chancellor, coroner, council, court, duke, exchequer, government, liberty, majesty, manor, mayor, minister, noble, parliament, peasant, prince, realm, revenue, royal, sir, sovereign, squire, tax, traitor, treasurer, treaty, tyrant

Religion
abbey, baptism, cardinal, cathedral, chant, charity, clergy, communion, confess, convent, creator, crucifix, friar, heresy, immortality, mercy, miracle, novice, ordain, pity, prayer, religion, saint, salvation, sermon, solemn, trinity, vicar, virgin, virtue

Law
accuse, adultery, arrest, arson, assize, attorney, bail, blame, convict, crime, decree, depose, evidence, felon, fine, gaol, heir, inquest, judge, jury, justice, larceny, legacy, pardon, plaintiff, plea, prison, punishment, sue, summons, verdict, warrant

Military
ambush, archer, army, battle, besiege, captain, combat, defend, enemy, garrison, guard, lance, lieutenant, moat, navy, peace, portcullis, retreat, sergeant, siege, soldier, spy, vanquish

Fashion
brooch, button, cloak, collar, diamond, dress, embroidery, emerald, fashion, gown, jewel, ornament, pearl, petticoat, robe

Food and drink
appetite, bacon, beef, biscuit, cruet, date, dinner, feast, fry, grape, gravy, jelly, lettuce, mackerel, mustard, mutton, orange, oyster, plate, pork, roast, salad, salmon, saucer, sausage, spice, supper, tart, taste, toast, treacle, veal, venison, vinegar

Learning and art
art, beauty, geometry, grammar, image, medicine, music, noun, painting, paper, pen, poet, romance, sculpture, story, surgeon

General
action, adventure, age, blue, brown, bucket, carol, carry, ceiling, certain, chair, chess, chimney, city, conversation, curtain, cushion, dance, debt, easy, flower, forest, foreign, gay, hour, joy, kennel, lamp, leisure, mountain, move, nice, ocean, ointment, pain, pantry, people, piece, please, real, reason, river, scarlet, spaniel, special, square, stomach, terrier, towel, use, usual, wait, wardrobe

As the new vocabulary arrived, there were many cases where it duplicated a word that existed already in English from Anglo-Saxon times. In such cases, there were two main outcomes. Either one word would supplant the other; or both would co-exist in the language, but with slightly different meanings. The first outcome was very common, in most cases the French word replacing an Old English equivalent. For example, Old English *leod* gave way to *people*, *wlitig* to *beautiful*, *stow* to *place*, and *herian* to *praise*. Hundreds of Old English words were lost in this way. But at the same time, Old English and

French words often both survived, and when this happened, their meanings would begin to differ. Thus, Old English *doom* and French *judgement* no longer mean the same thing, nor do *hearty* and *cordial*, *house* and *mansion*, *wish* and *desire*.

The fourteenth and fifteenth centuries were also a time when several thousand words came into the language directly from Latin (though it is often difficult to exclude an arrival route via French). The 1384 translation of the Bible initiated by John Wyclif, for example, contained over 1,000 Latin words not previously known in English. Most of these words were professional or technical terms, belonging to such fields as religion, medicine, law and literature – a selection is given below. They also include many words which were borrowed by a writer in a deliberate attempt to produce a high-blown style. Only a very small number of these 'aureate terms' entered the language (e.g. *mediation*, *oriental*, *prolixity*); the vast majority died almost as soon as they were born (e.g. *abusion*, *sempitern*, *tenebrous*).

Some Latin borrowings in Middle English

abject, adjacent, conspiracy, contempt, distract, genius, gesture, history, incarnate, include, incredible, incumbent, index, infancy, inferior, infinite, intellect, interrupt, legal, lucrative, lunatic, magnify, mechanical, missal, moderate, necessary, nervous, ornate, picture, polite, popular, private, prosecute, pulpit, quiet, reject, rosary, scripture, solar, spacious, subjugate, substitute, temperate, testimony, ulcer

---

The result of the simultaneous borrowing of French and Latin words led to a highly distinctive feature of modern English vocabulary – sets of three words which all express the same fundamental meaning, but which differ slightly in meaning or stylistic effect.

Old English	French	Latin
kingly	royal	regal
ask	question	interrogate
fast	firm	secure
rise	mount	ascend
holy	sacred	consecrated
time	age	epoch

The Old English word is often the more popular one, with the French word being literary, and the Latin word more learned. But more important than this, there are distinctions in the way the words are used. Thus we talk about *royal blue*, *a royal flush*, and the *Royal Navy*, but a *regal manner* and a *regal expression*. There is no *Kingly Navy* or *Regal Navy*! English has thousands of words which are almost synonymous, thanks to the co-existence of these parallel items, and it is because of this that English is said to have a larger core vocabulary than that of other modern languages.

GRAMMAR

Vocabulary was only one of the major changes affecting the language in the Middle English period. Less noticeable, but just as important, were the changes in grammar, some of which were becoming apparent in the Peterborough Chronicle. All but a few of the Old English noun endings finally died away during the period, and the corresponding 'modern' ways of expressing grammatical relationships, using prepositions and fixed patterns of word order, became established along the lines familiar to us today. Thus where Old English would have said *þæm scipum*, with a 'dative' ending on both the words for 'the' and 'ship', Middle English would have said *to the shippes*, using a preposition and the common plural ending only. The only noun case ending to survive into modern English was the genitive (*'s* or *s'* in writing). Some of the personal pronouns also kept the old accusative form: *he* v. *him*, *she* v. *her*, etc.

The endings of the verbs, however, remained close to those of Old English during this period. A typical verb *playe(n)* (play) would have the following forms (ignoring certain dialect differences, such as the northern use of *-es* instead of *-eth*);

	Present tense	*Past tense*
(I)	play(e)	played(e)
(thou)	playest	playedest
(he/she)	playeth	played(e)
(we/you/they)	playe(n)	played(en)

The final simplification to the modern system, where we have only *play* and *plays* in the present tense, and *played* throughout in the past, took place after the Middle English period.

Also at this time, new verb constructions began to appear, such as *hadde maked* (had made), and *shal be* (shall be) – the latter being a new way of expressing future time. The use of *to* to mark the infinitive form of the verb, instead of the *-an* ending found in Old English, was also current by the end of the period: *cuman* became *to come*.

One other important change at this time was the way many of the irregular forms of Old English lost their irregularity and began to follow the pattern of the regularly constructed words. For example, in Old English the plural of *boc* (book) was *bec*, and *broc* (breeches) was *brec*. These and several other forms adopted the regular *-s* ending during the early Middle English period, leaving just a handful of irregular plurals in modern English (*men*, *mice*, *oxen*, etc.). Similarly, many verbs which were irregular in Old English became regular: Old English *help* had a past tense *healp* and a past participle form *holpen*, but in Middle English we find the use of *helped*, which ultimately replaced the other forms.

SPELLING AND PRONUNCIATION

There were major changes in the way the language was spelled. The Norman scribes listened to the English they heard around them, and began to spell it according to the conventions they had previously used for French, such as *qu* for *cw* (*queen* for *cwen*) or *ch* for *c* (see p. 75). The distinctive Old English letters, þ, ð, ρ, and æ, also fell out

In writing Middle English, þ was often confused with *y* – a confusion which is commemorated still in such signs as 'Ye' Olde Tea Shoppe, where the originator misread the first letter of þe as if it were a *y*.

of use. Thorn was the last to be lost, being found until around 1400 before it was finally replaced by *th*.

Changes affected pronunciation too. The /h/ which appeared at the beginning of many Old English words, such as *hring* (ring) and *hnecca* (neck), was dropped early on in the Middle English period. The /v/ sound became much more important, because of its use in French loan words, and began to distinguish pairs of words, as it still does today (*fan* v. *van*, etc.) The *ng* sound /ŋ/ at the end of a word also began to distinguish word meanings at this time (*thing* v. *thin*, etc.). And the vowel qualities which originally distinguished the word endings – such as *stanes* (stone's) and *stanas* (stones) – no longer did so. The *e* ending of words was still sounded until around 1400 – words like *tunge* (tongue) were thus pronounced with two syllables, the final *e* having the sound /ə/ (as in the last syllable of *butter*).

'CLASSICAL' MIDDLE ENGLISH

The many linguistic developments which identify the period of Middle English are most clearly in evidence in the poetry and prose of the second half of the fourteenth century. There are several surviving prose texts, especially on religious themes, notably the Bible inspired by (and perhaps also translated by) John Wyclif – the first complete translation of this work into English. The passage overleaf, dating from around 1380, illustrates the state of the language at the time. It comes from one of Wyclif's treatises, where he defends the need for a new translation. There is no need for a full translation, but as an aid to better reading, the manuscript symbol *þ* has been changed to *th*, and *ȝ* to *y* or *gh*.

Naturally enough, most attention has been paid to the major poetic creations of the time. Among the best-known are the poems *Sir Gawayne and the Grene Knight* (written some time after 1350), the *Pearl* (about 1375), both by unknown authors, and William Langland's *Piers Plowman* (in manuscripts dating from around 1360). The universally recognized pinnacle of poetic achievement in Middle English, however, is the work of Geoffrey Chaucer, which – in addition to its creative brilliance – provides a wealth of information about medieval attitudes and society, and about contemporary linguistic structure and style.

From *Wyclif's Treatise*, De Officio Pastorali (*Chapter 15*)

Also the worthy reume [realm] of Fraunse, notwithstondinge alle lettingis [hindrances], hath translated the Bible and the Gospels, with othere trewe sentensis [writings] of doctours, out of Lateyn into Freynsch. Why shulden [should] not Engliyschemen do so? As lordis of Englond han [have] the Bible in Freynsch, so it were not aghenus resoun [against reason] that they hadden the same sentense in Engliysch; for thus Goddis lawe wolde be betere knowun, and more trowid [believed], for onehed [unity] of wit [understanding], and more acord be bitwixe [between] reumes.

And herfore [therefore] freris [friars] han taught in Englond the Paternoster in Engliysch tunge, as men seyen [say] in the pley of York, and in many othere cuntreys. Sithen [since] the Paternoster is part of Matheus Gospel, as clerkis knowen, why may not al be turnyd to Engliysch trewely, as is this part? Specialy sithen alle Cristen men, lerid and lewid [educated and uneducated], that shulen [shall] be sauyd [saved], moten algatis sue [must continually follow] Crist, and knowe His lore [teaching] and His lif. But the comyns [commoners] of Engliyschmen knowen it best in ther modir tunge; and thus it were al oon [all one] to lette siche [such] knowing of the Gospel and to lette Engliyschmen to sue [follow] Crist and come to heuene [heaven].

The poetic language of *The Canterbury Tales* is not of course a guide to the spoken language of the time: it is a variety of written language which has been carefully crafted, and constrained by the metrical pattern of the verse. It contains many variations in word order, especially, which are dictated by the rhythm of the lines, and many literary allusions and turns of phrase, which often make the language difficult to follow. It is no more typical of everyday Middle English than contemporary poetry would be of modern English. None the less, it provides a major source of information about medieval grammar, vocabulary, and (thanks to the rhymes used in the verse) sounds. And the opening lines of the Prologue to *The Canterbury Tales*, written in the 1390s, undoubtedly contain the most widely recognized words in the whole of Middle English.

Geoffrey Chaucer

Squier 2

Haue me excused if I speke amys
Thy wyl is good, and lo my tale is this

Heere bigynneth the Squieres tale

At Sarray, in the land of Tartarye
Ther dwelte a kyng that werreyed Russye
Thurgh which ther dyde many a doughty man
This noble kyng was cleped Cambyuskan
Which in his tyme was of so greet renoun
That ther was nowher in no regioun
So excellent a lord in alle thyng
Hym lakked nought that longeth to a kyng
And of the secte of which that he was born
He kepte his lay, to which that he was sworn
And therto he was hardy, wys, and riche
And pitous and just, alwey yliche
Sooth of his word, benigne, and honurable
Of his corage as any centre stable
Yong, fressh, strong, and in armes desirous
As any bacheler of al his hous
A fair persone he was and fortunat
And kepte alwey so wel roial estat
That ther was nowher swich another man
This noble kyng, this Tartre Cambyuskan
Hadde two sones on Elpheta his wyf
Of whiche the eldeste highte Algarsyf
That oother sone was cleped Cambalo
A doghter hadde this worthy kyng also
That yongest was and highte Canacee
But for to telle yow al hir beautee
It lyth nat in my tonge, n'yn my konnyng
I dar nat vndertake so heigh a thyng
Myn englissh eek is insufficient
It moste been a rethor excellent
That koude hise colours longynge for that art
If he sholde hir discryuen euery part
I am noon swich, I moot speke as I kan
And so bifel that whan this Cambyuskan
Hath twenty wynter born his diademe
As he was wont fro yeer to yeer, I deme
He leet the feeste of his natiuitee
Doon cryen thurgh out Sarray his citee
The laste Idus of March, after the yeer
Phebus the sonne ful ioly was and cleer
For he was neigh his exaltacion
In Martes face, and in his mansion.

The opening lines of the Squire's Tale, as recorded in the Ellesmere
manuscript

Whan that Aprille with hise shoures soote
When April with its sweet showers

The droghte of March hath perced to the roote
has pierced the drought of March to the root

And bathed euery veyne in swich licour
and bathed every vein in such liquid

Of which vertu engendred is the flour
from which strength the flower is engendered;

Whan Zephirus eek with his sweete breeth
When Zephirus also with his sweet breath

Inspired hath in euery holt and heeth
has breathed upon in every woodland and heath

The tendre croppes and the yonge sonne
the tender shoots, and the young sun

Hath in the Ram his half cours yronne
has run his half-course in the Ram,

And smale fowles maken melodye
and small birds make melody

That slepen al the nyght with open eye
that sleep all night with open eyes

So priketh hem nature in hir corages
(so nature pricks them in their hearts);

Thanne longen folk to goon on pilgrimages. . .
then long folk to go on pilgrimages . . .

Middle English does not stop suddenly in 1400, but major changes do take place in the language after this date. By the end of the fifteenth century, the advent of printing (see Chapter 11) had fundamentally altered the character and quantity of written texts. And the pronunciation of the language had radically changed. Soon after 1400, the six long vowels began to vary their sounds, in a series of changes known as the 'Great Vowel Shift'. Chaucer would have pronounced the vowel in the middle of the word *time* like that in modern *team*; *see* would have sounded more like *say*; *fame* like *farm* (without the '*r*'); *so* like *saw*; *do* like *doe*; and *now* like *noo*. These changes took place very quickly – within a couple of generations – and they amounted to a completely fresh 'sound' being given to the language. To get an impression of the cumulative effect of these changes, we need to 'translate' the long vowels of a sentence into their medieval equivalents. For example, the sentence

> so it is time to see the shoes on the same feet now

would have sounded more like this, in Middle English:

> saw it is team to say the shows on the sarm fate noo.

The loss of immediate intelligibility is striking.

The Great Vowel Shift marks the last major barrier between early English and the standard language of the present day. Once it was complete, there seems to be a lull in the pace of linguistic change. Sounds continue to change, but less dramatically. The grammar continues to develop, but in ways which do not affect the language's basic structure. Only in vocabulary are there further major developments, and these, when they come, are on a grand scale.

The Origins of Modern Standard English

The main dialect divisions of Middle English broadly correspond to those found in Old English (p. 156), but scholars have given different names to some of the dialects, and there has been one important development. Kentish remains the same, but West Saxon is now referred to as 'Southern', and Northumbrian as 'Northern'. Also, the Mercian dialect area has split in two: there is now an eastern dialect ('East Midland') and a western one ('West Midland').

How do we know these dialects existed? The evidence lies in the distinctive words, grammar, and spellings of the manuscript texts. For example, the spelling (and presumably the pronunciation) of several verb endings changed from area to area.

● The *-ing* ending (as in *running*) appears as *-and(e)* in Northern English; as *-end(e)* in parts of the East Midlands; as *-ind(e)* in parts of the West Midlands; and as *-ing* elsewhere.
● The *-th* ending (as in *goeth*) appears as *-s* in Northern English and the northern part of Midland dialects – a form that ultimately became standard.
● The verb ending used in the present tense with such forms as *we* and *they* also varied: it was *-es* in Northern English and the northern parts of the East Midlands; *-eth* in Southern, Kentish, and the southern parts of the West Midlands; and *-en* elsewhere. (None of these endings survived in modern English.)

There were several other reliable indicators, apart from verbs. *They*, *their* and *them* are found in Northern and West Midland English, but they appear as *hi*, *here* and *hem* in the south. *Shall*, *should*, and other such words appear without an *h* in Northern English (as *sal*, etc.), but keep the *h* elsewhere. And there were several distinctive uses of individual vowels and consonants. *Stane* in the north corresponded to

The dialects of Middle English

stone in the south; *for* in the north Midlands to *vor* in the south; *kirk* in the north to *church* in the south, and so on. Sometimes, sounds from different dialects survived into modern English: *fox* has an *f*, reflecting its Northern/Midlands origins; whereas *vixen* has a *v*, reflecting its origins as a Southern word.

Based on these criteria alone, it is possible to get a sense of the kind of linguistic detective work carried on by Middle English dialectologists. For example, this sentence is taken from 'Love is life', a poem probably written by Richard Rolle about 1400. Which dialect does it represent?

> Bot fleschly lufe sal fare as dose þe flowre in May
> And lastand be na mare þan ane houre of a day . . .
>
> *But carnal love shall fare as does the flower in May*
> *And lasting be no more than one hour of a day . . .*

We find *sal*, *dose*, *ane* and *lastand*. It must be Northern. On the other hand, there are many manuscripts where the solution is not at all obvious. Sometimes, a text seems to reflect a mixture of dialects, perhaps because an author lived in a boundary area, or had moved about the country. Quite often, the author is not particularly consistent – as would be likely to happen in a period when sounds and spellings were changing. Sometimes, most of the forms reflect one dialect, and there is a scattering of forms from another – suggesting that the person who was copying the manuscript came from a different part of the country from the original author. And analysts must always beware of the possibility that a form in a manuscript never had any linguistic existence at all – in other words, the copyist made a mistake!

Which of these dialects produced modern standard English? The modern language is in fact something of a mixture, but by far the most dominant influence was the dialect of the East Midlands. The map suggests why. The East Midland area was the largest of the dialect areas, and contained more of the population. In particular, it contained London, Cambridge, and (on the borders with Southern) Oxford – the main social and political centre, and the main seats of learning. The presence of the Court in London was a compelling attraction for those who wished for social prestige or career opportunities. The East Midlands 'triangle' was a wealthy agricultural area, and the centre of the growing wool trade. And it was also conveniently positioned between the Northern and Southern dialects, acting as a kind of communication 'bridge' between them. This last point was even recognized at the time. Here is a contemporary writer, the translator John of Trevisa, writing about 1387, and pointing out that

men of myddel Engelond, as hyt were parteners of the endes, vnderstondeth betre the syde longages, Northeron and Southeron, than Northeron and Southeron vnderstondeth eyther other.

The clinching factor was William Caxton, who in 1476 set up his printing press in Westminster, and chose to use the speech of the London area as the basis for his translations and spelling. By the end of the fifteenth century, the distinction between 'central' and 'provincial' life was firmly established. It was reflected in the distinction between 'standard' and 'regional' speech – the former thought of as correct, proper, and educated, the latter as incorrect, careless, and inferior – which is still with us today.

11

ʊ ʊ ʊ ʊ ʊ ʊ ʊ ʊ ʊ ʊ

Early Modern English

The pace of English language history quickens after William Caxton introduced the technology of printing into England in 1476, or so it seems. Apart from its role in helping to develop a standard form of English spelling and punctuation (p. 74), the new invention provided more opportunities for people to write, and gave their works much

'Shall I compare thee to a summer's day?
The Easter bonnet thing didn't work.'

Punch, 2 May 1984

wider circulation. As a result, more texts of the period have survived. Within the following 150 years, nearly 20,000 English books appeared. The story of English thus becomes more definite in the sixteenth century, with more evidence available about the way the language was developing, both in the texts themselves, and in a growing number of observations dealing with the grammar, vocabulary, and writing system. In this century, scholars seriously got down to talking *about* the English language.

Caxton himself was not a linguist or a literary scholar, but a merchant, who had lived abroad (in Belgium) for nearly thirty years. A large number of his first publications were translations from French or Dutch, and here he found himself faced with several major problems.

● Should he use foreign loan words in his translation or replace these by native English words? Some people wanted the former; some the latter.
● Which variety of English should be followed, given the great differences in regional dialect that existed?
● Which literary style should be used as a model? Chaucer? Thomas Malory (who wrote around 1470)? Something derived from the Latin authors?
● How should the language be spelled and punctuated, given the enormous scribal variations of the previous centuries?
● In publishing native writers, should he change their language to make it more widely understood?

If the books were to sell, the language they contained had to be understandable throughout the country – but, as he complained, although he wanted to satisfy everyone, how was this to be done? A famous extract from one of his Prefaces (see p. 191) gives a vivid account of the size of the problem. If even a simple little word like *eggs* couldn't be understood by everyone, what hope was there?

Caxton made his decisions, as did other publishers of the time, and gradually a consensus arose, based on the speech of the London area (see p. 187). The distinction between what was standard and what was non-standard became more clear-cut. Within 100 years, there was remarkable uniformity in the appearance of printed texts, though some matters of spelling and punctuation (such as the use of the

In 1490, Caxton decided to translate a classical work, *Eneydos*, from a French original, and in his Preface he talks about the kind of problem he was having to face (punctuation has been modernized):

And certaynly our langage now vsed varyeth ferre [far] from that whiche was vsed and spoken whan I was borne. For we Englysshe men ben [be] borne vnder the domynacyon of the mone [moon], which is never stedfaste but euer waueRynge [wavering], wexynge one season and waneth & dyscreaseth another season. And that comyn [common] Englysshe that is spoken in one shyre varyeth from a nother. In so moche that in my dayes happened that certayn marchauntes were in a shippe in Tamyse [Thames] for to have sayled ouer the see into Zelande [Zeeland], and for lacke of wynde thei taryed atte forlond [headland], and wente to lande for to refreshe them. And one of theym named Sheffelde, a mercer, cam in to an hows and axed for mete, and specyally he axyd after 'eggys'. And the good wyf answerde that she coude speke no Frenshe. And the marchaunt was angry, for he also coude speke no Frenshe, but wold haue hadde egges, and she vnderstode hym not. And thenne at last a nother sayd that he wolde haue 'eyren'. Then the good wyf sayd that she vnderstod hym wel. Loo! What sholde a man in thyse dayes now wryte, 'egges' or 'eyren'? Certaynly, it is harde to playse euery man by cause of dyuersite [diversity] & chaunge of langage. For in these dayes euery man that is in ony reputacyon in his countre wyll vtter his commynycacyon and maters in such maners & termes that fewe men shall vnderstonde theym. And som honest and grete clerkes haue ben wyth me and desired me to wryte the moste curyous termes that I coude fynde. And thus betwene playne rude & curyous I stande abasshed. But in my iudgemente the comyn termes that be dayli vsed ben lyghter to be vnderstonde than the olde and auncyent englysshe.

apostrophe) were not finally settled until the seventeenth century.

THE RENAISSANCE

The main factor promoting the flood of new publications in the sixteenth century was the renewed interest in the classical languages and literatures, and in the rapidly developing fields of science, medicine, and the arts – a period, lasting from the time of Caxton until around 1650, which later came to be called the 'Renaissance'.

This was also the age of the Reformation, of Copernicus, and the discovery of America. The effects of these fresh perspectives on the English language were immediate, controversial, and far-reaching.

The focus of interest was vocabulary. There were no words in the language to talk accurately about the new concepts, techniques, and inventions which were emerging in Europe, and so writers began to borrow them. Most of the words which came into the language at the time were taken from Latin, and a goodly number from Greek, French, Italian, Spanish and Portuguese. But the period of world-wide exploration was well under way, and words came into English from over fifty languages, including several American Indian languages and the languages of Africa and Asia. Some words came into English directly; others came by an intermediary language. Many words came indirectly from Latin or Italian by way of French.

Some writers went out of their way to find new words, in order (as they saw it) to 'enrich' the language. They saw their role as enabling the new learning – whether this was access to the old classical texts, or to the new fields of science, technology, and medicine – to be brought within the reach of the English public. There were many translations of classical works during the sixteenth century, and thousands of Latin or Greek terms were introduced, as translators searched for an English equivalent and could not find one. Often they would pause before a new word, and explain it, or apologize for it. 'I am constrained to vsurpe a latine word,' said Thomas Elyot in *The Governour* (1531), '. . . for the necessary augmentation of our langage'. He was talking about his intention to use the word *maturity* to apply to human behaviour:

whiche worde though it be strange and darke, yet by declaring the vertue in a fewe mo [more] wordes, the name ones [once] brought in custome shall be as facile to vnderstande as other wordes late commen out of Italy and France, and made denizins amonge vs.

Then, as now, the influx of foreign vocabulary caused hackles to rise. Purists objected to the way classical terms were pouring into the language. They called them 'inkhorn' terms, and condemned them for their obscurity and for the way they interfered with the development of native English vocabulary. Some writers (notably the poet Edmund Spenser) attempted instead to revive obsolete English

Some Renaissance foreign words

Latin and Greek

absurdity, adapt, agile, alienate, anachronism, anonymous, appropriate, assassinate, atmosphere, autograph, benefit, capsule, catastrophe, chaos, climax, conspicuous, contradictory, crisis, criterion, critic, disability, disrespect, emancipate, emphasis, encyclopedia, enthusiasm, epilepsy, eradicate, exact, exaggerate, excavate, excursion, exist, expectation, expensive, explain, external, extinguish, fact, glottis, habitual, halo, harass, idiosyncrasy, immaturity, impersonal, inclemency, jocular, larynx, lexicon, lunar, monopoly, monosyllable, necessitate, obstruction, pancreas, parenthesis, pathetic, pneumonia, relaxation, relevant, scheme, skeleton, soda, species, system, temperature, tendon, thermometer, tibia, transcribe, ulna, utopian, vacuum, virus

French

alloy, anatomy, battery, bayonet, bigot, bizarre, chocolate, colonel, comrade, detail, docility, duel, entrance, explore, grotesque, invite, moustache, muscle, passport, pioneer, probability, shock, ticket, vase, vogue, volunteer

Italian

balcony, ballot, cameo, carnival, concerto, cupola, design, fuse, giraffe, grotto, lottery, macaroni, opera, rocket, solo, sonata, sonnet, soprano, stanza, violin, volcano

Spanish and Portuguese

alligator, anchovy, apricot, armada, banana, barricade, bravado, cannibal, canoe, cockroach, cocoa, corral, embargo, guitar, hammock, hurricane, maize, mosquito, negro, potato, port (wine), rusk, sombrero, tank, tobacco, yam

Others

bazaar (Persian), caravan (Persian), coffee (Turkish), cruise (Dutch), easel (Dutch), harem (Arabic), keelhaul (Dutch), kiosk (Turkish), knapsack (Dutch), landscape (Dutch), pariah (Tamil), sago (Malay), shogun (Japanese), wampum (Algonquian), yacht (Dutch)

. . . And some of the words that didn't make it

cautionate (*caution*), deruncinate (*weed*), disacquaint (opposite of *acquaint*), emacerate (*emaciate*), expede (opposite of *impede*), mansuetude (*mildness*), uncounsellable words (what were sometimes called 'Chaucerisms'), and to make use of little-known words from English dialects – such as *algate* (always), *sicker* (certainly), and *yblent* (confused). Some (notably the scholar John Cheke) used English equivalents for classical terms whenever he could: in his translation of St Matthew's Gospel, we find *byword* for *parable*, *hundreder* for *centurion*, *crossed* for *crucified*, and *gainrising* for *resurrection*.

The rhetorician Thomas Wilson was one of the most ferocious critics of the new foreign words. In one of his works he cites a letter written, he claims, by a Lincolnshire gentleman asking for assistance in obtaining a vacant benefice (it is likely that the letter is Wilson's own concoction, but the words he makes use of seem to be genuine):

... I obtestate [beseech] your clemencie, to inuigilate [take pains] thus muche for me, accordyng to my confidence, and as you know my condigne merites, for suche a compendious [profitable] liuyng. But now I relinquishe [cease] to fatigate [tire] your intelligence with any more friuolous verbositie, and therfore he that rules the climates be euermore your beautreux [?buttress], your fortresse, and your bulwarke. Amen.

Dated at my Dome, or rather Mansion place in Lincolneshire, the penulte of the moneth Sextile. Anno Millimo, quillimo, trillimo.

He comments:

Among all other lessons this should first be learned, that wee never affect any straunge ynkehorne termes, but to speake as is commonly received: neither seeking to be over fine, nor yet living over-carelesse, using our speeche as most men doe, and ordering our wittes as the fewest have done. Some seeke so far for outlandish English, that they forget altogether their mothers language. And I dare sweare this, if some of their mothers were alive, thei were not able to tell what they say; and yet these fine English clerkes will say, they speake in their mother tongue, if a man should charge them for counterfeiting the Kings English.

Some went to the opposite extreme, and objected to the use of any English at all in the expression of new learning. English, they argued, could never compare with the standards of Latin or Greek, especially in such fields as theology and medicine. Better to stick to the old and tested languages, and leave English for the gutter.

Then, as now, purist opinion had no general influence on what happened. And the merits of English were strongly defended by such writers as Richard Mulcaster:

For is it not in dede a mervellous bondage, to becom servants to one tung for learning sake, the most of our time, with losse of most time, whereas we maie have the verie same treasur in our own tung, with the gain of most time? our own bearing the joyfull title of our libertie and fredom, the Latin tung remembring us of our thraldom and bondage? I love Rome, but London better; I favor Italie, but England more; I honor the Latin, but I worship the English.

The Mulcaster view triumphed. Latin continued to be used by several scientists during the sixteenth century, but went out of general use during the seventeenth, apart from its continuing status in the Roman Catholic Church.

Nor did purist opinion stem the influx of new words. What is interesting, though, and little understood, is why some words survived whereas others died. Both *impede* and *expede* were introduced, but the latter disappeared, whereas the former did not. Similarly, *demit* (send away) was replaced by *dismiss*, but *commit* and *transmit* stayed. In the extract from Wilson's letter, most of the new Latin words *clemency*, *invigilate*, *confidence*, *compendious*, *relinquish*, *frivolous*, and *verbosity* survived, but *obtestate* and *fatigate* for some reason died. It will probably never be possible to determine the reasons for such differences in the 'natural history' of these words.

The influx of foreign words was the most 'noticeable' aspect of the vocabulary growth in the Renaissance. At the same time, of course, the vocabulary was steadily expanding in other ways. In fact, far more new words came into English by adding prefixes and suffixes, or by forming new compounds. The following are examples of suffixes: *straightness*, *delightfulness*, *frequenter*, *investment*, *relentless*, *laughable*, *anatomically*, *anathemize*; of prefixes: *uncomfortable*, *uncivilized*, *bedaub*, *disabuse*, *forename*, *nonsense*, *underground*, *submarine*; and of compounds: *heaven-sent*, *chap-fallen*, *Frenchwoman*, *commander-in-chief*. In addition, increasing use was made of the process of 'conversion' (p. 39) – turning one word class into another without adding a prefix or suffix. Some examples from Shakespeare are given below.

New verbs from old nouns in Shakespeare

Season your admiration for a while
It *out-herods* Herod
the hearts that *spaniel'd* me . . .
No more shall trenching war *channel* her fields
Uncle me no uncle.

SHAKESPEARE AND THE BIBLE

All textbooks on the history of English agree that the two influences which dominate the final decades of the Renaissance are the works of William Shakespeare (1564–1616) and the King James Bible (the 'Authorized Version') of 1611. Dominate, that is, from a linguistic point of view. The question of their literary brilliance and significance is not an issue for this book. Our question is much simpler yet more far-reaching: what was their effect on the language?

This isn't just a matter of the way these works use language in a memorable way – the 'quotability', as some say. Certainly, extracts from both sources predominate in any collection of quotations. But quotations are different. 'To be or not to be' is a quotation, but it had no subsequent influence on the development of the language's grammar or vocabulary. On the other hand, Shakespeare's use of *obscene* is not part of any especially memorable quotation, but it is the first recorded use in English of this word, and it stayed in the language thereafter.

Of course, to say that Shakespeare, or anyone, is 'the first' to use a word, or to use it in a particular way, does not mean that this person actually invented the word or usage. It may already have been present in the spoken language, but never written down. However, this is really beside the point. Whether Shakespeare was the first to use a word or not, the fact remains that his use of it put the word into circulation, in a way that had not happened before.

Not all the new words in Shakespeare were taken into the language

Prince of Denmarke.

We will beſtow our ſelues;reade on this booke,
That ſhow of ſuch an exerciſe may collour
Your lowlineſſe;we are oft too blame in this,
Tis too much proou'd,that with deuotions viſage
And pious action,we doe ſugar ore
The Diuell himſelfe.

King, O tis too true,
How ſmart a laſh that ſpeech doth giue my conſcience?
The harlots cheeke beautied with plaſtring art,
Is not more ougly to the thing that helps it,
Then is my deede to my moſt painted word:
O heauy burthen:

Enter Hamlet,

Pol. I heare him comming,with-draw my Lord.
Ham. To be,or not to be,that is the queſtion,
Whether tis nobler in the minde to ſuffer
The ſlings and arrowes of outragious fortune,
Or to take Armes againſt a ſea of troubles,
And by oppoſing,end them:To die to ſleepe
No more:and by a ſleepe,to ſay we end
The hart-ake,and the thouſand naturall ſhocks
That fleſh is heire to ; tis a conſumation
Deuoutly to be wiſht to die to ſleepe,
To ſleepe,perchance to dreame,I there's the rub,
For in that ſleepe of death what dreames may come?
When we haue ſhuffled off this mortall coyle
Muſt giue vs pauſe,there's the reſpect
That makes calamity of ſo long life:
For who would beare the whips and ſcornes of time,

An extract from Shakespeare's First Folio, published in 1623 as a whole. Some that stayed were *accommodation*, *assassination*, *barefaced*, *countless*, *courtship*, *dislocate*, *dwindle*, *eventful*, *fancy-free*, *lack-lustre*, *laughable*, *premeditated* and *submerged*. Some that disappeared were *abruption*, *appertainments*, *cadent*, *conflux*, *protractive*, *questrist*, *tortive*, *ungenitured* and *vastidity*. A large number of idiomatic phrases are also found for the first time in his writing.

Some Shakespearian expressions

beggars all description (*Antony and Cleopatra*, II, ii)
a foregone conclusion (*Othello*, III, iii)
hoist with his own petard (*Hamlet*, III, iv)
in my mind's eye (*Hamlet*, I, ii)
it's Greek to me (*Julius Caesar*, I, ii)
salad days (*Antony and Cleopatra*, I, v)
more in sorrow than in anger (*Hamlet*, I, ii)
play fast and loose (*Antony and Cleopatra*, IV, xii)
a tower of strength (*Richard III*, V, iii)
make a virtue of necessity (*Pericles*, I, iii)
dance attendance (*Henry VIII*, V, ii)
cold comfort (*King John*, V, vii)
at one fell swoop (*Macbeth*, IV, iii)
to the manner born (*Hamlet* I, iv)
there are more things in heaven and earth . . . (*Hamlet*, I, v)
brevity is the soul of wit (*Hamlet*, II, ii)
hold the mirror up to nature (*Hamlet*, III, ii)
I must be cruel only to be kind (*Hamlet*, III, iv)

The Authorized Version of the Bible, similarly, introduced many idioms into the language. It is a more conservative language than is found in Shakespeare. The group of translators had been instructed to pay close attention to the English translations which had already appeared. As they say in their Preface, their aim was not to make a new translation, 'but to make a good one better, or out of many good ones, one principall good one, not iustly to be excepted against'. They aimed for a dignified, not a popular style, and often used older forms of the language, even when modern alternatives were available.

Some Biblical expressions

my brother's keeper (Gn 4)	an eye for an eye (Ex 21)
the apple of his eye (Dt 32)	the skin of my teeth (Jb 19)
the root of the matter (Jb 19)	eat sour grapes (Ezk 24)
the salt of the earth (Mt 5)	cast pearls before swine (Mt 7)
the strait and narrow (Mt 7)	in sheep's clothing (Mt 7)
whited sepulchre (Mt 23)	physician, heal thyself (Lk 4)
the signs of the times (Mt 16)	filthy lucre (1 Tm 3)
suffer fools gladly (2 Co 11)	new wine into old bottles (Mt 9)
rule with a rod of iron (Rv 2)	to kick against the pricks (Ac 9)

go from strength to strength (Ps 84)
heap coals of fire upon his head (Pr 25)
a lamb brought to the slaughter (Jr 11)
if the blind lead the blind (Mt 15)
out of the mouths of babes (Mt 21)
in the twinkling of an eye (I Co 15)
touch not, taste not, handle not (Col 2)

The Authorized Version of the Bible, then, does not contain large numbers of new words, as Shakespeare's plays did. The vocabulary looks backwards, rather than forwards. Compared with Shakespeare's vocabulary of over 30,000 words, this translation of the Bible is tiny, containing only about 8,000.

Similarly, the Authorized Version looks backwards in its grammar, and preserves many of the forms and constructions which were falling out of use elsewhere. Not that this period was one in which there was much basic change in grammar. The main developments – the loss of word endings and the fixing of word order – had largely run their course in the medieval period (see Chapter 10). In Early Modern English, what we see is the 'residue' of this period of radical change. It is most noticeable in a conservative style, such as that of the Bible, or the Book of Common Prayer (originally compiled in 1549, in a style which was largely preserved in the 1662 version still used today). In Shakespeare, on the other hand, much greater use is made of the newer forms and constructions. The religious sources, therefore, are a good way of displaying the differences between sixteenth century and modern English grammar. They show the distance the language still had to travel to reach its present-day norms.

William Shakespeare

● Many irregular verbs are found in their older forms: *digged* (dug), *gat* (got) and *gotten*, *bare* (bore), *spake* (spoke), *forgat* (forgot), *sware* (swore), *tare* (tore), *clave* (cleft), *strake* (struck) and *holpen* (helped).

● Older word orders are still in use: *follow thou me, speak ye unto, cakes unleavened, things eternal.* In particular, the modern use of *do* with negatives and in questions is missing: we find *they knew him not*, instead of *they did not know him*. By contrast, both old and new constructions are used in Shakespeare, and the *do* construction became standard by about 1700.

● The third person singular of the present tense of verbs is always *-eth*. Elsewhere, it is being replaced by *-s* – a northern form (p. 185) which was moving south in the sixteenth century. It is often found in Shakespeare along with the older ending: both *comes* and *cometh* are used, for example (the choice depending to some extent on the needs of the poetic metre).

● The second person pronouns were changing during this period. Originally, *ye* was the subject form, and *you* was the form used as object or after a preposition. This distinction is preserved in the Bible, as can be seen in such examples as *Ye cannot serue God and Mammon. Therfore I say vnto you* ... But in most other writing, by the end of the sixteenth century *you* was already being used for *ye*, and the latter form disappeared completely from standard English in the later seventeenth century.

Similarly, *thou* was originally used for addressing one person, and *ye/you* for more than one. But during this period, usage changed: *thou* became intimate and informal, and *ye/you* polite and respectful. The *thou* form ceased to be in general use at the end of the seventeenth century – though it continued in some regional dialects and religious styles, and notably in the language of the Quakers.

● *His* is used for *its*, as in *if the salt has lost his savour, wherewith shall it be salted?* Although *its* is recorded as early as the end of the sixteenth century, it does not become general until 100 years later. (It may be some solace to those struggling with rules of punctuation to learn that *its* was spelled with an apostrophe until the end of the eighteenth century.) Similarly, in nouns, the modern use of the genitive was still not established, as is clear from such usages as *for Jesus Christ his sake*.

● The auxiliary verb *shall* is used for all persons; *will* is not found in the Authorized Version, but it is used in Shakespeare, especially in informal speech.

● The most noticeable difference in the use of adjectives is the way they can occur in a 'double' superlative: *the most straitest sect, the most Highest*.

A page from the King James Bible.
The typography is in the style known as
'black letter' (or 'gothic').

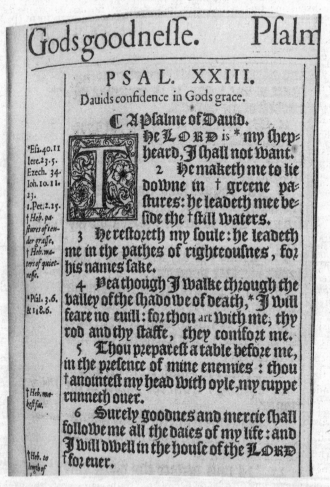

Gods goodneſſe.   Pſalm

PSAL. XXIII.

Dauids confidence in Gods grace.

¶ A Pſalme of Dauid.

HE LORD is * my ſhep-
heard, I ſhall not want.

2 He maketh me to lie
downe in † greene pa-
ſtures: he leadeth mee be-
ſide the † ſtill waters.

3 He reſtoreth my ſoule: he leadeth
me in the pathes of righteouſnes, for
his names ſake.

4 Yea though I walke through the
valley of the ſhadowe of death,* I will
feare no euill: for thou art with me; thy
rod and thy ſtaffe, they comfort me.

5 ¶ Thou prepareſt a table before me,
in the preſence of mine enemies : thou
† anointeſt my head with oyle, my cuppe
runneth ouer.

6 Surely goodnes and mercie ſhall
followe me all the daies of my life : and
I will dwell in the houſe of the LORD
† for euer.

*Eſa. 40. 11
Iere. 23. 5.
Ezech. 34.
Ioh. 10. 11.
23.
1. Pet. 2. 15.
† Heb. pa-
ſtures of ten-
der graſſe.
† Heb. wa-
ters of quiet-
neſſe.

*Pſal. 3. 6.
& 118. 6.

† Heb. ma-
keſt fat.

† Heb. to
length of

• Several prepositions have different uses from today: *the zeal of* (for) *thine house, tempted of* (by) *Satan, to you-ward* (towards you).

It is only natural to focus on Shakespeare and the King James Bible in discussing this period. But they were by no means alone. There were dozens of other dramatists writing at the time, some (such as Ben Jonson or Christopher Marlowe) of considerable stature. There were several other major biblical translations (such as Tyndale's and Coverdale's). The influence of these other writers and translators on the language is less obvious, but it can't be ignored. Likewise, there were innumerable tracts, sermons, pamphlets, letters, and other publications presenting a variety of styles of varying levels of formality and complexity. The great age of Elizabethan literature resulted in an unprecedented breadth and inventiveness in the use of the English language. But not everyone in the seventeenth century found this state of affairs satisfactory.

THE AGE OF THE DICTIONARY

The problem had been sensed in the sixteenth century, when (as we have seen) thousands of new words were entering the language. 'It were a thing verie praiseworthie', wrote Richard Mulcaster in 1582, 'if som one well learned and as laborious a man, wold gather all the words which we use in our English tung . . . into one dictionarie'. The task wasn't attempted until 1721, when Nathaniel Bailey published his *Universal Etymological English Dictionary*. But in the meantime, there were several attempts to do something about the main problem – the existence of new and learned words which many people did not understand.

The first 'dictionary of hard words' was published by Robert Cawdrey in 1604: *A Table Alphabeticall* was compiled 'for the benefit and helpe of Ladies, Gentlewomen, or any other unskilfull persons, Whereby they may the more easilie and better vnderstand many hard English wordes, which they shall heare or read in Scriptures, Sermons, or elsewhere, and also be made able to vse the same aptly themselues' (as it said on the title page). The book contained 3,000 'hard vsuall English wordes, borrowed from the Hebrew, Greeke, Latine, or French, &c. With the interpretation thereof by plaine English words'. It included such words as *aberration*, glossed 'a going astray, or wandering', *acquisition* 'getting, purchasing', and *paucitie* 'fewness or smale number'. It was a commercial success, and was followed by several other compilations along similar lines.

By the end of the seventeenth century, there was a strong feeling of unease about the way the language was going. The language was changing too fast, it was felt. Words such as 'unruly', 'corrupt', 'unrefined', and 'barbarous' came to be applied to it. There seemed to be no order in it – unlike Latin, which was viewed as a model of fixed, definite structure and use.

The critics were thinking of many things. They were worried about the uncontrolled way in which foreign words had come into the language. They could see no order in the creative way in which the Elizabethan dramatists and poets had used language, and they were uncertain whether to follow their example. They saw increasing variety in everyday usage – such as a fashion for new abbreviations (*ult* for *ultimate*, *rep* for *reputation*), or for new contracted forms (*disturb'd*, *rebuk'd*). Individual writers (and speakers) followed their own instincts. There were no norms of spelling or punctuation. Many people spelled words as they spoke, regardless of tradition (such as *sartinly* for *certainly*). Some had added extra letters to words, claiming that they were there in Latin (though in fact they were not): this is where the *s* in *island* or the *c* in *scissors* came from. An author might spell the same word in different ways on the same page, without anyone criticizing (or even noticing). The title page of Cawdrey's book spells *words* with an *e* and then without an *e*. Which was correct?

Many authors, in particular, were deeply worried. Given the pace at which English was changing, and the absence of any controls, would their work still be understandable in a generation or so? Jonathan Swift put it this way:

How then shall any man, who hath a genius for history equal to the best of the ancients, be able to undertake such work with spirit and cheerfulness, when he considers that he will be read with pleasure but a very few years, and in an age or two shall hardly be understood without an interpreter.

The poet Edmund Waller made a similar point:

> Poets that Lasting Marble seek
> Must carve in Latin or in Greek;
> We write in Sand . . .

Out of this developing sense of chaos and confusion came several lines of thought. Some scholars, such as John Hart (d. 1574), attempted to reform the spelling. Some, such as Bishop John Wilkins (1614–72), tried to develop a logical alternative to English, which would do away with all irregularity and inconsistency – a universal, artificial language. Some scientists tried to develop a plain, objective style, without rhetoric and classical vocabulary, more suitable to scientific expression. When the Royal Society was founded in 1662, this 'naked, natural way of speaking; positive expressions; clear senses' was said to be a hallmark of the founder members' style. But the issue which dominated discussion for several decades, well into the eighteenth century, was whether the English language should be placed in the hands of an Academy.

The first Academy was founded in Italy in 1582, and by 1612 it had produced a dictionary, which was seen as the first step on the road to 'purifying' the Italian language. A French Academy followed in 1635, and its dictionary appeared in 1694. During the same period, there came proposals for an English Academy which would look after the language in similar ways. The idea had been proposed by such men as John Dryden and Daniel Defoe, but it received its most vociferous support from Jonathan Swift. In 1712, he wrote a letter to the Lord Treasurer of England, 'A proposal for correcting, improving, and ascertaining the English tongue':

What I have most at heart is that some method should be thought on for ascertaining and fixing our language for ever, after such alterations are made in it as shall be thought requisite. For I am of opinion, it is better a language should not be wholly perfect, than that it should be perpetually changing.

Change, for Swift, and for many others in the early eighteenth century, was synonymous with corruption. Language was going downhill. It needed protection, and only dictionaries, grammars, and other manuals could provide it. The language needed to be purified and refined, its defects removed. It would then have its rules clearly stated, and would remain fixed, providing standards of correctness for all to follow.

Such opinions have appealed to every generation since, but they have never been implemented. The idea of an Academy never got off the ground, even though it received a great deal of support at the time. It was apparent to many that language could not be kept static, and that standards change. Even Latin and Greek had changed over the centuries when they were spoken. And not everyone felt that the work of the French or Italian Academies had been for the better. Dr Johnson summed up the alternative opinion in his typical style:

When we see men grow old and die at a certain time one after another, we laugh at the elixir that promises to prolong life to a thousand years; and with equal justice may the lexicographer be derided, who being able to produce no example of a nation that has preserved their words and phrases from mutability, shall imagine that his dictionary can embalm his language, and secure it from corruption and decay, that it is in his power to change sublunary nature, or clear the world at once from folly, vanity and affectation.

However, what the debate about language corruption did achieve was to focus public attention on the nature of the problem, and the need for a solution. And the first part of the solution, an English dictionary, came from Johnson himself, in 1755. Over a seven-year period, Johnson wrote the definitions of over 40,000 words, illustrating their use from the best authors since the time of the Elizabethans. In the words of his biographer, Boswell, the work 'conferred stability' on the language – at least in respect of the spelling and meaning of words. Its influence on the history of lexicography has been unparalleled (see illustrations, pp. 208–9).

At about the same time, the first attempts to define the field of English grammar began to appear. One of the most influential grammars of the time was Robert Lowth's *Short Introduction to English Grammar* (1762) – the inspiration for an even more widely used book, Lindley Murray's *English Grammar* (1794). Both grammars went through twenty editions in the years following their publication, and had enormous influence on school practices, especially in the USA. Murray's axiom was: 'Perspicuity requires the qualities of purity, propriety, and precision.'

It is in these books, and those they influenced, that we find the origins of so many of the grammatical controversies which continue to attract attention today (see Chapter 2). Should grammars (and, indeed, dictionaries) *reflect* usage, simply describing it, or should they *evaluate* usage, by prescribing certain forms as correct and proscribing others as incorrect? This is the age when many of the rules of 'correct' grammar were first formulated, such as those governing the use of *shall* and *will*, or the rule which states that sentences should not end with a preposition, or that two negatives make an affirmative. And these rules were as forcefully attacked as they were firmly formulated. Thus, on the one hand, we find Robert Lowth saying in 1762:

The principal design of a grammar of any language is to teach us to express ourselves with propriety in that language; and to enable us to judge of every phrase and form of construction, whether it be right or not.

And on the other hand, we have Joseph Priestley saying in 1761:

Our grammarians appear to me to have acted precipitately. It must be allowed that the *custom of speaking* is the original and only standard of any language. In modern and living languages, it is absurd to pretend to set up the compositions of any person or persons whatsoever as the standard of writing, or their conversation as the invariable rule of speaking.

That was the controversy in the 1760s, but the same sentiments, in almost the same language, can be found a hundred years later, and indeed are still widely expressed today. Even the examples are the same, as the arguments about double negatives, split infinitives, ending sentences with prepositions, and so on, continue to illustrate.

At the end of the eighteenth century, any English language history has to adopt a fresh perspective. It no longer makes sense to follow a single chronology, as we have in Chapters 9–11, plotting changes within a single community (England). The language of the eighteenth century is now very close to that of the present day, and there is very little by way of linguistic commentary that can be added. This part of the story is brought up to date in Chapter 13.

But first it is necessary to recognize that, in the early modern English period, it becomes increasingly unreasonable to focus on England alone as the basis of a historical account. There were important parallel developments in the rest of Britain, especially in Scotland and Ireland. And a new perspective is required in order to take account of the linguistic consequences of the discovery of America and other parts of the world – the colonization of some of these areas by English-speaking people, and the development of regional linguistic standards different from those in use in England.

HIG

The plenteous board *high-heap'd* with cates divine,
And o'er the foaming bowl the laughing wine.   *Pope.*

2. Raised into high piles.

I saw myself the vast unnumber'd store
Of brass, *high-heap'd* amidst the regal dome.   *Pope's Odyssey.*

HIGH-HE'ELED. Having the heel of the shoe much raised.
By these embroider'd *high-heel'd* shoes,
She shall be caught a∫ith a noose.   *Swift.*

HI'GH-HUNG. Hung aloft.
By the *high-hung* taper's light,
I could di∫cern his cheeks were glowing red.   *Dryden.*

HIGH-ME'TTLED. Proud or ardent of spirit.
He fails not in these to keep a stiff rein on a *high-mettled*
Pegasus; and takes care not to furfeit here, as he had done on
other heads, by an erroneous abundance.   *Garth.*

HIGH-MI'NDED. Proud; arrogant.
My breast I'll burst with training of my courage,
But I will cha∫ti∫e this *high-minded* trumpet.   *Shakes. H.VI.*
Because of unbelief they were broken off, and thou standest
by faith: be not *high-minded*, but fear.   *Rom. ii. 20.*

HIGH-PRI'NCIPLED. Extravagant in notions of politicks.
This seems to be the political creed of all the *high-principled*
men I have met with.   *Swift.*

HIGH-RE'D. Deeply red.
Oil of turpentine, though clear as water, being dige∫ted
upon the purely with fugar of lead, has in a ∫hort time af-
forded a *high-red* tincture.   *Boyle on Colours.*

HIGH-SE'ASONED. Piquant to the palate.
Be ∫paring al∫o of falt in the ∫ea∫oning of all his victuals,
and u∫e him not to *high-fea∫oned* meats.   *Locke.*

HIGH-SI'GHTED. Always looking upwards.
Let *high-fighted* tyranny range on,
Till each man drop by lottery ;
But if the∫e countrymen bear fire enough,
What need we any fpur but our own cau∫e?   *Shakespeare.*

HIGH-SPI'RITED. Bold; daring; in∫olent.

HIGH-STO'MACHED. Ob∫tinate; lofty.
High-ftomach'd are they both, and full of ire ;
In rage, deaf as the ∫ea, ha∫ty as fire.   *Shakespeare.*

HIGH-TA'STED. Gu∫tful; piquant.
Flatt'ry ∫till in ∫ugar'd words betrays,
And poi∫on in *high-tafted* meats conveys.   *Denham.*

HIGH-VI'CED. Enormou∫ly wicked.
As at a planetary plague, when Jove
Will o'er ∫ome *high-vic'd* city hang his poi∫on
In the ∫ick air.   *Shakespeare's Timon of Athens.*

HIGH-WROUGHT. Accurately fini∫hed ; nobly laboured.
Thou triumph'ft, victor of the *high-wrought* day,
And the plea∫'d dame, ∫oft ∫miling, lea∫t'ft away.   *Pope.*

HIGHLAND. *n. f.* [*high* and *land.*] Mountainous region.
The wood'ring moon
Beholds her brother's ∫teeds beneath her own ;
The *highlands* fmoak'd, cleft by the piercing rays.   *Addison.*
Ladies in the *highlands* of Scotland u∫e this di∫cipline to
their children in the mid∫t of Winter, and find that cold wa-
ter does them no harm.   *Locke.*

HIGHLA'NDER. *n. f.* [from *highland.*] An inhabitant of
mountains.
His cabinet council of *highlanders.*   *Addison.*

HI'GHLY. *adv.* [from *high.*]
1. With elevation as to place and ∫ituation.
2. In a great degree.
Whatever expedients can allay tho∫e heats, which break us
into different factions, cannot but be u∫eful to the publick,
and *highly* tend to its ∫afety.   *Addison's Freeholder.*
It cannot but be *highly* requi∫ite for us to ∫upport and en-
liven our faith, by dwelling often on the ∫ame con∫iderations.   *Atterbury's Sermons.*
3. Proudly; arrogantly; ambitiou∫ly.
What thou would∫t *highly*,
That thou would∫t holily ; would∫t not play fal∫e,
And yet would∫t wrongly win.   *Shakesp. Macbeth.*
4. With e∫teem ; with e∫timation.
Every man that is among you, not to think of him∫elf
more *highly* than he ought to think.   *Rom. xii. 3.*

HI'GHMOST. *adj.* [An irregular word.] Highe∫t; topmo∫t.
Upon the ∫un upon the *highmoft* hill
Of this day's journey ; and from nine 'till twelve,
Is three long hours.   *Shakesp. Romeo and Juliet.*

HI'GHNESS. *n. f.* [from *high.*]
1. Elevation above the ∫urface.
2. The title of princes, anciently of kings.
Mo∫t royal maje∫ty,
I crave no more than that your *highnefs* offer'd.   *Shakespeare.*
How long in vain had nature thriv'd to frame
A perfect princefs, ere her *highnefs* came?   *Waller.*
Beauty and greatne∫s are eminently joined in your royal
highnefs.   *Dryden.*
3. Dignity of nature ; ∫upremacy.
De∫truction from God was a terrour to me, and by rea∫on
of his *highnefs* I could not endure.   *Job xxxi. 23.*

HIGHT. [This is an imperfect verb, u∫ed only in the preterite

HIL

ten∫e with a pa∫∫ive ∫ignification : *hatan*, to call, Saxon; *he∫∫en*,
to be called, German.]
1. Was named ; was called.
The city of the great king *hight* it well,
Wherein eternal peace and happine∫s doth dwell.   *Fa. Queen.*
Within this home∫tead liv'd, without a peer
For crowing loud, the noble Chanticleer,
So *hight* her cock.   *Dryden's Nun's Prieft.*
2. It is ∫ometimes u∫ed as a participle pa∫∫ive, and ∫ignifies called ;
named. It is now ob∫olete, except in burle∫que writings.
Among∫t the re∫t a good old woman was,
Hight mother Hubberd.   *Hubberd's Tale.*

HIGHWA'TER. *n. f.* [*high* and *water.*] The utmo∫t flow of the
tide.
They have a good way in E∫∫ex of draining of lands that
lie below the *highwater*, and that are ∫omething above the low-
water mark.   *Mortimer's Husbandry.*

HIGHWA'Y. *n. f.* [*high* and *way.*] Great road ; publick path.
So few there be
That chu∫e the narrow path, or ∫eek the right :
All keep the broad *highway*, and take delight.   *Fairy Queen, b. i.*
With many rather for to go a∫tray.
Two in∫criptions give a great light to∫he hi∫tories of Appius,
who made the *highway*, and of Fabius the dictator.   *Addison.*
Ent'ring on a broad *highway*,
Where power and titles ∫catter'd lay,
He ∫trove to pick up all he found.   *Swift.*
I could mention more trades we have lo∫t, and are in the
highway to lo∫e.   *Child on Trade.*

HI'GHWAYMAN. *n. f.* [*highway* and *man.*] A robber that plun-
ders on the publick road.
'Tis like the friend∫hip of pickpockets and *highwaymen*,
that ob∫erve ∫trict ju∫tice among them∫elves.   *Bentley's Sermons.*
A remedy like that of giving my money to an *high-
wayman* before he attempts to take it by force, to prevent
the ∫in of robbery.   *Swift.*

HI'GLAPER. *n. f.* An herb.   *Ainsworth.*

HILA'RITY. *n. f.* [*hilaritas*, Latin] Merriment; gay∫ty.
Averrues re∫trained his *hilarity*, and made no more thereof
than ∫eneca commendeth, and was allowable in Cato; that is,
a ∫ober incaflecence from wine.   *Brown's Vulgar Errours.*

HILD, in *Ælrid's* grammar, is interpreted a lord or lady : fo
Hildbert is a noble lord ; *Mabtild*, an heroick lady ; and in
the ∫ame ∫en∫e in *Wiga* al∫o found.   *Gib. Camden.*

HI'LDING. *n. f.* [*hilo*, Saxon, ∫ignifies a lord : perhaps *hilding*
meant originally a *little lord* in contempt, for a man that has
only the delicacy or bad qualities of high rank ; or a term of re-
proach abbreviated from *hinderling*, degenerate. *Hughes's Sperf.*]
1. A ∫orry, paltry, cowardly fellow.
He was ∫ome *hilding* fellow, that had ∫ul'n
The hor∫e he rode on.   *Shakespeare's Henry IV. p. i.*
If your lord∫hip find him not a *hilding*, hold me no more in
your re∫pect.   *Shakef. All's well that ends well.*
You are curb'd from that enlargement by
The con∫equence o' th' crown, and mu∫t not foil
The precious note of it with a ba∫e ∫lave,
A *hilding* for a livery, a ∫quire's cloth.   *Shak. Cymbeline.*
This i∫le toy, this *hilding* ∫corns my power,
And fets us all at naught.   *Rowe's Jane Shore.*
2. It is u∫ed likewi∫e for a mean woman.
Laura, to his lady, was but a kitchen wench ;
Helen and Hero, *hildings* and harlots.   *Shak. Rom. and Jul.*

HILL. *n. f.* [hɩl, Saxon.] An elevation of ground le∫s than a
mountain.
My ∫heep are thoughts, which I both guide and ∫erve ;
Their pa∫ture is fair *hills* of fruitle∫s love.   *Sidney, b. ii.*
Jeru∫alem is ∫eated on two *hills*,
Of height unlike, and turned fide to fide.   *Fairfax.*
Three fides are fure imbar'd with crags and *hills*,
The re∫t is ea∫y, ∫cant to ri∫e e∫py'd;
But mighty bulwarks fence the plainer part :
So art helps nature, nature ∫trengtheneth art.   *Fairfax, b. iii.*
When our eye ∫ome pro∫pect would pur∫ue,
De∫cending from a *hill*, looks round to view.   *Granville.*
A *hill* is nothing but the ne∫t of ∫ome metal or mineral,
which, by a pla∫tick virtue, and the efficacy of ∫ubterranean
fires, converting the adjacent earths into their ∫ub∫tance, do
increa∫e and grow.   *Cheyne's Phil. Princ.*

HI'LLOCK. *n. f.* [from *hill.*] A little hill.
Yet weigh this, alas! great is not great to the greater :
What, judge you, doth a *hillock* ∫how by the lofty Olympus!   *Sidney, b. i.*
Sometime walking not un∫een
By hedge-row elms, on *hillocks* green.   *Milton.*
This mountain, and a few neighbouring *hillocks* that lie
∫cattered about the bottom of it, is the whole circuit of the∫e
dominions.   *Addison on Italy.*

HI'LLY. *adj.* [from *hill.*] Full of hills; unequal in the ∫ur-
face.
Towards the *hilly* corners of Druina remain yet her very
Aborigines, fatally thru∫t among∫t an a∫∫embly of mountains.   *Howel's Vocal Forreft.*

Climbing

Samuel Johnson

W. Evans sculpsit.

Left: a page from Johnson's dictionary. Note the careful attention paid to the different senses of a word, the copious use of quotations to support the definition, and the personal element in the writing. The last point is best known from such definitions as *lexicographer* 'a writer of dictionaries, a harmless drudge', or *oats* 'a grain, which in England is generally given to horses, but in Scotland supports the people'.

Indeed, given the statistics on the use of English described in Chapter 1, it is likely that, in another century or so, the influence of some of these other areas on the future development of the language will be critical (see Chapter 14). In Chapter 12, therefore, we look at English linguistic history on a world scale.

Words Then and Now

Language changes when society changes. And while it is true to say
that there have been no fundamental alterations in the structure of
the language during the past 300 years, that mustn't be taken to imply
that English has stood still. The vast social and technological changes
since the Industrial Revolution have had their linguistic consequences
in the form of thousands of new words. (Pronunciation and grammar,
by comparison, have changed very little in that time; but some of the
changes which *have* taken place – several of them resulting in disputes
about usage – are described in Chapters 2–4.)

Scientific terms in English

Eighteenth century

anaesthesia (1731), antiseptic (1751), dicotyledon (1727), fallopian
(1706), fauna (1771), hydrogen (1791), molecule (1794), nitrogen
(1794), nucleus (1704), oxygen (1790), pistil (1718), thyroid (1726)

Nineteenth century

accumulator (1877), allotropy (1849), barograph (1865), centigrade
(1812), chromosome (1890), dynamo (1882), gyroscope (1856),
micron (1892), ozone (1840), pasteurize (1881), protoplasm
(1848)

Twentieth century

allergy (1913), biochemistry (1902), decaffeinate (1934), gene (1909),
hormone (1902), ionosphere (1913), millibar (1912), penicillin (1929),
photon (1926), quantum (1910), radar (1942), sputnik (1957), vitamin
(1912)

Since the seventeenth century, the flow of new words into the language has continued without interruption, especially in the fields of science and technology. Scientific and technical terms now comprise well over half the vocabulary of English. A few examples from each century are given on p. 211 (dates are of the earliest recorded usage).

Vocabulary change is always the most frequently noticed aspect of language development, and it affects all sections of society – as is suggested by this random selection of words which began to be widely used in various fields of English during the 1960s and 1970s:

aerobics, Afro, biofeedback, blue movie, brain-drain, childproof, command module, computer graphics, disco, disinformation, frisbee, gay, hovercraft, jogging, male chauvinist, neutron star, ombudsman, fibre optics, privatize, quasar, RAM, sexploitation, skateboard, skyjacking, software, VAT, windsurfing, zip code

Not all of these words refer to new concepts or inventions, of course. There will, for instance, have been objects in Victorian times which were capable of withstanding the attacks of young children – but they would not have been characterized as *childproof*. And Victorian homosexuals were not *gay*.

But looking at new words from our own generation does not provide a strong sense of the recent history of vocabulary. An easier way is to look back at the literature of previous generations, and to note which words or senses have gone *out* of use – such as the fashionable slang of the twenties and thirties (*tosh, what-ho, old top, ripping*), or the names of early carriages (*gig, sociable, brougham, surrey*, etc.). Novels written a generation or so ago usually provide excellent examples:

'It won't do, old top. What's the point of putting up any old yarn like that? Don't you see, what I mean is, it's not as if we minded. Don't I keep telling you we're all pals here? I've often thought what a jolly good feller old Raffles was – regular sportsman. I don't blame a chappie for doing the gentleman burglar touch. Seems to me it's a dashed sporting —.'

P. G. Wodehouse, *A Gentleman of Leisure* (1910)

Dated, archaic, or unfamiliar old words are easy to spot. And similarly, the contrast between old and modern meanings is usually clear: no one has failed to notice that *gay*, for example, has developed a new meaning in recent years. But there are aspects of vocabulary change which are much more difficult to sense – in particular, the way in which words have changed their social status, coming into favour, or falling out of favour, among a particular social group.

Probably the most widely known attempt to discuss words in terms of their social prestige was carried out by the British linguist A. S. C. Ross, in an article published in 1954. The ideas were popularized by the novelist Nancy Mitford, and the terms 'U' and 'non-U' came into being. 'U' stood for 'upper-class usage' in Britain; 'non-U' for other kinds of usage. The idea was to draw attention to the way that words, pronunciations and other forms could demarcate upper-class people (or people who aspired to the upper class) from those belonging to other classes. Since the 1950s, of course, society and usage have profoundly altered; but many of the words considered to be U and non-U in those days still carry noticeable social overtones (though it is by no means easy to say precisely what these are):

Words said to be 'U'	*Words said to be 'non-U'*
luncheon	dinner
sick	ill
writing-paper	note-paper
table-napkin	serviette
lavatory	toilet
vegetables	greens
pudding	sweet
riding	horse-riding
looking-glass	mirror
Scotch	Scottish

Some of the U/non-U distinctions have been a source of debate for decades. The question of whether we should call females *ladies* or *women*, and males *men* or *gentlemen*, is still raised today – just as it was over a century ago. Here is an extract from a Victorian book of etiquette, *Society Small Talk, or What to Say and When to Say it* (1879):

In common parlance a man is always a man to a man and never a gentle-man; to a woman he is occasionally a man and occasionally a gentleman; but a man would far oftener term a woman 'a woman' than he would term her 'a lady'. When a man makes use of an adjective in speaking of a lady, he almost invariably calls her a woman: thus he would say, 'I met a rather agreeable woman at dinner last night'; but he would not say, 'I met an agreeable lady' . . . but he might say, 'A lady, a friend of mine, told me', when he would not say 'A woman, a friend of mine, told me'. Again, a man would say, 'Which of the ladies did you take in to dinner?' He would certainly not say, 'Which of the women . . .?'

Why not? The author does not go into the matter. And even today, the factors governing our preferences in this area of usage are little understood, as debates over *cleaning lady/woman, ladies'/women's final, young lady/woman*, and so on continue to show.

Some Victorian views about 'woman' and 'lady'

Uncle Julius turned round, and in a voice of thunder, audible to every one on the road, exclaimed, 'Ignorant and presumptuous young woman!' He had never seen her till that day. As she said to me years after, when she was a wife and mother, 'That the Archdeacon should call me ignorant and presumptuous was trying, but I could bear that very well; but that he should call me a *young woman* was not to be endured!'

Augustus Hare, *The Story of My Life*

'I'm sure she's clever'. 'Yes, I think she's clever.' 'And, and – *womanly* in her feelings.' Mrs Gresham felt that she could not say *ladylike*, though she would fain have done so, had she dared.

Anthony Trollope, *Framley Parsonage*

How often he had spoken scornfully of that word 'lady'! Were not all of the sex women? What need for that hateful distinction?

George Gissing, *Demos*

[Mrs Brattle] was a modest, pure, high-minded woman – whom we will not call a lady, because of her position in life, and because she darned stockings in a kitchen.

Anthony Trollope, *The Vicar of Bullhampton*

12

ᚼᚼᚼᚼᚼᚼᚼᚼᚼᚼ

English Around the World

Historical approaches to the English language inevitably begin with
'Englalond', and largely restrict their story to what took place in
educated standard English in southern Britain (Chapters 9–11). But,
from the late Old English period, it is necessary to broaden the
perspective. Other things happened to English, apart from what
went on in London and the south-east of England. In due course,
there developed other standard varieties of English as a mother
tongue, each with its own complex social history.

"Not the full translation, just the gist of what they're saying."

SCOTLAND

The first developments occurred in Scotland. After the fifth century invasions, what is now the north-east of England and the south-east of Scotland came to be occupied by the Angles, whose way of speech gradually led to a distinctive variety of English – the Northumbrian dialect (see p. 155). During the Old English period, most of Scotland was Celtic-speaking (primarily the variety known as Gaelic), but the number of English speakers in the southern part of the country was much increased in the eleventh century, following the French invasion of 1066. Many English noblemen became refugees, and fled north, where they were welcomed by the Scots King Malcolm III (most widely known as the slayer of Macbeth, as recounted by Shakespeare).

During the twelfth century, the move north continued, with many southern families being invited to settle in the area by King David I – notably in the new chartered royal estates known as *burhs* (such as Aberdeen and Edinburgh). These places were largely English-speaking, and gradually, English spread through the whole lowlands area, with Gaelic remaining beyond the Highland line.

This Scots English became increasingly different from that used in England, especially in pronunciation and vocabulary, and many of these differences are still heard today. In pronunciation, for example, there was the use of the *ch* sound in the middle of such words as *nicht* ('night'). The vowel in such words as *guid* ('good') was often made longer, and produced further forward in the mouth than it was in southern English. A distinction is made between the first sound of *which* and *witch*. A common spelling difference is that, where southern English writes *wh-*, older Scots used *quh-*. There were also some distinctive grammatical endings, such as the use of *-it* for the past tense (*trublit* for *troubled*). Many Gaelic words were assimilated, such as *bog*, *cairn*, *corrie*, *glen*, *loch*, *pibroch* and *whisky*. And there were a number of words from other languages which did not enter the standard English of England, such as *bonny* (beautiful, handsome), from French *bon*, and *ashet* (a serving dish) from *assiette*.

In the thirteenth century, these and other differences amounted to a considerable divergence between the English of Scotland and that of England, and this was increased by the split between the nations which followed Edward I of England's attempt at annexation, and the subsequent long period of conflict. By the late Middle Ages, Middle Scots had evolved as far from Old English as had the Middle English of England, and in a different direction. It is often said that the two varieties were as far apart then as, say, Danish and Swedish are now. And, as a result, some writers on the period refer to the two varieties as distinct 'languages' – and continue to do so, when discussing modern Scots. The point is controversial, as the question of whether two kinds of speech are one language or two depends as much on social and political considerations as on linguistic ones.

Verses from William Dunbar's *Lament for the Makaris* (*Elegy for the Poets*), written about 1505. The Latin line is taken from the Office of the Dead, and translates 'The fear of death troubles me'.

> The stait of man dois [does] change and vary,
> Now sound, now seik [sick], now blith, now sary [sorry],
> Now dansand [dancing] mery, now like to dee [die];
> Timor mortis conturbat me.

> No stait in erd [earth] heir standis sickir [secure]
> As with the wynd wavis [waves] the wickir [willow],
> Wavis this warldis [world's] vanité;
> Timor mortis conturbat me.

From the end of the fourteenth century to the beginning of the seventeenth, there was a flowering of literature in Scots, a period which reached its peak in the poetry of the fifteenth-century authors Robert Henryson and William Dunbar. But during the seventeenth century, the Scots literary language began to decay, as it fell increasingly under the influence of the southern standard. The main factor was the uniting of the crowns of Scotland and England in 1603, and the move to London of James VI and the Scottish Court – a move which led in due course to the adoption among the upper classes of southern English norms of speech. As James I of England, the new King ordered that the Authorized Version of the Bible (see p. 198) be used in Scotland, thus spreading further the influence of the southern standard as a prestige form.

The gap between Scots and southern English is well illustrated by this story, written probably by Andrew Boorde about 1540, about a Scot who went to live in the south, and who wanted to have a carpenter make him a boar's head sign. The author spells some of the words to represent the Scots pronunciation.

And he wente to London to haue a Bores head made. He dyd come to a Caruer (or a Joyner) saying in his mother tongue, I saye spek, kens thou meke me a Bare heade? Ye said the Caruer. Then sayd the skotyshman, mek me a bare head anenst Yowle [before Yule], an thowse bus [you shall] haue xx pence for thy hyre. I wyll doe it sayde the Caruer. On S. Andrewes daye before Chrystmas (the which is named Yowle in Scotland, and in England in the north) the skottish man did com to London for his Bores heade to set at a dore for a signe. I say speke said the skotish man, haste thou made me a Bare head? Yea, said the Caruer. Then thowse a gewd fellow. The Caruer went and did bryng a mans head of wod that was bare and sayd, syr here is youre bare head. I say sayde the skotyshman, the mokyl deuill [great devil], is this a bare head? Ye said the caruer. I say sayd the Skotishman, I will have a bare head, syk [such] an head as doth follow a Sew [sow] that hath Gryces [piglets]. Syr said the caruer, I can not tel what is a Sew, nor what is a Gryce. Whet herson [whoreson], kenst thou not a sew that wil greet and grone, and her gryces wil run after her and cry a weke a weke. O said the Caruer, it is a pigge. Yea said the skotish man, let me haue his fathers head made in timber . . .

Here a man maye see that euerye man doth delight in his owne sences. . . .

Lowland Scots (or 'Lallans', as it is often called) was kept alive in literature, notably in the poetry of Robert Burns (1759–96), and the tales of Walter Scott (1771–1832), and there is today a considerable re-awakening of interest in it, in literature, scholarship, and to some extent the media. But in the educated spoken language, it was largely replaced by standard southern English, spoken with any of a wide range of Scots accents, and containing a few grammatical differences and varying amounts of regional vocabulary and idiomatic phrasing. It is this variety which is these days referred to as standard Scottish English.

Some words and phrases from everyday Scottish English

aye	yes	*loch*	lake
brae	slope, hillside	*outwith*	outside
burn	stream	*pinkie*	little finger
dram	drink (usually of whisky)	*provost*	mayor
dreich	dull	*rone (pipe)*	drainpipe
janitor	caretaker	*wee*	small

Away to your . . .   Go to your . . .
Do you mind when . . .?   Do you remember when . . .?
I doubt she's not in   I expect she's not in
I'm finished it   I'm finished
the back of 3 o'clock   soon after 3 o'clock

IRELAND

The history of English involvement in Gaelic-speaking Ireland dates from the twelfth century, with the invasion of the country by Anglo-Norman knights, and the subsequent rule of King Henry II. English law was introduced almost immediately. The new settlers, however, were to adopt Irish ways of living, and despite attempts to halt this trend, the area of English control (known as the 'Pale') was still relatively small by the end of the sixteenth century.

But during the sixteenth century, renewed efforts were made by the Tudor monarchs to establish English control throughout the country. Plantation schemes were set up to encourage English settlers in the south, and support was given to promote the spirit of the Reformation. The Irish chiefs were defeated in a series of wars during the reign of Elizabeth I, and this was followed by a renewed influx of Protestant settlers, mainly from the Scottish Lowlands. James I made available large tracts of land in the north of Ireland, and over 100,000 came to develop plantations there. Further campaigns to quell Irish rebellion took place in the seventeenth century – notably the one led by Oliver Cromwell in 1649–50. Then in 1803 the Act of Union made Ireland part of the United Kingdom – a situation which remained until the 1920s, when there was partition between north (Ulster) and south.

The areas of differing linguistic influence in Scotland and Ireland

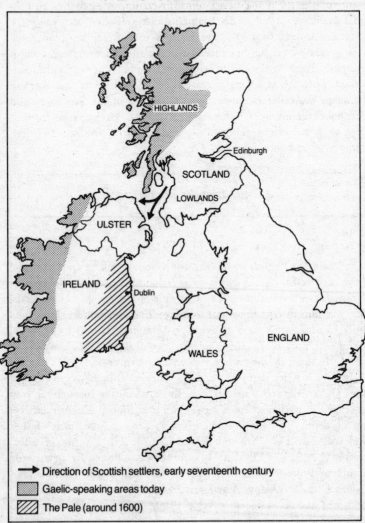

→ Direction of Scottish settlers, early seventeenth century

Gaelic-speaking areas today

The Pale (around 1600)

The linguistic consequence of these events was a steady development in the use of English, and a corresponding decline in the use of Gaelic, except among the poorer sections of the population.

Today, English is used everywhere, with Gaelic found only in certain rural parts of the west – notwithstanding its status as an official language in the Irish Republic alongside English. Since the nineteenth century, there have been several attempts to encourage the spread of Gaelic, but these have not affected the dominance of English. Even in the north, where the conflict was originally identified with the two languages, nowadays both sides use English (though the different linguistic backgrounds of the Protestant and Catholic communities – Lowland Scots and Gaelic respectively – are to some extent reflected in distinct styles of pronunciation, grammar, and vocabulary).

Some Irish English words

afeared	afraid	*delph*	crockery
airy	light-hearted	*garda*	police
blather	talk nonsense	*mannerly*	well-mannered
bold	naughty	*shore*	drain
cog	(to) cheat	*yoke*	thingummy

Some grammatical features of Southern Irish

- The use of *let* in commands: *Let you have a try* (You have a try).
- The use of *after* to express recent past time: *I'm after going to town* (I've just gone to town).
- The use of the *-ing* ending in certain verbs: *It's belonging to me* (It belongs to me).
- The use of Gaelic-influenced word orders: *Is it ready you are?* (Are you ready?)

A few Northern Ireland usages

- The use of *but*, meaning 'though': *I never went there, but.*
- The use of *from*, meaning 'since': *He's been here from he left the navy.*
- The use of *whenever*, meaning 'when': *I bought it whenever I was living in Belfast.*

And a fragment of Dublin speech, according to James Joyce

'But still and all he kept on saying that before the summer was over he'd go out for a drive one fine day just to see the old house again where we were all born down in Irishtown, and take me and Nannie with him. If we could only get one of them new-fangled carriages that makes no noise that Father O'Rourke told him about, them with the rheumatic wheels, for the day cheap – he said, at Johnny Rush's over the way there and drive out the three of us together of a Sunday evening. He had his mind set on that . . . Poor James!'

'The Lord have mercy on his soul!' said my aunt.

'The sisters', *Dubliners*, 1914

There is as yet little sign of a regionally distinctive educated standard in Ireland; but there are many cases of words, idioms, and grammatical patterns in informal, non-standard speech which are characteristic of the area, some of which have been influenced by Gaelic. Much that is special about Irish English has been given literary expression in the poetry of W. B. Yeats (1865–1939), the plays of J. M. Synge (1871–1909) and the novels of James Joyce (1882–1941), and the interest these authors generated in this variety continues to be found in the work of contemporary authors.

AMERICA

The most significant step in the progress of English towards its status as a world language took place in the last decades of the sixteenth century, with the arrival of the expeditions commissioned by Walter Raleigh to the 'New World'. The first venture was a failure. In 1584 the first group of explorers landed near Roanoke Island, in what is today called North Carolina, and established a small settlement. But conflict with the Indians followed, and it proved necessary for a ship to return to England for help and supplies. By the time those arrived, in 1590, none of the original group of settlers could be found. The mystery of their disappearance has never been solved.

The first permanent English settlement dates from 1607, when an expedition arrived in Chesapeake Bay, and called the settlement Jamestown, after James I. Further settlements quickly followed along the coast, and also on the nearby islands – Bermuda, and later the Bahamas. Then, in 1620, the first group of Puritan settlers arrived on the *Mayflower* – the 'Pilgrim Fathers' – searching for a land where they could found a new religious kingdom 'purified' from the practices which they found unacceptable in the English Church of the time. They landed at Cape Cod, in Plymouth, Massachusetts, and established a settlement there (a way of life which has in recent times

Early English-speaking settlement areas in America

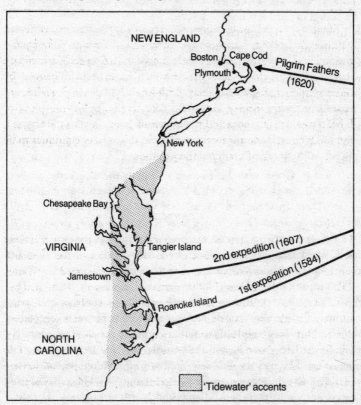

been lovingly recreated by a group of 'living history' enthusiasts). By 1640 around 25,000 people had settled in the area.

It's important to appreciate that these two patterns of settlement resulted in different linguistic consequences. The southern explorers came mainly from the West Country, and brought with them the characteristic west-country accent, with its 'Zummerzet' voicing of *s* sounds, and the *r* pronounced after vowels. Strong hints of this accent can still be heard in the speech of communities living in some of the isolated valleys and islands in the area, such as Tangier Island in Chesapeake Bay. These 'Tidewater' accents, as they are called, will have changed somewhat over the past 300 years, but not as rapidly (because of the relative isolation of the speakers) as elsewhere in the country. They are sometimes said to be the closest we will ever get to the sound of Shakespearean English.

In contrast, the Puritans came mainly from East Anglia and the surrounding counties, and their accent was quite different – notably lacking an *r* after vowels (as in present-day standard English). This tendency not to 'pronounce the *r*' is still a main feature of the speech of people from the New England area today.

Other features of the dialects of seventeenth-century England can be identified in modern American speech, such as the short, 'flat' *a* vowel, where British Received Pronunciation later developed the 'long' *a*, in such words as *dance*. British English also later pronounced such words as *not* with lip-rounding, but in the USA the earlier unrounded vowel remained ('nat'). American speech kept *gotten* for *got*, and *ate* (pronounced 'eight') for *ate* (pronounced 'et'). And several older words or meanings were retained, such as *mad* (angry) and *fall* (autumn). A phrase such as *I guess*, which often attracts condemnation as an Americanism by British purists, in fact can be traced back to Middle English (see further pp. 246–50).

The separateness of the colonies remained for much of the seventeenth century, but during this time increasing contacts and new patterns of settlement caused the sharp divisions between accents to begin to blur. New shiploads of settlers brought people with a variety of linguistic backgrounds, and the 'middle' Atlantic areas began to be opened up. The area around New York saw rapid development. From 1681, Pennsylvania came to be settled mainly by Quakers, whose origins were mostly in the Midlands and North of England. By 1700,

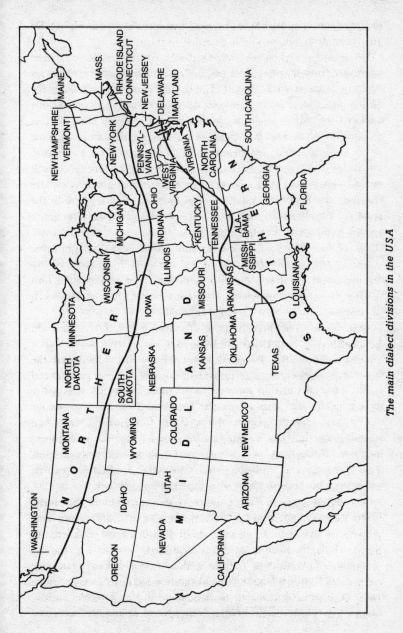

The main dialect divisions in the USA

the immigrant population of the continent had increased to around a quarter of a million.

In the early eighteenth century, there was a vast wave of immigration from northern Ireland. The Irish had been migrating to America from around 1600, but the main movements took place during the 1720s, when around 50,000 Irish and Scots-Irish immigrants arrived. By the time Independence was declared in 1776, it is thought that no less than one in seven of the American population was Scots-Irish. Many stayed along the coast, especially in the area of Philadelphia, but most moved inland through the mountains in search of land. They were seen as frontier people, with an accent which at the time was described as 'broad'. The opening up of the South and West was largely due to the pioneering spirit of this group of settlers – a spirit well captured in the tales of the frontiersman Davy Crockett (1786–1836), who was one of many with a Scots-Irish background.

By the time of the first census, in 1790, the population of the continent was around four million, most of whom lived along the Atlantic coast. A century later, after the opening up of of the West, the population numbered over fifty million, spread all over the continent. Much of the movement west had been led by the Scots-Irish. The accent which emerged can now be heard all over the so-called 'Sunbelt', and is the accent most commonly associated with present-day American speech.

The main population movements to some extent preserved the three major dialect areas of the east coast: the New England people moved west into the region of the Great Lakes; the southerners moved along the Gulf Coast, and into Texas; and the midlanders spread out throughout the whole of the vast, mid-western area, across the Mississippi and ultimately into California. The dialect picture was never a neat one, because of widespread north–south movements within the country, and the continuing inflow of immigrants from different parts of the world. There are many mixed dialect areas, and 'pockets' of unexpected dialect forms. But the main divisions of North, Midland and South are still demonstrable today.

An important aspect of American life, its cosmopolitan character, was present from the beginning, and this had linguistic consequences too. The Spanish had occupied large areas in the west and south-west of the country. The French were present in the northern territories, around the St Lawrence, and throughout the middle regions (French Louisiana) as far as the Gulf of Mexico. The Dutch were in New York (originally New Amsterdam) and the surrounding area. Large numbers of Germans began to arrive at the end of the seventeenth century, settling mainly in Pennsylvania and its hinterland. And there were increasing numbers of blacks in the south, as a result of the slave trade from Africa, which dramatically increased in the eighteenth century: a population of little more than 2,500 blacks in 1700 had become about 100,000 by 1775, far outnumbering the southern whites.

During the nineteenth century, these immigration patterns increased, with many people fleeing the results of revolution and famine in Europe. Large numbers of Irish came following the potato famine in the 1840s. Germans and Italians came, escaping the consequences of the failure of the 1848 revolutions. And as the century wore on, there were increasing numbers of Central European Jews, especially fleeing from the pogroms of the 1880s. In the decades around the turn of the century, the United States welcomed five million Germans, four million Italians, and two and a half million Jews.

The origins of American state names

Alabama Choctaw 'I open the thicket' (i.e. one who clears land)
Alaska Eskimo 'great land'
Arizona Papago 'place of the small spring'
Arkansas Sioux 'land of the south wind people'
California Spanish 'earthly paradise'
Colorado Spanish 'red' (i.e. colour of the earth)
Connecticut Mohican 'at the long tidal river'
Delaware named after the English governor Lord de la Warr
Florida Spanish 'land of flowers'
Georgia named after King George II
Hawaii Hawaiian 'homeland'
Idaho Shoshone 'light on the mountains'
Illinois French from Algonquian 'warriors'
Indiana English 'land of the Indians'
Iowa Dakota 'the sleepy one'
Kansas Sioux 'land of the south wind people'

Kentucky Iroquois 'meadow land'

Louisiana named after King Louis XIV of France

Maine named after a French province

Maryland named after Henrietta Maria, Charles I's queen

Massachusetts Algonquian 'place of the big hill'

Michigan Chippewa 'big water'

Minnesota Dakota Sioux 'sky-coloured water'

Mississippi Chippewa 'big river'

Missouri probably French from Algonquian 'muddy water'

Montana Spanish 'mountainous'

Nebraska Omaha 'river in the flatness'

Nevada Spanish 'snowy'

New Hampshire named after Hampshire, England

New Jersey named after Jersey (Channel Islands)

New Mexico named after Mexico

New York named after the Duke of York

North Carolina named after King Charles II

North Dakota Sioux 'friend'

Ohio Iroquois 'beautiful water'

Oklahoma Choctaw 'red people'

Oregon possibly Algonquian 'beautiful water' or 'beaver place'

Pennsylvania named after Quaker William Penn + Latin for 'woodland'

Rhode Island Dutch 'red clay' island

South Carolina named after King Charles II

South Dakota Sioux 'friend'

Tennessee name of a Cherokee settlement – unknown origin

Texas Spanish 'allies'

Utah possibly Navaho 'upper land' or 'land of the Ute'

Vermont French 'green mountain'

Virginia named after Queen Elizabeth I

Washington named after George Washington

West Virginia derived from Virginia

Wisconsin possibly Algonquian 'grassy place' or 'beaver place'

Wyoming Algonquian 'place of the big flats'

The chief linguistic result of this multilingual setting was a large number of loan words, which added to the many new words that were introduced as a consequence of the first period of settlement. In that early period, most of the words had been to do with new fauna and flora, or with notions deriving from contact with the Indian tribes – words like *wigwam* and *skunk*. Now, there were many words from Spanish, French, German, Dutch, and the other immigrant languages, which were increasingly becoming part of the American environment.

New words and phrases in American English

From Indian languages
chipmunk, hickory, how!, moccasin, moose, opossum, papoose, pemmican, pow-wow, racoon, skunk, tomahawk, totem, wigwam

From Dutch
boss, caboose, coleslaw, cookie, snoop

From French
bayou, butte, cache, caribou, cent, chowder, crevasse, gopher, levee, poker, praline, saloon

From German
and how, cookbook, delicatessen, dumb, frankfurter, hoodlum, kindergarten, nix, no way, phooey, pretzel, sauerkraut, spiel

From Italian
capo, espresso, mafia, minestrone, pasta, pizza, spaghetti, zucchini

From Spanish
bonanza, cafeteria, canyon, coyote, lassoo, loco (mad), marijuana, mustang, plaza, ranch, rodeo, stampede, tacos, tornado, vamoose

From Yiddish
gonif, kosher, mazuma, mensch, nosh, schmaltz, schmuck, schnoz, scram, shlemiel; Enjoy!, You should worry!, Get lost!, Crazy she isn't!

Noah Webster

The patriotism of the newly independent United States of America found its linguistic expression in the teacher Noah Webster (1758–1843). His first books, on English spelling and grammar, were extremely successful – his *American Spelling Book* selling around eighty million copies in the century following its publication. In 1828, he published *An American Dictionary of the English Language*, in two volumes – what in later revisions has come to be known simply as *Webster's*. This work was the foundation of American lexicography, and was held in similar esteem to Johnson's *Dictionary* in England. Webster's aim was to show the way the language was developing independently in America: 'our honour', he wrote, 'requires us to have a system of our own, in languages as well as in government. Great Britain, whose children we are, should no longer be *our* standard; for the taste of her writers is already corrupted, and her language on the decline.' He introduced several spelling reforms – one of the few people ever to have done so successfully – which resulted in such spellings as *color*, *center*, *defense*, and *traveler*. Some, such as his proposal to spell *medicin*, *examin*, etc. without the *e*, did not succeed; on the other hand, his spelling of *music*, *logic*, etc. without a final *k* has since become standard.

The many stages in the history of the country are reflected in its remarkable variety of place names:

Indian names, like Oshkosh, Saratoga, Tallahassee, Weewahitchka.
European names, like Athens, Berlin, London, Paris.
Personal names, like Dallas, Houston, Jackson, Washington.
French names in -*ville*, like Higginsville, Louisville, Nashville, Niceville, Washingtonville.
'Poetic' names, like Arcadia, Aurora, Belvedere, Meadowvale.
Landmarks, like Little Rock, Pine Bluff, South Bend.
Animal names, like Beaver City, Buffalo, Eagletown, Elkton.
Spanish names, like Las Vegas, Los Angeles, Rio Grande, Sacramento.

At the same time, an enormous number of coinages were introduced – words and phrases based on earlier English elements which reflected the many social and cultural developments in American history. Specific events and activities, such as cattle ranching, the railroad, gambling, the gold rush, and the new political system added thousands of new words, senses, and idioms to the language:

bartender, bluff (promontory), bootleg, caucus, congress, corn (maize), cowboy, eggplant, freight, groundhog, maverick, popcorn, prairie, prospector, stagecoach, steamboat, bite the dust, bury the hatchet, face the music, go off the rails, go on the warpath, hit the jackpot, stake a claim, strike it rich, the real McCoy, up the ante.

Many of these words and phrases have entered the standard language, and are used wherever English is spoken. But there remains a substantial distinctive vocabulary restricted to the United States, along with several features of grammar, spelling and pronunciation that combine to set 'American English' off from 'British English' and the other varieties in the world. These are reviewed on pp. 246–50.

CANADA

The roots of Canadian English can be found in the events which followed the American Revolution of 1776. Those who had supported Britain found themselves unable to stay in the new United States, and most went into exile in the Ontario region of Canada. From there they spread to all parts of the country. They were soon followed by many thousands who were attracted by the cheapness of land. Within fifty years, the population of Upper Canada (above Montreal) had reached 100,000 – mainly people from the United States.

In the east, the Atlantic Provinces had been settled with English speakers much earlier (the first contacts were as early as 1497, when the British explorer John Cabot claimed Newfoundland), but even today these areas contain less than 10 per cent of the population, so that they have only a marginal role in the development of the Canadian 'norm'. In Quebec, the use of French language and culture remains from the first period of exploration, with the majority of people using French as a mother-tongue: here, English and French coexist uneasily.

Because of its origins, Canadian English has a great deal in common with the rest of the English spoken in North America – and is often difficult to distinguish for people who live outside the region. To British people, Canadians may sound American; to Americans, they may sound British. Canadians themselves insist on not being identified with either, and certainly there is a great deal of evidence in support of this view.

The vocabulary looks very 'mixed', with American and British items coexisting – such as *tap* (US *faucet*) and *porridge* (US *oatmeal*) alongside *gas* (Br *petrol*) and *billboard* (Br *hoarding*). Vehicle terms are typically American: *trucks*, *fenders*, *trunks*, *cabooses*, etc. There is a greater likelihood of encountering British spellings, though the American model is gradually becoming more widespread, especially in popular publications: such words as *curb*, *jail*, and *tire* are normally spelled in the American way. Newspapers tend to use American spellings, and learned journals and school textbooks to use British.

In pronunciation, Canadian English has several important identifying features – notably the sound of the *ou* diphthong, which in words like *out* sounds more like *oat* (in Received Pronunciation, p. 52); moreover there is a contrast between such words as *out* and *house* and those such as *loud* and *houses*. Most Canadians rhyme such pairs as *cot* and *caught* (as do many US speakers and most Scots). There is also a social preference for the British pronunciation of

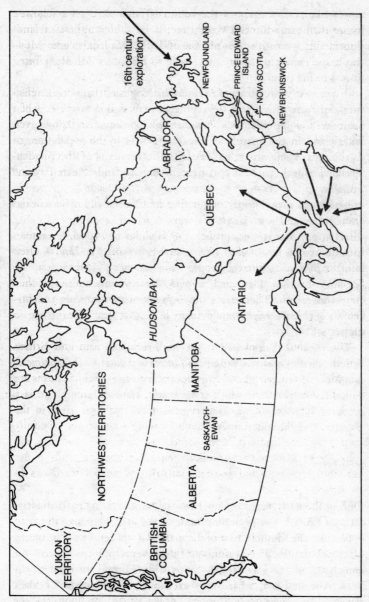

The direction of English-speaking immigration in Canada

words like *tune*, *due* and *news*, with a [j] after the first consonant, rather than using the US 'toon', 'do', 'nooz' (though the latter pronunciations are native to many Canadians). This has become one of the usage issues in the country, with broadcasters' attention being drawn to the point.

A commonly cited feature of Canadian English occurs in conversation – the use of *eh?* as a tag with rising intonation at the end of a sentence (*So she went into Lincoln, eh?*). However, although it is widespread in the speech of Canadians, it is by no means unique to the area, being also found in several other parts of the English-speaking world, such as Scotland, New Zealand, Australia, and Jamaica.

There are many words originating in Canada, often borrowings from American Indian languages, some of which have entered English directly, and sometimes through the medium of French. Examples include *caribou*, *chesterfield* (sofa), *kayak*, *kerosene*, *mukluk* (Eskimo boot), *parka*, *reeve* (mayor), *riding* (constituency), *skookum* (strong). Ice-hockey terminology, such as *puck*, *face-off*, *rush* and *slot*, comes from this region. There are around 10,000 words listed in the *Dictionary of Canadianisms*, though many of these are restricted to certain dialect areas.

The regional dialects of Canada, both rural and urban, have been little studied. There is a widespread impression that Canadian speech is uniform from one end of the continent to the other, but this is a superficial impression, which ignores important differences in such areas as Newfoundland, Quebec, the more isolated parts of the country, and the inner cities.

BLACK ENGLISH

During the early years of American settlement, a highly distinctive form of English was beginning to develop in the islands of the West Indies and the southern part of the mainland, spoken by the incoming black population. The beginning of the seventeenth century saw the emergence of the slave trade. Ships from Europe travelled to the West African coast, where they exchanged cheap goods for black slaves. The slaves were shipped in barbarous conditions to the

Caribbean islands and the American coast, where they were in turn exchanged for such commodities as sugar, rum, and molasses. The ships then returned to England, completing an 'Atlantic triangle' of journeys, and the process began again. Britain and the United States had outlawed the slave trade by 1865, but by that time, nearly 200 years of trading had taken place. By the middle of the nineteenth century, there were over four million black slaves in America.

The policy of the slave-traders was to bring people of different language backgrounds together in the ships, to make it difficult for groups to plot rebellion. The result was the growth of several pidgin forms of communication (see p. 12), and in particular a pidgin between the slaves and the sailors, many of whom spoke English. Once arrived in the Caribbean, this pidgin English continued to act as a major means of communication between the black population and the new landowners, and among the blacks themselves. Then, when children came to be born, the pidgin became their mother tongue, thus producing the first black creole speech in the region. This creole English rapidly came to be used throughout the cotton plantations, and in the coastal towns and islands. Similarly, creolized forms of French, Spanish and Portuguese emerged in and around the Caribbean.

The different Caribbean islands have since developed their own varieties of creole English, and display a range of dialects which have been influenced by the standard language to varying degrees. In the varieties furthest away from the standard, there are many identifying features of pronunciation, grammar, and vocabulary. In Jamaican English, for example, there is no distinction between the [a] and [ɒ] vowels, so that such words as *pat* and *pot* rhyme, both being pronounced with an [a]. A very noticeable feature is the way syllables tend to be equally stressed, so that a word like *Jamaica* comes out with three more-or-less equal beats. This rhythmic difference is the main problem for people who are used only to standard British or American English (with its 'te-tum, te-tum' rhythm) when they listen to West Indian speakers. Amongst the grammatical differences, nouns often do not mark plurals (*three book*) or possessives (*that man house*), verbs do not use the -s ending (*he see me*), and *be* may be absent (*he going home*). There is a large regional vocabulary: the

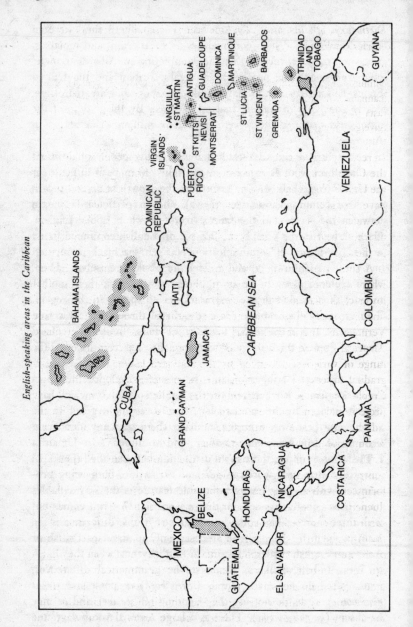

English-speaking areas in the Caribbean

Dictionary of Jamaican English (1967) contains around 15,000 entries, including:

chillum (pipe), dreadlocks (Rastafarian hair style), duppy (ghost), ganja (cannabis), Jah (God), John Canoe (chief dancer), lick (hit), quashie (fool), rasta (Rastafarian), something (thing), so-till (until), susumba (plant), trust (give/get credit)

In recent years, of course, West Indian speech has moved well outside the Caribbean, with large communities now to be found in Canada, the United States and Britain. As we might expect, these new locations have brought new speech styles; there are now noticeable differences between the speech of the children of those living in London (many of whom have never been to the West Indies) and their counterparts in the Caribbean.

A similar pattern of development is found in the United States, where one contemporary variety in particular – the language used by lower-class blacks in urban communities – has been the focus of linguistic study in recent decades, under the heading of 'Black English Vernacular'. It is thought that some 80 per cent of present-day black Americans speak this variety of the language. The remainder use a range of varieties influenced by the standard language, reflecting a gradual process of integration and the rise of a black middle class. Creole English is not apparent in the public speech of many black professionals and politicians, though several maintain two dialects side by side, standard and creole – something which has often been recommended by black educationists.

The history of black English in the United States is complex, controversial, and only partly understood. Records of the early speech forms are sparse. It is unclear, for example, exactly how much influence black speech has had on the pronunciation of southern whites; according to some linguists, generations of close contact resulted in the families of the slave owners picking up some of the speech habits of their servants, which gradually developed into the distinctive southern 'drawl'. Information is clearer after the American Civil War (1861–5), when the slaves received civil rights for the first time. There was a widespread exodus to the industrial cities of the northern states, and black culture became known throughout the

---

Some grammatical features of Black English Vernacular

- No final *-s* in the third-person singular form of the present tense, e.g. *he walk*, *she come*.
- No use of forms of the verb *be* in the present tense, when it is used as a 'linking' verb within a sentence, e.g. *They real fine, If you interested*.
- The use of the verb *be* to mark habitual meaning, but without changing its grammatical form, e.g. *Sometime they be asking me things*.
- Use of *been* to express a meaning of past activity with current relevance, e.g. *I been know your name*.
- Use of *be done* in the sense of 'will have', e.g. *We be done washed all those things soon*.
- Use of double negatives involving the auxiliary verb at the beginning of a sentence, e.g. *Won't nobody do nothing about that*.

---

country, especially for its music and dance. The result was a large influx of new, informal vocabulary into general use, as whites picked up the racy speech patterns of those who sang, played, and danced – from the early spirituals, through the many forms of jazz and blues to the current trends in soul music and break-dancing. And in recent years, the linguistic effects of freedom fighting and integration can be seen in any representative list of black English vocabulary:

beat (exhausted), cat (jazz musician), chick (girl), dig (understand), groovy, hep, hepcat, hip, honkey (white person), jam (improvise), jive-talk, nitty-gritty, pad (bed), rap (street talk), right on!, sit-in, solid (great), soul, soul brother, square (dull)

AUSTRALIA AND NEW ZEALAND

The remaining major areas where English is used as a mother tongue are in the Antipodes. Australia was discovered by James Cook in 1770, and within twenty years Britain had established its first penal colony at Sydney, thus relieving the pressure on the overcrowded gaols of England. From 1788, for over fifty years, about 130,000 prisoners were transported. 'Free' settlers, as they were called, began to enter the country from the very beginning, but they did not achieve substantial numbers until the mid-nineteenth century. From then on, the immigrants came in increasing numbers. By 1850, the population of Australia was about 400,000, and by 1900 nearly four million.

Australia and New Zealand

In New Zealand, the story started later and moved more slowly. A few Europeans settled in the country in the 1790s, but the official colony was not established until 1840. There was then a considerable increase – from around 2,000 Europeans in 1840 to 25,000 in 1850, and to three quarters of a million by 1900.

The main source of settlers, and thus the main influence on the language, was Britain. Many of the convicts came from London and Ireland, and features of Cockney and Irish English can be traced in the characteristic pronunciation patterns (the Australian 'twang') still heard today. Many of the words now thought of as Australian in fact started out in Britain, and some can still be heard in British local dialects – such as *dinkum*, *cobber*, *tucker* (cf. tuck shop) and *joker* (person). On the other hand, in recent years the influence of American English has been apparent, so that the country now displays a curious lexical mixture, in some ways resembling that found in Canada (see p. 232). Thus we find American *truck*, *elevator*, and *freeway* alongside British *petrol*, *boot* (of a car) and *tap*.

People usually think of Australian English as characterized by such Aboriginal borrowings as *boomerang*, *billabong*, *dingo*, *kangaroo*, *koala*, *kookaburra*, *wallaby*, and *wombat*; but in fact the English settlers took very few words from the native languages spoken in the two countries. There were various reasons for this. Neither the Aborigines of Australia nor the Maoris of New Zealand were very numerous when the Europeans arrived – perhaps 200,000 of each race at the beginning of the nineteenth century. The Aborigines were nomadic, contact was occasional, and there were many language differences (over 200 languages were in use at the time). As a result, hardly any Aboriginal words came into English, most of the ones that did being plant and animal names. (On the other hand, about a third of Australian place names are unmistakably Aboriginal: Wolloomooloo, Bugarribbee, Warragumby.) Similarly, there are few Maori words in New Zealand English: among the exceptions are *hongi* (way of greeting), *haka* (war dance), *kiwi*, *pakeha* (a European), and *whare* (small house). The number seems to be increasing.

In relation to pronunciation, Australians and New Zealanders can tell each other apart, though the differences are not readily apparent to outsiders, nor are they very great (mainly a matter of slight changes in vowel quality). But within each country, few regional dialectal differences have been noted – which is surprising, considering the vast distances between the centres of population in Australia, and the considerable size of some of the cities. The country is some thirty times the size of Britain, with large tracts of uninhabited desert, and the bulk of the population is concentrated in the fertile areas near the coasts. Today, two cities (Sydney and Melbourne) contain nearly half the population.

The absence of dialect differences within Australia and New

Some Australian words and phrases

this arvo (this afternoon), ball-up (in Australian football), bathers (swimming costume), beaut (expression of approval), biggie (big one), bushman, bush telegraph, crook (unwell, irritable), drongo (fool), flying doctor, footpath (pavement), frock (dress), goodday (hello), lay-by (hire purchase), lolly (sweet), outback, paddock (field of any size), sheep-station, sheila (girl), singlet (vest), washer (face-cloth), weekender (holi-day cottage); bald as a bandicoot, better than a kick in the tail, scarce as rocking-horse manure, starve the crows

Some New Zealand words

bach (holiday cottage), fantail (type of bird), gully (valley), lancewood (type of tree), section (housing plot), tramping (hiking), waxeye (type of bird)

Zealand may be more apparent than real, given that very little detailed regional study has taken place. Where major geographical boundaries exist (such as between Western Australia and the rest of the country, or between North Island and South Island in New Zealand), we would expect dialects to develop. People do sometimes claim to be able to tell that someone comes from a certain part of the country, but few systematic variations have yet been described. One clear case is the use of a rolled *r* in parts of South Island, where the influence of early Scots settlement can still be heard.

A few regional lexical differences have been noted – for example, a small ice cream carton is a *pixie* in Victoria, and a *bucket* in New South Wales; a child's push-chair is a *stroller* in New South Wales, and a *pusher* in South Australia. This kind of variation should be on the increase as cities grow, and immigrants arrive. The non-English-speaking immigrants, in particular, may well exercise some influence on the development of Australian English: some 20 per cent of the population now comes from a background where English is a foreign language.

Although there seems to be little regional speech variation, factors to do with social prestige are important. In particular, Received Pronunciation (see p. 62) continues to exert a considerable influence. The variety known as 'cultivated' Australian English, used by about 10 per cent of the population, shows this most strongly: in some speakers the accent is very close to educated southern British, with just a hint in certain vowels and in the intonation of its Australian origin. At the opposite extreme there is the 'broad' Australian accent, used by some 30 per cent, and most clearly identified as 'Australian' in the popular mind abroad from the characters portrayed by such comedians as Paul Hogan and Barry Humphreys. In between, there is a continuum of accents often called simply 'general' Australian, used by the majority of the population. A similar situation exists in New Zealand, though that country tends to be rather more conservative in speech style, with R P-influenced accents more dominant, and it lacks the extremely broad accent found in Australia.

The accent variations have provoked not a little controversy in recent years, with the broad Australian accent in particular having its critics and its defenders. There is ongoing debate about whether Australians should be proud of their distinctive speech, and stress its features, or whether they should aspire to use a more conservative style, associated with the traditional values of educated British speech. The picture has been complicated by a generation of Australian comedians who exaggerate and satirize the accent, and whose work has become universally known through the medium of television. When all that other people have to go on is an amalgam of Crocodile Dundee and Edna Everage, it becomes difficult for outsiders to begin to distinguish stereotype from reality.

SOUTH AFRICA

One further area where there is a substantial number of mother-tongue speakers of English is South Africa. Although Dutch colonists arrived in the Cape as early as 1652, British involvement in the region dates only from 1795, during the Napoleonic Wars, when an expeditionary force invaded. British control was established in 1806, and a policy of settlement began in earnest in 1820, when some 5,000 British were given land in the eastern Cape. English was made the official language of the region in 1822, and there was an attempt to anglicize the large Dutch- (or Afrikaans-) speaking population. English became the language of law, education, and most other aspects of public life. Further British settlements followed in the 1840s and 1850s, especially in Natal, and there was a massive influx of Europeans following the development of the gold and diamond areas in the Witwatersrand in the 1870s. Nearly half a million immigrants, many of them English-speaking, arrived in the country during the last quarter of the nineteenth century.

South Africa

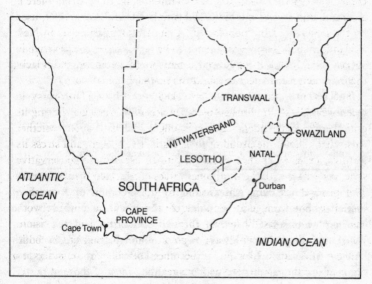

The English language history of the region thus has many strands. There was initially a certain amount of regional dialect variation among the different groups of British settlers, with the speech of the London area predominant in the Cape, and Midlands and Northern speech strongly represented in Natal; but in due course a more homogeneous accent emerged – an accent that shares many similarities with the accents of Australia, which was also being settled during this period. At the same time, English was being used as a second language by the Afrikaans speakers, and many of the Dutch colonists took this variety with them on the Great Trek of 1836, as they moved north to escape British rule. An African variety of English also developed, spoken by the black population, who had learned the language mainly in mission schools, and which was influenced in different ways by the various language backgrounds of the speakers. In addition, English came to be used, along with Afrikaans and often other languages, by those with an ethnically mixed background (Coloureds); and it was also adopted by the many immigrants from India, who arrived in the country from around 1860.

Some South African English words and phrases

aardvark, Afrikaner (white Afrikaans-speaking South African), apartheid, bakkie (type of truck), biltong (strips of dried meat), braai (barbecue) busy with (engaged in), camp (paddock), classify (assign to a racial group), commandeer, commando, dinges (thingummy), dorp (village), fundi (expert), gogga (insect), homeland (area set aside for an African population), indaba (meeting), just now (in a little while), kloof (ravine), kraal, land (cultivated field), lekker (nice), location (black residential area), reference book (identity papers carried by Africans), robot (traffic light), spoor, trek, veld, voorskot (advance payment to a farmer)

Present–day South African English thus comprises a range of varieties, but from a social point of view they are unified by the tension which exists between the use of English and the use of Afrikaans. English has always been a minority language in South Africa. Afrikaans, which was given official status in 1925, is the first language of the majority of whites, including most of those in power, and acts as an important symbol of identity for those of Afrikaner background. It is also the first language of most of the Coloured population. English is used by the remaining whites (of British background) and by increasing numbers of the majority black population (blacks outnumber whites by over four to one). There is thus a linguistic side to the political division which has marked South African society in recent decades: Afrikaans is perceived by the black majority as the language of authority and repression; English is perceived by the white government as the language of protest and self-determination. Many blacks see English as a means of achieving an international voice, and uniting themselves with other black communities.

On the other hand, the contemporary situation regarding the use of English is more complex than this opposition suggests. For the white authorities, too, English is important as a means of international communication, and 'upwardly mobile' Afrikaners have become increasingly bilingual, with fluent command of an English that often resembles the British-influenced variety. The public statements by South African politicians, seen on world television, illustrate this ability. As a result, a continuum of accents exists, ranging from those that are strongly influenced by Afrikaans to those that are very close to Received Pronunciation (see p. 62); and there are corresponding variations in grammar and vocabulary. Such complexity is inevitable in a country where the overriding issue is social and political identity, and people strive to maintain their deeply held feelings of national and ethnic identity in the face of opposition.

British and American English

There is no definitive survey of all the differences between American English (AmE) and British English (BrE). The only safe statement is that there are far more of them than are usually recognized. A small number have entered the standard written language of each nation, and these are quite well-known. But they form just a fraction of the thousands of non-standard and regionally restricted words in daily spoken use which would be totally unknown outside each country. Informal idiomatic phrases are particularly numerous – as this author found to his cost when he first encountered egg-ordering procedure at breakfast-time in a US hotel. Having asked for ham and eggs, the question 'How would you like your eggs?' left him nonplussed, as he was unaware of the linguistic (let alone the culinary) possibilities expected of him – such as (immediately learned, due to hunger) *once over easy* and *sunny-side up*. Culture-specific phrases of this kind are often absent from dictionaries, and they are very numerous.

PRONUNCIATION

Apart from the regular differences, such as the pronunciation of /r/ after vowels in much of AmE (see p. 224), there are several individual words which are pronounced differently. Here are some of the frequently used ones. In each case the contrast is with Received Pronunciation (see p. 62).

● *Schedule* begins with two consonants in AmE (as in *skin*), but with one in BrE (as in *shin*).
● The middle vowel of *tomato* rhymes only with *car* in BrE, but also with *mate* in AmE.
● The first syllable of *lever* rhymes only with *leaver* in BrE, but also with that of *level* in AmE.

● Conversely, the first syllable of *leisure* rhymes only with the vowel of *let* in BrE, but also rhymes with *lee* in AmE.

● *Route* rhymes with *out* for many AmE speakers; it is always like *root* in BrE.

● *Vase* rhymes only with cars in BrE, but also with *vase* or *days* in AmE.

● *Docile* is 'doss-ile' in AmE, but 'doe-sile' in BrE. The *-ile* ending regularly changes in this way: *missile* is often pronounced like *missal* in AmE, and similarly *fertile*, *hostile*, etc.

● *Herb* is pronounced without the initial *h* in AmE, but with the *h* in BrE; however, some *herb*- words do have *h* in AmE, such as *herbivore*, *herbicide*.

● Many AmE speakers stress certain words differently from BrE speakers:

AmE	ballet	debris	address	inquiry	magazine
BrE	ballet	debris	address	inquiry	magazine

And several words which have one main stress in BrE have two in AmE:

AmE	auditory	secretary	laboratory	Birmingham (US city)
BrE	auditory	secretary	laboratory	Birmingham

SPELLING

Some typical examples of spelling differences follow. However, the picture is complicated by the fact that some American spellings are now in use in BrE (e.g. *judgment*, *inquire*, *encyclopedia*) and some BrE spellings are used in the US (e.g. *enclose*, *judgement*).

BrE	-ou-	colour	honour	labour	mould	smoulder
AmE	-o-	color	honor	labor	mold	smolder

BrE	en-	enclose	endorse	enquiry	ensure
AmE	in-	inclose	indorse	inquiry	insure

BrE	-ae/oe-	anaesthetic	encyclopaedia	foetus	manoeuvre
AmE	-e-	anesthetic	encyclopedia	fetus	maneuver

BrE	-re	centre	litre	theatre	fibre
AmE	-er	center	liter	theater	fiber

| *BrE* | *-ce* | defence | offence | licence (*noun*) | | |
| *AmE* | *-se* | defense | offense | license (*noun/verb*) | | |

| *BrE* | *-ll-* | libellous | quarrelling | travelled | jewellery | woollen |
| *AmE* | *-l-* | libelous | quarreling | traveled | jewelry | woolen |

| *BrE* | *-l-* | fulfil | skilful | instalment |
| *AmE* | *-ll-* | fulfill | skillful | installment |

And there are many individual items (but usage can vary):

| *BrE* | cheque | gaol | kerb | moustache | plough | storey | tyre |
| *AmE* | check | jail | curb | mustache | plow | story | tire |

| *BrE* | tsar | pyjamas | programme | kidnapper | draught |
| *AmE* | czar | pajamas | program | kidnaper | draft |

Non-standard spellings are much more in public use in AmE in advertisements, shop signs, road signs, etc.:

donuts   hi/lo   tonite   thru   thruway   kool

GRAMMAR

There are many small points of difference in the grammar of the two varieties, though the influence of AmE on BrE is such that many of the usages which were once restricted to the former now appear in the latter. Also, some of the BrE usages are found in AmE, with varying preference, depending on dialect and style.

BrE	*AmE*
twenty to four	twenty of four
five past eight	five after eight
River Thames	Hudson River
really good	real good
different to/from	different than/from
behind the building	in back of the building
half an hour	a half hour
in future, . . .	in the future, . . .
I burnt it	I burned it
He's got off the chair	He's gotten off the chair
I sneaked out quietly	I snuck out quietly
I shan't tell anyone	I won't tell anyone
I'd like you to go now	I'd like for you to go now
I'm visiting her tomorrow	I'm visiting with her tomorrow

BrE	AmE
I'll go and get the car	I'll go get the car
Come and take a look	Come take a look
I've just eaten	I just ate
I asked him to leave	I asked that he leave
The government is/are stupid	The government is stupid
I want to get out	I want out
They've one innings left (*cricket*)	They've one inning left (*baseball*)
There were six millions	There were six million
He's in hospital	He's in the hospital
I've not seen it yet	I didn't see it yet
I'll see you at the weekend	I'll see you over the weekend
Look out of the window	Look out the window
I'll go in a moment	I'll go momentarily
I haven't seen her for ages	I haven't seen her in ages
On Mondays we take the bus	Mondays we take the bus
I'll start on March 1st	I'll start March 1st
Monday to Friday inclusive	Monday through Friday

VOCABULARY

There are many words which are used in both AmE and BrE, but with a difference of meaning. Several of the AmE uses have come to be used in BrE in recent years.

	AmE	BrE
billion	a thousand million	a million million (now archaic)
dumb	stupid, mute	mute
homely	plain (people)	domestic
knock up	get a woman pregnant	get someone to answer
nervy	cheeky	nervous
pants	trousers	underpants
pavement	any paved surface	pedestrian path
school	any educational institution	mainly primary and secondary levels
smart	intelligent	intelligent *or* groomed

In the following list, the words have the same meaning (in certain contexts of use). However, some BrE terms are found in AmE, and several of the AmE terms are now widely used in BrE.

AmE	BrE	AmE	BrE
alumnus	graduate	billboard	hoarding
apartment	flat	biscuit	scone
attorney	solicitor/barrister	broil	grill
automobile	motor car	buffet	sideboard
baby buggy/carriage	pram	cab	taxi
ballpoint	biro	call (phone)	ring
bar	pub	call collect	reverse the charges

AmE	BrE	AmE	BrE
can	tin	outlet	point (power)
candy	sweets	overalls	dungarees
changepurse	purse	overpass	flyover
check (mark)	tick	pacifier	dummy
checkers	draughts	pants	trousers
closet	cupboard	pantyhose	tights
corn	maize/sweet corn	peek	peep
couch	sofa	pitcher	jug
cracker	biscuit (savoury)	potato chips	crisps
crib	cot	pullman car	sleeping car
custard	egg custard	public school	state school
davenport	sofa	purse	handbag
dessert	sweet/pudding	railroad	railway
detour	diversion	raise (salary)	rise
diaper	nappy	realtor	estate agent
dish towel	tea towel	schedule	timetable
drug store	chemist	second floor	first floor
eggplant	aubergine	sedan	saloon car
elevator	lift	shorts (men)	underpants, shorts
fall	autumn	sick	ill
faucet	tap	sidewalk	pavement
fender	wing/mudguard	sneakers	plimsolls, trainers
first floor	ground floor	sophomore	second-year student
flashlight	torch	spigot	tap (outdoors)
garbage	rubbish	station wagon	estate car
garter	suspender	suspenders	braces
gas	petrol	term paper	essay (school)
gear shift	gear lever	thread	cotton
generator	dynamo	thumbtack	drawing pin
grade school	primary school	tightwad	miser
hobo	tramp	traffic circle	roundabout
hood (car)	bonnet	transportation	transport
intersection	crossroads	trash	rubbish
janitor	caretaker	trashcan	dustbin
Jello	jelly	truck	lorry
jelly	jam	trunk (car)	boot
kerosene	paraffin	tuxedo	dinner jacket
lawyer	solicitor/barrister	underpants	knickers/pants
line	queue	undershirt	vest
liquor store	off-licence	vacation	holidays
mail	post	vest	waistcoat
mailbox	pillar-box	washcloth	face flannel
math	maths	windshield	windscreen
molasses	treacle	wrench	spanner
mortician	undertaker	yard	garden
movie	film	yield (road sign)	give way
movies	cinema	zero	nought
muffler	silencer	zipper	zip
oil pan	sump	zucchini	courgettes

13

ଓଓଓଓଓଓଓଓଓଓ

English Today

Two main themes can be traced through the earlier chapters in this book: the regional and the social diversification of the English language. English has never been a totally homogeneous language, but its history is primarily the story of the way it has become increasingly heterogeneous in its sounds, grammar, and vocabulary, as it has come to be adopted by different communities around the world, and

'But am I a person, Cynthia?'

Punch, 21 March 1984

adapted by them to meet their social needs. At the same time, each community has had to respond to the pressure of social change, both from within – from its members – and from outside. Different social groups make demands on society for recognition, and use distinctive language as a means of achieving public identity. And everyone is affected by the political, economic, and cultural pressures which come from abroad, causing societies to change in unprecedented ways, and to adopt the language that comes with such change.

ENGLISH LOAN WORDS

The best-known current example of external influence causing language change is the 'Americanization' of world culture, which has caused English words to appear prominently in city streets all over the world, reflecting the dominance of that culture's popular songs, films, television, high finance, food and drink, and consumer goods. The American way of life is considered modern, fashionable, and desirable to the younger, trend-setting generations of society found in all developed countries, and the language associated with these trends is eagerly taken up. The effect is most noticeable in popular music. Foreign groups (such as the Swedish pop-stars Abba) often record in English, and the words are picked up and rehearsed in the same language everywhere, even by children who otherwise have little or no command of the language. I once met a Brazilian child of about ten who could count 'one, two, three', but only by adding the words 'o'clock, four o'clock rock' at the end.

Depending on your point of view, therefore, English loan words are a good or a bad thing. People who do not approve of American values or who are disturbed by rapidity of change are often strongly critical of the impact of English on their language – especially when an English word supplants a traditional word. For example, in Spanish, *planta* ('plant', in the sense of 'factory') is often used where *fabrica* (factory) was used before, and this has been criticized in the press and on television. Similarly, in Dutch *mistletoe* is now often found where *maretak* was used before. In 1977, France passed a law banning the use of English words in official contexts if an equivalent French expression existed – but the law seems to be honoured more in the breach than in the observance.

English loan words in Europe

All the words below have been found in various European languages without any translation being given. The spelling below is standard English; different countries may re-spell a word according to its own conventions, e.g. *boxing* becomes *boksing* in Norwegian, *goal* becomes *gowl* in Spanish. Also several languages adapt English words to their own grammar, e.g. Italian *weekendista*, *cocacolonizzare* (coca-cola-colonize).

Sport: baseball, bobsleigh, clinch, comeback, deuce, football, goalie, jockey, offside, photo-finish, semi-final, volley, walkover

Tourism, transport etc.: antifreeze, camping, hijack, hitchike, jeep, joyride, motel, parking, picnic, runway, scooter, sightseeing, stewardess, stop (sign), tanker, taxi

Politics, commerce: big business, boom, briefing, dollar, good-will, marketing, new deal, senator, sterling, top secret

Culture, entertainment: cowboy, group, happy ending, heavy metal, hi-fi, jam session, jazz, juke-box, Miss World (etc.), musical, night-club, pimp, ping-pong, pop, rock, showbiz, soul, striptease, top twenty, Western, yeah-yeah-yeah

People and behaviour: AIDS, angry young man, baby-sitter, boy friend, boy scout, callgirl, cool, cover girl, crack (drugs), crazy, dancing, gangster, hash, hold-up, jogging, mob, pin-up, reporter, sex-appeal, sexy, smart, snob, snow, teenager

Consumer society: air conditioner, all rights reserved, aspirin, bar, best-seller, bulldozer, camera, chewing gum, coca cola, cocktail, coke, drive-in, eye-liner, film, hamburger, hoover, jumper, ketchup, kingsize, kleenex, layout, Levis, LP, make-up, sandwich, science fiction, Scrabble, self-service, smoking, snackbar, supermarket, tape, thriller, up-to-date, WC, weekend

And of course: OK

However, not everyone is critical. In particular, commercial firms and advertisers are well aware of the potential selling power that the use of English vocabulary can bring. There have been several reports of an increase in sales once a firm has given a product an English name (in much the same way as some products are given foreign names in Britain – such as French names for scent). In Japan, English is even used in television commericals, despite the fact that the majority of viewers would not understand exactly what was being said: the prestige connotations attached to the mere use of English are apparently enough to commend the strategy to the advertisers. Nor is it purely a matter of commerce. In one Dutch town, the leader of a youth club gave his club an English name, and there was a immediate increase in the active interest of the boys in the area.

Most of the influence of English is upon the vocabulary of foreign languages; but surveys are slowly bringing to light several cases where word order or word structure has been affected. In Spanish, for example, a standard invitation might begin *El señor X y señora* . . . ('Mr X and Mrs . . .'); but nowadays one often sees *El señor y la señora X* ('Mr and Mrs X'), following English word order. Sentences of the type 'The book sells well', using an active construction for a passive meaning, have begun to appear in Danish (*Bogen sælger godt*). Several languages keep the English plural ending when they make use of a loan word, and do not translate it into the native form, e.g. *drinks, callgirls, cocktails*. An indefinite article is sometimes used in Swedish sentences like *Han är en läkare* (He is a doctor), where previously it would not have appeared. English word endings some- times compete with foreign ones (e.g. *eskalation* alongside *eskalering* in Danish). There are many other such cases.

When English words and constructions are frequently used by foreign speakers, we sometimes get the impression that a 'mixed' language has emerged, and this is often given a name which reflects the mixture, such as Franglais, Angleutsch, Spanglish, Swedlish, Japlish, Wenglish (Welsh–English), Anglikaans, and so on. The phenomenon happens only in communities where there is regular contact between people of different language backgrounds who have varying degrees of knowledge of each other's language. For example, in the parts of Texas bordering on Mexico, the phenomenon of Tex- Mex is often heard – an informal speech style in which English and Spanish words and phrases are combined, as in this fragment of dialogue:

Dónde está el thin-sliced bread? Where is the thin-sliced bread?
Está en aisle three, sobre el second shelf, en el wrapper rojo. It's in aisle three,
  on the second shelf, in the red wrapper.

A similar language-mixing was heard at a Welsh railway station:

Mae'r train o Liverpool yn five minutes yn late. The train from Liverpool is
  five minutes late.

Hybrids of this kind are only now beginning to be seriously studied
to determine whether there are rules governing the language 'switching' that occurs, and what function these switches have. As evidence
accumulates, it appears that switching is much more widespread than
was previously imagined; indeed, it is probably to be found, in varying
degrees, in bilingual communities everywhere, enabling communication to take place satisfactorily. None the less, it is frequently
mocked or attacked by purists as an incoherent or debased form of
language.

SOCIAL IDENTITY

Apart from their use as a means of communication, linguistic hybrids
such as Tex-Mex perform an important social identifying function.
In one study of a group of business people having lunch, the solidarity
between two members of the group showed itself by the way they
slipped the occasional Spanish word or phrase into their English
when they addressed each other – something they never did when
they talked to the remaining members, who came from outside the
area. The same kind of thing happens when a group of English
speakers with different dialect backgrounds come together (see p.
86). People unconsciously vary their speech as they go through the
day, depending on whom they are addressing, the formality of the
occasion, and so on. There is a strong tendency for people to express
their identity by emphasizing features of their accent or dialect which
convey where they are from – especially when it's a question of
'taking sides' in a conversation.

But regional identity is only one factor. Also important are the
other facets of a person's background, which may find expression in

linguistic form, such as age, occupation and, in particular, sex. Probably the most important change which has happened to English since 1970 has to do with the attitude society has adopted towards the practices and consequences of sexism. There is now an awareness, which was lacking a generation ago, of the way in which language identifies social attitudes towards men and women. The criticisms have been mainly directed at the biases that constitute a male-orientated view of the world, which have led to unfair sexual discrimination and the low status of women in society. All of the main European languages have been affected, but English more than most, because of the impact of early American feminism.

Both grammar and vocabulary have been affected. In vocabulary, attention has been focused on the replacement of 'male' words by neutral words – *chairman*, for example, becoming *chair* or *chairperson*, *salesman* becoming *sales assistant*. In certain cases, the use of sexually neutral language has become a legal requirement (such as in job descriptions). There is continuing debate between extremists and moderates as to how far such revisions should go – whether they should affect traditional idioms such as *man in the street* and *stone-age man*, or apply to parts of words where the male meaning of *man* is no longer dominant, such as *manhandle* and *woman*. The vocabulary of marital status has also been affected – notably in the introduction of *Ms* as a neutral alternative to *Miss* or *Mrs*.

In grammar, the focus has been on the lack of a sex-neutral third person singular pronoun in English, which becomes a problem when it is used after sex-neutral nouns (such as *student*) or after indefinite pronouns (such as *someone*). The difficulty can be seen in such sentences as the following, where the blanks would traditionally be filled by the pronouns *he* or *his*:

> If anyone wants to see me, — should come at 4 o'clock.
> A student should see — tutor at the beginning of term.

To avoid the *he* bias, various alternatives have been suggested. *He or she* is sometimes used (or, in writing, forms such as *(s)he*), but this is often stylistically awkward. In informal speech, *they* is widespread after words like *anyone*, but this usage attracts criticism from those who feel that a plural word should not be made to agree with a singular one. A common strategy is to recast the sentence structure to avoid the problem (*People wanting to see me should . . .*), or to turn the singular noun into a plural (*Students should see their tutors . . .*). And there have been many proposals for brand-new pronouns to be added to the word-stock of English (such as *co, mon, heesh, hesh, hir, na, per* and *po*), but none of these have achieved any real currency.

The linguistic effect of these changes in social attitudes has been far more noticeable in writing than in speech – and in certain kinds of writing, in particular. One study compared the frequency with which such forms as *he* and *man* were used in American English between 1971 and 1979: the frequency fell from around twelve per 5,000 words to around four per 5,000 words during that period. Women's magazines showed the steepest decline, followed by science magazines, with newspapers further behind, and congressional records least of all. The trend is likely to continue, and become more pervasive. Publishing companies now usually issue guidelines recommending that authors should avoid sexist language, as do several national bodies, such as the American Library Association. It will take much longer before we can say whether the changes are having any real impact on the spoken language, with its greater spontaneity. If I inadvertently introduce a sexist pronoun in the draft of this book, I (or a sub-editor) will doubtless spot it and replace it. But there are no such controls available in the rush of conversational speech. How long it takes for spoken language to respond to fresh social pressures so that a new usage becomes automatic throughout a community, no one knows.

NEW REGIONAL ENGLISHES

In recent decades, increasing attention has been drawn to the emergence of new varieties of English around the world, spoken by people for whom English is a second language (see p. 2). In India, Pakistan, Bangladesh, Sri Lanka, Singapore, Malaysia, the countries of West and East Africa, and many other areas which retain links with the era of British colonialism, the English language is used officially or semi-officially as a means of communication. Large numbers of people are involved; and, as a consequence, there is an inevitable tendency to develop new local norms of usage that in the course of time become adopted by educated speakers and thus form new local standards – the same process as affected the development of new mother-tongue varieties of English (see Chapter 12). The emergence of these second-language varieties, and the uneasy relationship which sometimes exists between them and the standard British or American varieties, is a major feature of the current world English-language situation.

The English of the subcontinent of India – sometimes called South Asian English – provides the clearest example of the way these developments have affected the language (for numbers of speakers, see p. 5). There are many varieties of English spoken within the region, ranging from pidgin English to a standard English that is very close to British, including the use of Received Pronunciation. Some of these varieties have developed over a long period of time, deriving from the period of colonial rule (from the end of the eighteenth century until 1947). As a result, there are hundreds of distinctive lexical items; some derive from local Indian languages, some are new combinations of English words, or British English words which have been given new senses. Especially when the subject matter is specialized – for instance, in relation to religion, agriculture, politics – a newspaper account can appear unintelligible to outside eyes (see opposite).

There are marked differences in pronunciation, due mainly to the different rhythm of the Indian languages native to the area: the syllables in Indian English are typically spoken with equal weight ('rat-tat-tat'), and do not fall into the kind of strong and weak ('tum-te-tum') patterns found in British English. Certain sounds, such as the 'retroflex' *t* and *d*, pronounced with the tip of the tongue curled back, are a highly distinctive feature of Indian English.

In grammar, there are several points of difference, but few have been studied in detail. They include:

● The use of the 'progressive' form of such verbs as *have, know, think,* or *understand*: *I am understanding it now, He is knowing the answer.*
● The use of repeated forms (mainly in Sri Lanka): *Who and who left early? They went running running.*
● Collective nouns are often made plural: *litters* (waste paper), *fruits* (fruit), *aircrafts.*

'Familiar' English words and phrases from India

bandana, brahmin, bungalow, calico, cheroot, chintz, chutney, coolie, curry, guru, juggernaut, jungle, jute, pundit, purdah, rajah, sahib, tiffin, verandah

brother-anointing ceremony, caste-mark, cow-worship, cousin-sister, nose-screw (ornament for a woman's nose), waist-thread (ritual thread tied round the waist)

And some less familiar words and phrases

ayah (nurse), bandh (labour strike), crore (10 million), demit (resign), dhobi (washerman), durzi (tailor), godown (warehouse), goondah (hooligan), jawan (soldier), kukri (curved knife), lakh (a hundred thousand), lathi (baton), ryot (farmer), stir (demonstration), stepney (spare wheel), swadeshi (indigenous)

backward class (deprived groups), Himalayan blunder (grave mistake), military hotel (non-vegetarian hotel), pin-drop silence (dead silence), swadeshi hotel (native restaurant)

Extracts from Indian newspapers (compiled by Braj Kachru) show the potential distinctiveness (and corresponding unintelligibility to outsiders) of standard Indian English:

● Dharmavati was chosen for Ragam, Tanam and Pallavi. Singing with an abandon, M.S. set off the distinct character of the mode and followed with methodically improvised Pallavi. The swaraprastara was full of tightly knit figures.
● Urad and moong fell sharply in the grain market here today on stockists offerings. Rice, jowar and arhar also followed suit, but barley forged ahead.
● In Karachi Quran khawani and fateha was held at the Cifton residence . . .
● Wanted well-settled bridegroom for a Kerala fair, graduate Baradwaja gotram, Astasastram girl . . . Subsect no bar. Send horoscope and details.

- Unfamiliar compound nouns appear: *chalk-piece*, *key-bunch*, *schoolgoer*.
- Prepositions are sometimes used in different ways: *pay attention on*, *accompany with*, *combat against*.
- The word order of certain constructions can vary: *Eggs are there* (for British *There are eggs*), *Who you have come to see?* (Who have you come to see?)
- Tense usage may alter: *I am here since this morning.*
- *Isn't it?* is often used at the end of a sentence in an invariable way (like *n'est-ce pas* in French): *You're going now, isn't it?*

Because of the length of the British presence in India, and the countries' vast populations, South Asian English has developed to a more distinctive level than is found in other countries where English is used as a second language. But this may be only a temporary situation. Any country which relies on English as its primary medium of communication sooner or later will find itself developing its own norms of pronunciation, grammar and vocabulary. And at that point, a critical question of identity is posed, which must be answered at various levels – in particular, by government officials in charge of educational programmes, and by writers wishing to express their identity, and the identity of their country, in a literary way. Which variety should they use? In the case of teaching, should they choose the internationally recognized standard English as a model for teachers to follow in class, or should they recommend the use of the regional standard, which is the one the children will hear and see around them? In the case of literary expression, should authors opt for standard English, which will guarantee them a readership throughout the world, or should they write in their regional standard, which will give them a more authentic and personal 'voice'? Or should they stay with their mother tongue, and not write in English at all?

These questions are fiercely and emotionally debated in all parts of the world where new varieties of second-language English are emerging. There is a great deal of stylistic experiment, and several distinct genres have developed. The problem is greatest for poets, novelists, and dramatists in the newly independent nations, where there is often considerable antagonism towards English, seen as a symbol of colonial oppression. The dilemma is acute. Should they

The Indian poet Kamala Das adopts a pragmatic view of the language situation. For her, the language used is unimportant; what counts is 'the thought contained in the words'.

> . . . I am Indian, very brown, born in
> Malabar, I speak three languages, write in
> Two, dream in one. Don't write in English, they said,
> English is not your mother-tongue. Why not leave
> Me alone, critics, friends, visiting cousins,
> Every one of you? Why not let me speak in
> Any language I like? The language I speak
> Becomes mine, its distortions, its queernesses
> All mine, mine alone. It is half English, half
> Indian, funny perhaps, but it is honest.
> It is as human as I am human, don't
> You see? It voices my joys, my longings, my
> Hopes, and it is useful to me as cawing
> Is to crows or roaring to the lions . . .
> *The Old Playhouse and Other Poems* (1973)

use the 'enemy's' language, with all the alien awkwardness that comes with the use of a second language for literary expression, in order to achieve an international audience? Or should they use their mother tongue, for which they have an immediate sensitivity, but which will place severe constraints on their potential readership? The solution, many writers maintain, is to concentrate on developing the English of their own region, making it into a language which belongs to them, and with which they can identify. 'Our method of expression', wrote the Indian author Raja Rao, 'has to be a dialect which will some day prove to be as distinctive and colorful as the Irish or the American . . . The tempo of Indian life must be infused into our English expression.' And the call for new Englishes, personal, evocative, and dynamic, has been echoed by second-language writers around the world, in South-east Asia, East and West Africa, and by first-language writers in Jamaica, South Africa, and New Zealand.

WORLD STANDARD ENGLISH

Meanwhile, as English-speaking communities and individuals strive to make the language different, to reflect their own backgrounds and experiences, there is a strong, persistent pull in the opposite direction. The demand for a language medium which is universally intelligible is widely felt, and frequently voiced. At present, English is the only language in a position to adopt the role of the world's first language. Chinese has many more mother-tongue speakers, but is currently too isolated (and its main writing system too unfamiliar) to attract much external interest.. Russian is little used outside the Eastern bloc countries. French, the world language of the eighteenth century, is an important lingua franca in many countries, but does not have the regional or occupational spread of English. Spanish is important in South America, and increasingly so in the United States, but has little further potential outside Spain. No language other than English carries universal appeal. And auxiliary languages, such as Esperanto, have to date made very slow progress in persuading world authorities to pay attention to their claims.

At present, due primarily to the economic superiority of the United States, there is no competitor for English as a world language. And therefore a great deal of attention is being paid to devising standards of language use which will transcend regional differences and guarantee intelligibility when people from different English-speaking parts of the world communicate with each other. There has been a veritable information explosion, as researchers and popularizers draw attention to the differences between dialects and styles of English, and attempt to explain them. In the last twenty years, we have seen a remarkable growth in reference works, including the publication of more general and specialized dictionaries, grammars, and manuals of style than have ever appeared before. Information networks, term-inology banks, computer-assisted translation, speech synthesis and recognition by machine, and other computationally controlled systems all bring people together, and presuppose shared norms of usage in order to be successful. Many projects aimed at standardizing usage and eliminating differences have been the result, in such fields as science, finance, industry, medicine, government, transport, and advertising.

Two specific examples will illustrate the application of this point. English is the official language of air traffic control, but it is widely recognized that this fact alone does not solve all communication problems. There have been several accidents in which an inadequate command of English by air crew has been cited as a causative factor. Reactions to this problem have been various. There are reports that some flights now talk to ground control in languages other than English – to the discomfiture of other aircraft in the vicinity. There have been proposals to replace English by Esperanto, though there is no evidence that the problems of communication are due to those irregularities of English structure which artificial languages avoid. Most promising is the ongoing research into the factors which hinder intelligibility in the air. Some of the difficulty must be due to the considerable levels of noise and interference which are present in ground-to-air transmission, which will affect foreign-language learners more than native speakers. And it is likely that improvements could be made to the actual patterns of Airspeak, which pilots are recommended to use.

Improvements of this kind have already taken place in the form of English used as the international medium of communication at sea. Here, too, it is essential that the language should follow clear rules, to reduce the possibilities of ambiguity and confusion when sending or receiving messages. Bridge officers come from a variety of language backgrounds. Shipping routes often alter, and new problems of traffic flow are always present. Larger and faster ships present greater navigational hazards.

In 1980 a British project was set up to produce Essential English for International Maritime Use – known as Seaspeak. The project extended the coverage of the Standard Maritime Navigational Vocabulary already in existence, and allowed the communication of longer messages than was previously possible. The guidelines relate mainly to communication by VHF radio, and include procedures for initiating, maintaining and terminating conversations, as well as a recommended grammar, vocabulary, and structure for messages on a wide range of topics. But the language is still much more restricted than everyday English.

Seaspeak recommends a set of standard phrases, to avoid the many alternative ways of expressing a meaning in everyday language. For example, 'What did you say?', 'I can't hear you', 'Please repeat that', and several other possibilities are all replaced by the single sentence 'Say again'. The range of meanings expressed by such conjunctions as *because*, *so that*, *in order to*, *as* and *to* are replaced by the word

A Seaspeak conversation

Part of a typical conversation between two ships, taken from the Seaspeak project report. Standard phrases are shown in italics.

NIPPON MARU: Gulf Trader, Gulf Trader. *This is* Nippon Maru, Juliet-Sierra-Alpha-Alpha. Nippon Maru, Juliet-Sierra-Alpha-Alpha. *On VHF channel* one-six. *Over.*

GULF TRADER: Nippon Maru, Juliet-Sierra-Alpha-Alpha. *This is* Gulf Trader, Alpha-Six-Zulu-Zulu. *Over.*

NIPPON MARU: Gulf Trader. *This is* Nippon Maru. *Switch to VHF channel* zero-six. *Over.*

GULF TRADER: Nippon Maru. *This is* Gulf Trader. *Agree VHF channel* two-six. *Over.*

NIPPON MARU: Gulf Trader. *This is* Nippon Maru. *Mistake. Switch to VHF channel* zero-six. *I say again. Switch to VHF channel* zero-six. *Over.*

GULF TRADER: Nippon Maru. *This is* Gulf Trader. *Correction. Agree VHF channel* zero-six. *Over.*

Call signs in Seaspeak (as in several other areas) use a standard alphabet in which each letter is given a name spoken in a fixed pronunciation. Stressed syllables are in **bold** type.

A	Alpha	**AL**FAH	N	November	NO**VEM**BER
B	Bravo	**BRAH**VOH	O	Oscar	**OSS**CAH
C	Charlie	**CHAR**LEE	P	Papa	PAH**PAH**
D	Delta	**DELL**TAH	Q	Quebec	KEY**BECK**
E	Echo	**ECK**OH	R	Romeo	**ROW**MEOH
F	Foxtrot	**FOKS**TROT	S	Sierra	SEE**AIR**RAH
G	Golf	**GOLF**	T	Tango	**TANG**GO
H	Hotel	HOH**TELL**	U	Uniform	**YOU**NEEFORM
I	India	**IN**DEEAH	V	Victor	**VIK**TAH
J	Juliet	**JEW**LEE**ETT**	W	Whiskey	**WISS**KEY
K	Kilo	**KEY**LOH	X	Xray	**ECKS**RAY
L	Lima	**LEE**MAH	Y	Yankey	**YANG**KEY
M	Mike	**MIKE**	Z	Zulu	**ZOO**LOO

'Reason', as in, 'I intend to enter stern first. Reason: my port thruster is damaged'. A question is always preceded by the word 'Question', a warning by the word 'Warning', and so on. Each message has its reply-marker: 'Answer', 'Instruction Received'. Bearings and courses using the 360-degree figure notation are always spoken in three-figure values: 'oh-oh-five degrees', not 'five degrees'. Dates are signalled using prefixes, such as 'day one-three, month zero-two, year one-nine-eight-eight'. Special marker words are used for such messages as urgency (PAN-PAN) and distress (MAYDAY).

Systems such as Seaspeak are but a fraction of the way English is being used for international purposes. The degree of refinement and standardization in this case is extreme; but a similar tendency to eradicate idiosyncrasy and to opt for the most widely understood features of language is common to all areas of international communication. These pressures themselves foster the development of new varieties of the language, of course. Examples from other areas include the linguistic constraints which affect us all when we wish to interact with computers. Indeed, given the fundamental nature of the computer revolution, with the formation of international databases and all kinds of man–machine interaction, from medical diagnosis to supermarket shopping, it is difficult to predict the shape of international English in the twenty-first century. But it seems likely that more rather than less standardization will result. In which case, the gap between the desire for an English which will identify ourselves and our loyalties and an English which will be understood by all will become even wider. We may, in due course, all need to be in control of two standard Englishes – the one which gives us our national or local identity, and the one which puts us in touch with the rest of the human race. In effect, we may all need to become bilingual in our own language.

Plain English

One of the most important trends in contemporary language use is the move towards developing a 'plain' English in official speech and writing. The main aim of the Plain English campaigns in Britain and the USA is to attack the use of unnecessarily complicated language (often called 'gobbledegook') by government departments, businesses, and any other group whose role puts them in linguistic contact with the general public. Application forms, safety instructions, official letters, licences, contracts, insurance policies, hire-purchase documents, guarantees, and other documents, the campaigners argue, should be presented clearly, using language that people are likely to understand.

The movements are very recent, growing up only in the late 1970s. But already they have played an important part in promoting public awareness of the problems, and they have helped to form a climate of opinion which has led several organizations to change their practices. In the UK, the campaign was launched in 1979 by a ritual shredding of government forms in Parliament Square. By 1985, over 21,000 forms had been revised, and a further 15,000 withdrawn. In the USA, President Carter issued an order in 1978 requiring that regulations be written in plain English; the order was revoked by President Reagan in 1981, but it none the less promoted a great deal of local legislation throughout the country, and an increase in plain English usage among corporations and consumers.

Today, the influence of the campaigns continues to grow. In addition, several research projects into the typographical design of forms have helped to improve current practice. Annual publicity is given to the Plain English Awards in the UK, which commend organizations that have produced the clearest documents, and criti-

An example of one of the new generation of official letters, written as plainly as it is possible to imagine.

NATIONAL
SAVINGS

Your reference

Our reference

National Savings Bank
Boydstone Road
GLASGOW
G58 1SB

Telephone 041–649 4555 ext

Date

Dear Sir/Madam

Thank you for telling us your bank book is missing.

If you have since found the book, please

◆ complete question 1 overleaf and return this form to me.

If the book is still missing, please

◆ answer both questions overleaf
◆ sign the enclosed declaration
◆ return both forms to me.

I enclose a post free envelope for return of the form(s).

Yours faithfully

howard

R S Watts
Controller

---

cize those whose materials are least intelligible (the Golden Bull awards). In the USA, there is similar interest in the annual Doublespeak Awards given by the National Council of Teachers of English to 'American public figures who have perpetrated language that is grossly unfactual, deceptive, evasive, euphemistic, confusing, or self-contradictory'.

By contrast, an extract from an old-style letter about housing rents (from the collection of the Plain English Campaign):

Dear/Sir Madam,

I am writing to inform you that the City Council at their meeting on 25th July, 1979, in accordance with the duty imposed by Section 113(1A) of the Housing Act, 1957, to review rents from time to time and to make such changes, either of the rents generally or of particular rents, as circumstances may require, decided that the net rents (i.e. exclusive of rates) of all Council-owned dwellings should continue to be related to Gross Rateable Values and adopted a general basis of 130% of Gross Rateable Value as the level at which the net rents should be set.

Net rents are at present based on 100% of Gross Rateable Values and, as a first step towards achieving the new basis of assessment, the Council have decided that those rents which are below 130% of Gross Rateable Value should be increased with effect from the rent week beginning Monday, 1st October, 1979, by 60p per week, or by such appropriate lesser amount as is required to bring them up to the level of 130% of Gross Value, and that current rents which are in excess of 130% Gross Value should remain unchanged.

The campaigners stress that clear language does not simply benefit the recipient; it can also save organizations time and money. They cite cases where unclear letters and instructions have led to so many complaints and questions that staff had to be specially employed to answer them. Another common problem is the return of application forms which have been filled in wrongly because the instructions were too complex or ambiguous. On the positive side, there are firms (such as insurance companies, and do-it-yourself manufacturers) who have benefited from increased sales, once their publicity or instructional literature was revised in this way.

More than money is involved: health and safety are affected. One focus of the Plain English Campaign's concern is the kind of language found on medical labels. Instructions such as 'Use sparingly' or 'Take after meals' were found, in one survey, to be extremely ambiguous. Some patients thought that taking a tablet 'after a meal' could mean anything up to immediately before the next meal. 'Take 2 tablets 4-hourly' was interpreted in all kinds of ways, such as 'Take one tablet every two hours', and 'Take eight tablets every hour.'

The movement towards plain English has not been without its critics, especially from within the legal profession. It has been pointed out that everyday language is itself very prone to ambiguity, and that if this language were used in official or legal documents, there could be problems. The public, it is argued, needs to have confidence in legal formulations, and that confidence can come only from using language that has been tried and tested in the courts over the years. So far, these fears seem to be without foundation: there has been no sudden increase in litigation as a result of the emergence of plain English materials. On the other hand, it is too early to be sure that these radical changes in communicative practice are going to be problem-free. But there is no doubting the widespread beneficial effects of the campaign, and it looks very much as if the 1980s will come to be seen as a stylistic turning point in the kind of written language used in officialese.

The address of the Plain English campaign:

Vernon House,
Whaley Bridge,
Stockport SK12 7HP,
UK

A US organization with similar aims is:

Document Design Center,
American Institutes for Research,
1055 Thomas Jefferson Street, NW,
Washington, DC 20007,
USA

DO YOU WRITE PLAIN ENGLISH?

It is not easy to devise precise, consistent, and acceptable guidelines for writing plain English. Several of the authors who write on this subject disagree as to what counts as 'plain' and what does not. Certain recommendations do, however, recur, such as the preference for short words and paragraphs, the use of concrete rather than abstract words, and the avoidance of the passive voice (*You should send this form* rather than *This form should be sent*). In *Politics and the English Language* (1947), George Orwell gave six rules to be followed in everyday language:

- Never use a metaphor, simile, or other figure of speech which you are used to seeing in print.
- Never use a long word when a short one will do.
- If it is possible to cut a word out, always cut it out.
- Never use the passive where you can use the active.
- Never use a foreign phrase, a scientific word, or a jargon word if you can think of an everyday English equivalent.
- Break any of these rules sooner than say anything outright barbarous.

WHAT'S YOUR READABILITY SCORE?

In recent years there has been a vogue for rating the readability of written material using simple mathematical formulae. Such formulae, because they rely on very basic notions, such as the relative length of words and sentences, cannot capture all the linguistic complexity of a text. It is possible to have a text written in short words and sentences which is quite difficult to understand because the thought being expressed is complex. And two texts can have the same 'score', but one be more complex than the other, because it uses a more complicated syntax. For example, these two sentences have the same number of words of the same length (in syllables), but the first is much easier than the second:

I can see the man and the cat and the dog and the cow.
The man, who saw the dog that chased the cat, is near the cow.

It is not wise, therefore, to rely exclusively on readability scores in grading the difficulty of texts (as one might in a reading scheme for schools, for example). But there is no harm in keeping an eye on your word and sentence length in this way, as there is no doubt that, all else being equal, short is sweet.

An influential reading test in the USA was devised by Rudolf

Flesch. The test scores from 0 (practically unreadable) to 100 (extremely easy to read). Most states require that insurance documents, for example, should score between 40 and 50 on this test. According to the English language researcher James Dayananda, the *Reader's Digest* scores 65, *Time* magazine 52, and the *Harvard Law Review* 32. You can try it out on anything you have written – even something as everyday as a letter.

- Count the words in your text.
- Count the syllables in the words.
- Count the sentences. (A sentence here means anything followed by a full-stop, colon, semi-colon, dash, question mark, or exclamation mark.)
- Divide the number of syllables by the number of words (thus working out the average number of words per sentence).
- Multiply the average word length by 84.6.
- Multiply the average sentence length by 1.015.
- Add the two numbers, and subtract them from 206.835.
- The result is your readability score.

There are always a few problems in interpreting instructions of this kind. As we have seen (p. 33), it is not easy to say what counts as a word: for example, different people will write *ashtray* or *ash tray*. And punctuation varies greatly from person to person. You will often find yourself making a few arbitrary decisions. But the results are always interesting.

To illustrate the procedure, here is the readability score for the first two paragraphs of Chapter 1:

A Total words: 154
B Total syllables: 244
C Total sentences: 8

$$B \div A = 1.584 \times 84.6 = 134.006 +$$
$$A \div C = 19.25 \times 1.015 = 19.539$$

$$153.545$$

$$206.835 - 153.545 = \underline{53.29}$$

Not in *Reader's Digest*'s league, but slightly better than *Time*, it seems. On the other hand, this criterion shows considerable variation in my style. The first two paragraphs of the present section (p. 266) produced a score of 27.9, lower than the *Harvard Law Review*.

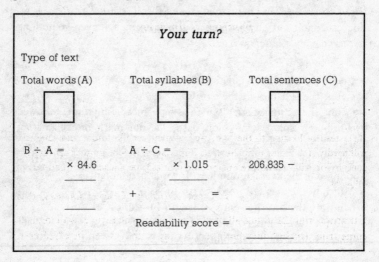

Your turn?

Type of text

Total words (A)   Total syllables (B)   Total sentences (C)

$B \div A =$ $A \div C =$

        $\times 84.6$ $\times 1.015$ $206.835 -$

        $+$ $=$

Readability score =

14

ԑՑ ԑՑ ԑՑ ԑՑ ԑՑ ԑՑ ԑՑ ԑՑ ԑՑ ԑՑ

English Tomorrow

If, instead of looking to the past, we speculate on the future, our language
will hardly sink in our estimate of its importance. Before another century has
gone by, it will, at the present rate of increase, be spoken by hundreds of
millions.

> E. Guest, *A History of English Rhythms*, 1838

Guest was right. But not all predictions about the future of a language
come true. In the nineteenth century, as we have seen in Chapter 1,

'Funny how you soon forget his regional accent.'

Punch, 27 June 1984

several people were confidently claiming that, within 100 years, British and American English would be mutually unintelligible. The same prediction continues to be made today. Again, in the nineteenth century, people were citing split infinitives and other 'errors' (see p. 25) as evidence of the decline of the language, and giving English only a few years to live if drastic reform were not undertaken. The same prediction continues to be made today.

The future of a language is closely bound up with the influence and prestige of its speakers – and who can predict such things? What will be the balance of power among the major nations of the world a century from now? Will American supremacy continue to underwrite the role of English? Or will some momentous political or economic event motivate people to look elsewhere for their world language? The role of English has developed to such an extent, unprecedented in world history, that it is difficult to see how it can now be dislodged. But people must have thought that way about Latin once.

The break-up of Latin into the modern Romance languages is often referred to by prophets of linguistic doom. They point to the way new varieties of English are rapidly developing in different parts of the world (see Chapters 12 and 13). They quote the many voices in newly independent nations who argue the need for further language change in order to provide a badge of political, social, and literary identity. They conclude that within a generation or two international standard English will have fragmented into a range of only partly intelligible dialects.

On the other hand, it is just as often pointed out that those who promote the cause of language change are underestimating the massive unifying forces at work in the world. Sociologists and economists affirm that progress of any kind today depends as never before on a network of international relations – in particular, those mediated by the United Nations and the World Bank. Communications analysts point out that the existence of the world media introduces an element into the situation which has never existed before. New varieties, when they emerge, no longer develop in isolation over long periods of time, as happened to Old French or Old English. Speakers of Australian, Indian, Jamaican or other Englishes can be heard at almost any time, simply by turning on the radio or television, or by going to the cinema. There is inevitably a 'levelling' which takes place in such circumstances. There is a greater interchange of words, and an enhancing of the levels of mutual comprehension. Whatever the features of regional English are, they are tiny compared with the mass of vocabulary and structure of 'world standard' English, which is within easy reach of all.

But no one wants to lose their identity in a world melting-pot. It therefore seems likely that, in the course of the next century, we will see the emergence of a more universal 'bidialectism' on the part of those who play a role in the international community. People will use one variety of the language at home, and slip into another variety when they communicate with those from different communities. It already happens, of course, when people with different regional dialect backgrounds meet. I was part of a conversation recently where someone from Scotland and someone from Wales were discussing a point. Although both speakers have strongly dialectal speech patterns when they are at home, the conversation was remarkably free of regional vocabulary or idiom; and when the speakers did introduce local phrases, they were often accompanied by a comment which acknowledged that the other might not follow – such as 'as we say', or 'are you with me?'. I recall a similar conversation with an American. There is no real difference between intra-national and inter-national varieties of English, in this respect.

So maybe in a century or so we shall all be bilingual in our own language, with our home variety of English co-existing with an English international lingua franca. And in the course of time, maybe 'bilingual' will not be too strong a word; for it is likely that the home varieties will develop along different lines from those followed by this lingua franca. There could well come a day, indeed, when the home languages of Indians, Americans, Jamaicans, and others are mutually unintelligible, but the whole community is bound together by the continuing existence of the lingua franca. Such a situation is not fantasy: there is an analogy today in China, where the several spoken Chinese 'dialects' are mutually unintelligible, but written Chinese is understood by all.

In the meantime, those who have invested a childhood, or adult time and money, in successfully acquiring the English language would do well to maintain an active interest in the language's progress. The more we learn about where the language has been, how it is structured, how it is used, and how it is changing, the more we will be able to judge its present course and help to plan its future. For many people, this will mean a conscious altering of attitude. Language variation and language change – the two aspects of English which are at the centre of its identity, and which are most in the public eye – are too often blindly condemned. If just a fraction of the nervous energy which is currently devoted to the criticism of split infinitives and the intrusive *r* were devoted to the constructive promotion of forward-looking language activities, what might not be achieved?

It is easy to forget the many areas where the language, and those who are professionally involved with it, need the active support of the general public. Adult literacy programmes, plain English campaigns, immigrant teaching, the BBC World Service, provision for the language handicapped, library and information services, the language arts: domains such as these need public support, in the form of money, time, and resources, if they are to succeed in their operation. The history, structure, and use of the English language is a fascinating topic in its own right; but the story does not end there. Rather, it should lead us to consider the unfulfilled linguistic needs of communities at home and abroad, and in particular the plight of the millions who are handicapped by their inadequate command of English, whether in speaking, listening, reading, or writing. For them, the story is only beginning.

Appendix A

ᛮ ᛮ ᛮ ᛮ ᛮ ᛮ ᛮ ᛮ ᛮ ᛮ

Some Events in English Language History

449	Invasion by Angles, Saxons, and Jutes
450–80	Earliest runic inscriptions in Old English
597	Augustine brings Christianity to Kent
680	Approximate earliest date for the composition of *Beowulf*
700	Approximate dating of earliest Old English manuscripts
735	Death of the Venerable Bede
787	Viking raids begin
871	Alfred becomes King of Wessex
886	Danelaw boundaries settled
950–1000	Approximate dates of the main Old English poetry collections
1016–42	Cnut and his sons reign
1066	Norman Conquest
1150–1200	Earliest texts in Middle English
1171	Henry II's invasion of Ireland
1204	France reconquers Normandy
1250–1300	Edward I's campaigns against the Welsh and Scots
1362	English first used at the opening of Parliament
1375–1400	Chaucer's main works written
1384	Wyclif's translation of the Bible
1400–1450	The Great Vowel Shift
1400–1600	Main period of older Scots literature
1476	Introduction of printing
1475–1650	Renaissance loan words into English
1549	Book of Common Prayer written
1560–1620	English plantation settlements in Ireland
1584	Roanoke settlement in America
1590–1616	Shakespeare's main works written
1600	East India Company established trading posts in India

1603	Act of Union of the crowns of England and Scotland
1604	Publication of Robert Cawdrey's *A Table Alphabeticall*
1607	First permanent English settlement in America
1609	First English settlement in the Caribbean
1611	Authorized Version of the Bible
1619	Arrival of first African slaves in North America
1620	Arrival of the Pilgrim Fathers in America
1623	First Folio of Shakespeare's plays published
1627	British established in Barbados
1655	British acquire Jamaica from Spain
1707	Union of the Parliaments of England and Scotland
1712	Jonathan Swift's proposal for an English Academy
1713	British control in eastern Canada recognized
1721	Publication of Nathaniel Bailey's *Universal Etymological English Dictionary*
1755	Publication of Samuel Johnson's *Dictionary of the English Language*
1762	Publication of Robert Lowth's *Short Introduction to English Grammar*
1765–1947	British Raj in India
1776	American independence declared
1780–1800	First wave of emigration to Canada from the USA
1783	Loss of American colonies of Britain
1788	Establishment of first penal colony in Australia
1791	Establishment of Upper and Lower Canada
1794	Publication of Lindley Murray's *English Grammar*
1800–1910	Main period of European emigration to the USA
1802	Ceylon and Trinidad ceded to Britain
1803	Act of Union between Britain and Ireland
1806	British control established in South Africa
1808	Sierra Leone made colony
1814	Tobago, Mauritius, St Lucia and Malta ceded to Britain
1816	Colony of Bathurst (Gambia) established
1819	British established Singapore
1828	Publication of Noah Webster's *American Dictionary of the English Language*
1840	Official colony established in New Zealand
1842	Hong Kong ceded to Britain
1861	Lagos (Nigeria) established as colony
1865–1900	Movement of blacks to northern parts of the USA after the American Civil War

1867	Independence of Canada
1874	Gold Coast (Ghana) established as colony
1884–1928	Publication of the *Oxford English Dictionary*
1888–94	British protectorates established in Kenya, Zanzibar, Uganda
1901	Independence of Australia
1907	Independence of New Zealand
1910	Union of South Africa established
1919	Tanganyika ceded to Britain
1922	Partition of Northern Ireland and Eire
1922	Establishment of the BBC
1925	Afrikaans given official status in South Africa
1931	British Commonwealth recognized
1947	Independence of India
1948	Independence of Ceylon (Sri Lanka)
1957	Independence of Ghana
1957–63	Independence of Malaysia
1960	Independence of Nigeria
1940–75	Main period of immigration to Britain from Europe, Caribbean and Asia
1961	Independence of Sierra Leone and Cyprus
1962	Independence of Jamaica, Trinidad and Tobago, Uganda
1963	Independence of Kenya
1964	Independence of Tanzania, Malawi, Malta, Zambia
1965	Independence of The Gambia, Singapore
1966	Independence of Guyana, Botswana, Lesotho, Barbados
1968	Independence of Mauritius, Swaziland, Nauru
1970–84	Independence of possessions in Caribbean and Pacific
1972	Independence of Bangladesh
1975	Independence of Papua New Guinea
1977	*Voyager* spacecraft leaves with English message

Appendix B

ଓ ଓ ଓ ଓ ଓ ଓ ଓ ଓ ଓ ଓ

A Guide to the Guides

In recent years there have been many accounts written of the language. Here is a selection of them, with an indication of their coverage and emphasis.

Richard W. Bailey and Manfred Görlach (ed.), *English as a World Language* (University of Michigan Press, 1982, Cambridge University Press, 1984, 496 pp.). A collection of essays, aimed at the serious student, outlining the political and social history of English language development around the world, and illustrating the variations which have taken place in each region.

Charles Barber, *Early Modern English* (The Language Library, Blackwell/Deutsch, 1976, 360 pp.). A detailed account of the history of English between 1500 and 1700, with particular attention to the attitudes to the language expressed during that period.

Albert C. Baugh and Thomas Cable, *A History of the English Language* (Prentice-Hall, and Routledge and Kegan Paul, 1978, 3rd edition, 438 pp.). The standard textbook on the history of the language, giving copious illustration of each stage of development, and a thorough discussion of the social and political history; particularly strong on American English.

W. F. Bolton, *A Living Language: The History and Structure of English* (Random House, 1982, 461 pp.). A scholarly treatment paying particular attention to the nature of English linguistic change, and to the history of ideas in English language studies; there are several illustrations from the texts of each period, and the account incorporates an explanation of relevant concepts from linguistics.

Whitney F. Bolton and David Crystal (ed.), *The English Language* (Sphere History of the English Language, Vol. 10, 2nd edition 1987, 362 pp.). A collection of essays introducing what is involved in the study of English sounds, grammar, vocabulary, and style, and providing a historical account from both linguistic and sociolinguistic points of view.

Robert Burchfield, *The English Language* (Oxford University Press, 1985, 194 pp.). A largely historically organized account from the former editor of the Oxford English Dictionary; particular attention paid to the development of vocabulary, and to the history of dictionaries and grammars.

English Today, edited by Tom McArthur (Cambridge University Press, four issues yearly since 1985). An international review of the English language, aiming to provide a popular but responsible account of important issues in English language development and use around the world; contains articles, reviews, discussion pieces, a correspondence column, and many illustrations of English in use.

Stuart Berg Flexner, *I Hear America Talking* (Simon and Schuster, 1976). A popular account of the social history behind many American English words, thematically organized and copiously illustrated.

Sidney Greenbaum (ed.), *The English Language Today* (Pergamon Press, 1985, 345 pp.). A collection of scholarly essays on the social contexts which have given rise to changes in the language, with particular reference to past and present-day beliefs and attitudes about all aspects of English structure and use.

Braj B. Kachru, *The Alchemy of English* (Pergamon Press, 1986, 200 pp.). A scholarly study of the spread of non-native varieties of English, with particular reference to their impact on other languages, the emergence of new standards, and their role in literary creativity.

Roger Lass, *The Shape of English: Structure and History* (J. M. Dent, 1987, 384 pp.). A synthesis of ideas and techniques relating to the history and present structure of the language. Particular reference is made to grammar and pronunciation, and to regional and social varieties.

Dick Leith, *A Social History of English* (Routledge and Kegan Paul, 1983, 224 pp.). An introductory account of the development of the language, paying particular attention to the historical and social circumstances that affect linguistic change; makes use of relevant concepts in sociolinguistics.

Robert McCrum, William Cran and Robert McNeil, *The Story of English* (Faber and Faber, and BBC Publications, 1986, 384 pp.). The book based on the BBC television series, with full-colour maps and illustrations, emphasizing the regional and social diversification of spoken English, and especially the varieties which have developed in recent years.

Leonard Michaels and Christopher Ricks (ed.), *The State of the Language* (University of California Press, 1980, 609 pp.). A collection of essays and poems on all aspects of the contemporary language; a mixture of objective and subjective observations contributed by linguists, novelists, broadcasters, critics, and many others. Second edition, 1989.

J. Platt, H. Weber and M. L. Ho, *The New Englishes* (Routledge and Kegan Paul, 1984, 225 pp.). A thematic treatment of the way new varieties of

English have developed in non-native situations, giving detailed analyses and illustrations of the linguistic characteristics of several varieties.

Randolph Quirk, *The Use of English* (Longman, 2nd edition, 1968, 370 pp.). A standard introductory text, giving an account of the structure and uses of the modern language, with particular reference to the realities of English usage and the styles and varieties which are to be observed.

Randolph Quirk and H. G. Widdowson (ed.), *English in the World* (Cambridge University Press, and The British Council, 1985, 275 pp.). A collection of papers by linguistic and literary scholars on the teaching of English language and literature around the world; a text which stresses the history of ideas and current trends in analysis.

Peter Trudgill and Jean Hannah, *International English: A Guide to Varieties of Standard English* (Edward Arnold, 1982, 130 pp.). A succinct account of the main differences in pronunciation, spelling, grammar, and vocabulary in the chief regional varieties of English; largely devoted to description and illustration of these differences.

Wolfgang Viereck and Wolf-Dietrich Bald (ed.), *English in Contact with Other Languages* (Akadémiai Kiado, 1986, 570 pp.). A collection of scholarly essays dealing with the way English sounds, spellings, vocabulary and grammar have influenced foreign languages all over the world.

Appendix C

ᎶᎶᎶᎶᎶᎶᎶᎶᎶᎶ

Data Sources

The following sources of data are referred to in the book.

p. 60 Robert Burchfield, *The Spoken Word: A BBC Guide*. London: BBC Publications, 1981.

p. 89 The sociolinguistic data is from J. K. Chambers and P. Trudgill, *Dialectology*. Cambridge: CUP, 1980.

p. 96. G. N. Leech, *English in Advertising*. London: Longman, 1966.

p. 100 W. O'Barr, *Linguistic Evidence: Language, Power and Strategy in the Courtroom*. London: Academic Press, 1982.

p. 103 J. Kettle-Williams, 'CB Rubber Duck. 10–10'. *Language Monthly*, 13, 1984, 20–22.

p. 109 R. K. Gordon, *Anglo-Saxon Poetry*. London: Dent, 1926.

p. 111 Afferbeck Lauder, *Let Stalk Strine*. Sydney: Ure Smith, 1965.
Frank Shaw, Fritz Spiegl and S. Kelly, *Lern Yerself Scouse*. Liverpool: The Scouse Press, 1966.
Jim Everhart, *The Illustrated Texas Dictionary of the English Language*, Vol. 2. Lincoln: Cliff's Notes, 1968.
Sam Llewellyn, *Yacky dar moy bewty!* London: Elm Tree Books, 1985.

p. 112 Eric Partridge, *Comic Alphabets*. London: Routledge and Kegan Paul, 1961.

p. 127 A. Ellegård, *Who was Junius?* Stockholm: Almqvist and Wiksell, 1962.

p. 128 C. B. Williams, *Style and Vocabulary: Numerical Studies*. London: Griffin, 1970.

p. 130 J. Svartvik, *The Evans Statements: A Case for Forensic Linguistics*. Gothenburg: Almqvist and Wiksell, 1968.

p. 140 A. Zettersten, *A Statistical Study of the Graphic System of Present-day American English*. Lund: Studentlitteratur, 1968.

p. 141 Written word-count data from Thorndike and Lorge (see p. 138), and R. Edwards and V. Gibbon, *Words Your Children Use*. London: Burke Books, 2nd edn., 1973. Spoken data from surveys carried out at Lund University and Reading University.

p. 163 Bengt Odenstedt, *The Inscription on the Undley Bracteate and the Beginnings of English Runic Writing*. Umeå University, 1983.

p. 213 A.S.C. Ross, 'U and non-U', in Nancy Mitford (ed.), *Noblesse Oblige*, London: Hamish Hamilton, 1956.

p. 257 R. L. Cooper, 'The avoidance of androcentric generics', *International Journal of the Sociology of Language*, 50 (1984), 5–20.

p. 259 B.B. Kachru, 'South Asian English', in Bailey and Görlach (see p. 280).

p. 264 F. Weeks, A. Glover, P. Strevens and E. Johnson, *Seaspeak Reference Manual*. Oxford: Pergamon, 1984.

p. 271 J. Dayananda, 'Plain English in the United States'. *English Today*, 5, 1986, 13–16.

Index

a, pronunciation of, 87–8
abbreviations, 36, 39, 204; scribal, 149
Aboriginal borrowings, 240
Academy, 205–6
accents, 63, 86–9, 111–13, 242; *see also*
    pronunciation
acrostics, 114
adjectives, use of, 30–31
advertising, 132, 253–4
Africa, English in, 3
air-traffic control, 262–3
Alfred, King, 153, 168
alliteration, 134–5
American English, 222–31; dialects of,
    225–7; *v.* British English, 74, 230, 246–
    50, 274; State names, 227–8
anagrams, 115
Anglo-Saxon, *see* Old English
Anglo-Saxon Chronicle, 168
assimilation, 55–7
assonance, 134–5
aureate terms, 176
Australian English, 111, 238–42
Authorized Version of the Bible, 196,
    198–203, 217
authorship research, 126–31
aygo-paygo speech, 120

back slang, 120
Bacon *v.* Shakespeare, 128–9
Bailey, Nathaniel, 203
BBC English, 58–61, 63, 88
Bede, the Venerable, 145–7
Beowulf, 153–5
between you and I, 27
Bible translation, 176, 198–203
bidialectism, 275
bilingualism in English, 265, 275
Black English, 234–8;Vernacular, 237–8
'Blankety Blank', 113
Bombaugh, C. C., 117
Book of Common Prayer, 198
Boorde, Andrew, 218
borrowing, 37–8, 77, 157–60, 174–7, 192–
    5, 229–31; in Europe, 252–5
Britain, early languages of, 152–3
Burchfield, Robert, 60
Burns, Robert, 218

Cædmon story, 147–8
'Call My Bluff', 113

calypso, 109
Canadian English, 231–4
Caribbean English, 234–7
Carroll, Lewis, 117, 124
Cawdrey, Robert, 203–4
Caxton, William, 75, 188–91
CB codes, 103
Celtic languages, 152–3, 216
centre slang, 120
Chaucer, Geoffrey, 179–83
Chaucerisms, 194
Cheke, John, 194
China, English in, 6
clichés, 41
code games, 120
comic alphabets, 112
complaints about grammar, 27–9
compound words, 39
confusions (word), 77–8
consonants, 53–7
conversation, 22–3, 92
conversion, 39, 195
courtroom strategies, 100–101
creoles, 15–16, 235–8
crosswords, 113–14
cummings, e. e., 131–2

Danes, 157–60
Das, Kamala, 261
Dayananda, James, 271
deafness, 133
decimate, use of, 42
Defoe, Daniel, 205
description *v.* prescription, 26–7, 206–7
deviant English, 131–7
dialects, 34–5, 89–92, 225–6, 234, 241,
    255; jokes about, 111–13; Middle Eng-
    lish, 185–8; Old English, 155–6
diction, poetic, 136–7
dictionary, 203–10, 230–31; choosing, 47–
    9
different from/to/than, 27–8
Donne, John, 132
doublets, 117
Dryden, John, 205
duels, linguistic, 109–10
Dunbar, William, 109–10, 217

Early Modern English, 189–214
eggy-peggy speech, 120
Eliot, T. S., 135

elision, 55–7
Elizabethan literature, 203, 204
Ellegård, Albar, 127
Elyot, Thomas, 192
English Now, 27, 61
etymological fallacy, 42–3
etymology, 37–8, 76, 227–8
Evans, Timothy, 129–30
Exeter Book, 109

feminism, 256–7
Flower, Kathy, 6
flyting, 109–10
Follow Me, 6
foreign-language use, 4–7
forensic linguistics, 128–31
Franglais, etc., 254–5
French: English influence on, 252–4;
    influence on English, 75, 172–6, 192–3
future of English, 10–11, 273–6

g dropping, 59
Gadsby, 116–17
Gaelic, 216–22
gematria, 118–19, 121
gobbledegook, 266
Golden Bull Awards, 268
Gowers, Ernest, 41–2
graffiti, 107
grammar, 19–31; Middle English, 170–
    71, 177–8; Old English, 150–52; prefer-
    ences in, 30–31; regional, 221, 237–8,
    248–9, 258; sexism and, 256–7
grammars, early, 25, 206–7
Graves, Robert, 137
Great Vowel Shift, 75–6, 183–4
Greek borrowings, 192–3
grid games, 118
Guardian, the, 93
Guest, E., 273

h dropping, 59, 89
Hart, John, 205
Henryson, Robert, 217
Herbert, George, 134
history of English, 143–279
Hogan, Paul, 242
hopefully, use of, 28
Hopkins, Gerard Manley, 137
humour, 105–13, 132
Humphreys, Barry, 242

identity, 10, 94–101, 255–61
idioms, 33, 198–9
Indian English, 4, 258–61
inflections, 20–22, 151–2, 170, 177–8,
    201, 238, 254

information explosion, 262
inkhorn terms, 192–5
intelligibility, 10–22, 262–76
intrusive *r*, 58–9
Irish English, 219–22; Northern, 221
irregular words, 178
-ize verbs, 41–2

Jamaican English, 235–7
John of Trevisa, 188
Johnson, Samuel, 205–9
jokes, 105–7
Joyce, James, 136–7, 222
Junius letters, 127–8

Kentish, 155, 185
King James Bible, 196, 198–203
'knowing about' grammar, 23–9

Lallans, 218
Langland, William, 179
Latin, 11, 20, 42, 74, 76, 149, 152–3, 156–
    7, 176–7, 192–5, 274
law, language of, 98–101
Leech, Geoffrey, 96
Lern Yerself Scouse, 111
Let Stalk Strine, 111
letters, silent, 76
letters *v.* sounds, 52, 58
lines of poetry, 133–4
linking *r*, 57
lip rounding, 56
lipograms, 116
literature, 131–7
Liverpool, 35, 111
Lowth, Robert, 25, 206–7

man, etc., 256
meaning, changes in, 40–41
Mendenhall, T. G., 128
Mercian, 155
Middle English, 166–88; history of, 172–
    4; spelling, 75; *v.* Old English, 172
Midland, East, 170, 185–6
Midland, West, 185–6
Milton, John, 135
missionaries, 153, 156
Mitford, Nancy, 213
morphology, 21
Morse, Samuel, 140
mother-tongue use, 2
Mulcaster, Richard, 195, 203
Murray, Lindley, 25, 206

names, 36–7, 158; *see also* place names
negatives, double, 28–9, 170–71, 238
New Zealand English, 239–42

nice, use of, 42
none, use of, 27
Norman invasion, 172–3
normative thinking, 204–7
Northern, 185–7
Northumbrian, 155
Nue Spelling, 80

O'Barr, William, 100–101
Odenstedt, Bengt, 163
Old English, 145–65; history of, 152–60; spelling, 74–5
only, use of, 27
onomatopoeia, 122
Orwell, George, 270

palindromes, 116
pangrams, 116
Partridge, Eric, 112
pauses and punctuation, 93
personal English, 125–41
Peterborough Chronicle, 167–72
phonetic transcription, 52–4
pidgins, 12–16, 235
pig Latin, 120
Pilgrim Fathers, 223–4
Pitman, James, 80
place names, 153, 157–60, 227–31
Plain English, 266–72
playing with English, 105–24
poetry, 132–7, 180, 183
Pope, Alexander, 135
prefixation, 39
prepositions at end of sentences, 28
Priestley, Joseph, 207
printing, 75, 188–91
pronouns and sexism, 256–7
pronunciation, 50–65; complaints about, 57–61; controversies, 60; history of, 150, 179, 183–4; regional standards of, 216, 224, 234, 235, 240, 242, 243–4, 246–7, 258
punctuation, 93
puns, 110
purism, 25, 40, 58, 192, 195, 205–7
Puritan settlers, 223–4

r, pronunciation of, 57–9, 87
Rao, Raja, 261
rapping, 108–9
readability scores, 270–72
rebus, 115–16
Received Pronunciation, 52–3, 62–5, 86, 242, 245
regional varieties, *see* dialects
religious language, 97, 132, 156–7
Renaissance, 191–6

rhyme, 134–5
rhythm, 133–4, 237, 258
riddles, 107–9
Roanoke settlement, 222–3
Rolle, Richard, 187
Ross, A. S. C., 213
Royal Society, 205
rules of grammar, 24–9, 206–7
runes, 153, 161–5
Ruthwell Cross, 164–5

Scandinavian names, 157–60
Schonell, F., 71
scientific vocabulary, 211–12
Scots English, 216–19
Scott, Walter, 218
Scrabble, 118–19
Seaspeak, 263–5
second-language use, 2–4, 257–61
sexism and language, 256–7
Shakespeare, William, 26, 196–200; authorship of, 128–9
shall/will, use of, 24, 28
Shavian, 80–81
Shaw, George Bernard, 80–81, 86
slang, 34–5, 94, 212
social status, 61–5, 212–14, 242, 245, 252–61
sound symbolism, 122–4
South African English, 242–5
South Asian English, 258–61
Southern, 185–8
speakers of English, 1–7
spectrogram, 55
speech rate, 50–57
speech *v.* writing, 22–3, 52–4, 92–4, 141
spelling, 66–81, 247–8; correct, 75; deviant, 76, 135, 248; history of, 74–7; irregular, 66–70; Middle English, 171, 178–9; Old English, 149–50, 155; reading *v.* 70; reform, 79–81; rules of, 70–74; teaching of, 69–72
Spenser, Edmund, 192
split infinitives, 27
standard English, 15–16, 185–8, 190–91; regional, 214–50, 257–61; teaching of, 260–61; world, 261–5, 273–6
statistical laws, 138–41
stressed syllables, 73, 247
structure, 17–81
style, 96–7, 125–41, 205
suffixation, 39
Survey of English Dialects, 90–91
Svartvik, Jan, 130
Swift, Jonathan, 115, 204–6
switching, language, 254–5
syllables per minute, 51

synonymy, 176–7
syntax, 21
Synge, J. M., 222
syzygies, 117

technical terms, 37, 67, 211–12
telestich, 114
television advertising, 96
terminology, grammatical, 24–9
Tex-Mex, 254–5
Thomas, Dylan, 136
Thorndike, E. L. and Lorge, I., 138
thou V. you, 201
't-ing in i', 120
Tok Pisin, 14–16
Tolkien, J. R. R., 164
tongue twisters, 116
trade names, 76
trucker talk, 102–4

U *v.* non-U, 213–14
Undley bracteate, 163
univocalics, 117
uses of English, 83–141

Van Buren, Paul, 132
varieties, 85–104; *see also* dialects
Viking invasions, 157
vocabulary, 32–49, 211–14; complaints about, 40–42, 204; Early Modern English, 192–9; estimating your own, 44–7; frequency of, 140–41; Middle English, 171–2; Old English, 150; regional, 34,

219, 221, 234, 237–8, 240–41, 244, 249–50, 258–60; total size of, 32–7; types of, 37–42
vowels, 52; short *v.* long, 73–4

Waller, Edmund, 204
Webster, Noah, 230
Wenglish, 254–5
West Saxon, 155
who/whom, use of, 28
Wilkins, Bishop John, 205
Wilson, Thomas, 194
Wood, Clement, 119
word endings, *see* inflections
word games, 113–21
word order, 21–2, 150–52, 170–71, 177, 200–201, 254
word squares, 114–15
words in English, 32–7; types and tokens, 68–9
words within words, 118
World English, 215–50, 273–6
Wright, Ernest, 116
writing, *see* speech *v.* writing
Wyclif, John, 176, 179–80
Wynne, Arthur, 113

Yacky dar moy bewty!, 111
ye, 178
Yeats, W. B., 222

Zettersten, Arne, 140
Zipf, George, 138–9

FOR THE BEST IN PAPERBACKS, LOOK FOR THE 🐧

In every corner of the world, on every subject under the sun, Penguin represents quality and variety – the very best in publishing today.

For complete information about books available from Penguin – including Puffins, Penguin Classics and Arkana – and how to order them, write to us at the appropriate address below. Please note that for copyright reasons the selection of books varies from country to country.

In the United Kingdom: Please write to *Dept E.P., Penguin Books Ltd, Harmondsworth, Middlesex, UB7 0DA.*

If you have any difficulty in obtaining a title, please send your order with the correct money, plus ten per cent for postage and packaging, to *PO Box No 11, West Drayton, Middlesex*

In the United States: Please write to *Dept BA, Penguin, 299 Murray Hill Parkway, East Rutherford, New Jersey 07073*

In Canada: Please write to *Penguin Books Canada Ltd, 2801 John Street, Markham, Ontario L3R 1B4*

In Australia: Please write to the *Marketing Department, Penguin Books Australia Ltd, P.O. Box 257, Ringwood, Victoria 3134*

In New Zealand: Please write to the *Marketing Department, Penguin Books (NZ) Ltd, Private Bag, Takapuna, Auckland 9*

In India: Please write to *Penguin Overseas Ltd, 706 Eros Apartments, 56 Nehru Place, New Delhi, 110019*

In the Netherlands: Please write to *Penguin Books Netherlands B.V., Postbus 195, NL–1380AD Weesp*

In West Germany: Please write to *Penguin Books Ltd, Friedrichstrasse 10–12, D–6000 Frankfurt/Main 1*

In Spain: Please write to *Longman Penguin España, Calle San Nicolas 15, E–28013 Madrid*

In Italy: Please write to *Penguin Italia s.r.l., Via Como 4, I-20096 Pioltello (Milano)*

In France: Please write to *Penguin Books Ltd, 39 Rue de Montmorency, F-75003 Paris*

In Japan: Please write to *Longman Penguin Japan Co Ltd, Yamaguchi Building, 2–12–9 Kanda Jimbocho, Chiyoda-Ku, Tokyo 101*

FOR THE BEST IN PAPERBACKS, LOOK FOR THE 🐧

PENGUIN REFERENCE BOOKS

The New Penguin English Dictionary

Over 1,000 pages long and with over 68,000 definitions, this cheap, compact and totally up-to-date book is ideal for today's needs. It includes many technical and colloquial terms, guides to pronunciation and common abbreviations.

The Penguin Spelling Dictionary

What are the plurals of *octopus* and *rhinoceros*? What is the difference between *stationary* and *stationery*? And how about *annex* and *annexe*, *agape* and *Agape*? This comprehensive new book, the fullest spelling dictionary now available, provides the answers.

Roget's Thesaurus of English Words and Phrases   Betty Kirkpatrick (ed.)

This new edition of Roget's classic work, now brought up to date for the nineties, will increase anyone's command of the English language. Fully cross-referenced, it includes synonyms of every kind (formal or colloquial, idiomatic and figurative) for almost 900 headings. It is a must for writers and utterly fascinating for any English speaker.

The Penguin Dictionary of Quotations

A treasure-trove of over 12,000 new gems and old favourites, from Aesop and Matthew Arnold to Xenophon and Zola.

The Penguin Wordmaster Dictionary
Martin H. Manser and Nigel D. Turton

This dictionary puts the pleasure back into word-seeking. Every time you look at a page you get a bonus – a panel telling you everything about a particular word or expression. It is, therefore, a dictionary to be read as well as used for its concise and up-to-date definitions.

FOR THE BEST IN PAPERBACKS, LOOK FOR THE 🐧

PENGUIN REFERENCE BOOKS

The Penguin Guide to the Law

This acclaimed reference book is designed for everyday use and forms the most comprehensive handbook ever published on the law as it affects the individual.

The Penguin Medical Encyclopedia

Covers the body and mind in sickness and in health, including drugs, surgery, medical history, medical vocabulary and many other aspects. 'Highly commendable' – *Journal of the Institute of Health Education*

The Slang Thesaurus

Do you make the public bar sound like a gentleman's club? Do you need help in understanding *Minder*? The miraculous *Slang Thesaurus* will liven up your language in no time. You won't Adam and Eve it! A mine of funny, witty, acid and vulgar synonyms for the words you use every day.

The Penguin Dictionary of Troublesome Words   Bill Bryson

Why should you avoid discussing the *weather conditions*? Can a married woman be *celibate*? Why is it eccentric to talk about the *aroma* of a cowshed? A straightforward guide to the pitfalls and hotly disputed issues in standard written English.

A Dictionary of Literary Terms

Defines over 2,000 literary terms (including lesser known, foreign language and technical terms), explained with illustrations from literature past and present.

The Concise Cambridge Italian Dictionary

Compiled by Barbara Reynolds, this work is notable for the range of examples provided to illustrate the exact meaning of Italian words and phrases. It also contains a pronunciation guide and a reference grammar.

FOR THE BEST IN PAPERBACKS, LOOK FOR THE 🐧

PENGUIN DICTIONARIES

Abbreviations
Archaeology
Architecture
Art and Artists
Biology
Botany
Building
Business
Chemistry
Civil Engineering
Computers
Curious and Interesting
  Words
Curious and Interesting
  Numbers
Design and Designers
Economics
Electronics
English and European
  History
English Idioms
French
Geography
German

Historical Slang
Human Geography
Literary Terms
Mathematics
Modern History 1789-1945
Modern Quotations
Music
Physical Geography
Physics
Politics
Proverbs
Psychology
Quotations
Religions
Rhyming Dictionary
Saints
Science
Sociology
Spanish
Surnames
Telecommunications
Troublesome Words
Twentieth-Century History